The Secular State Under Siege

The Secular State Under Siege

Religion and Politics in Europe and America

Christian Joppke

polity

First published in 2015 by Polity Press

Polity Press
65 Bridge Street
Cambridge CB2 1UR, UK

Polity Press
350 Main Street
Malden, MA 02148, USA

ISBN-13: 978-0-7456-6541-2
ISBN-13: 978-0-7456-6542-9(pb)

A catalogue record for this book is available from the British Library.

Library of Congress Cataloging-in-Publication Data

Joppke, Christian.
    The secular state under siege : religion and politics in Europe and America / Christian Joppke. – 1
      pages cm
    ISBN 978-0-7456-6541-2 (hardback) – ISBN 978-0-7456-6542-9 (paperback)   1. Religion and politics–Europe.   2. Religion and politics–United States.   3. Religion and state–Europe.   4. Religion and state–United States.   5. Secularism.   6. Islam.   7. Christianity.   I. Title.
    BL65.P7J67 2015
    322′.1094–dc23
                              2014025938

Typeset in 10/12 Sabon
by Toppan Best-set Premedia Limited
Printed and bound in the UK by Clays Ltd, St Ives PLC

The publisher has used its best endeavours to ensure that the URLs for external websites referred to in this book are correct and active at the time of going to press. However, the publisher has no responsibility for the websites and can make no guarantee that a site will remain live or that the content is or will remain appropriate.

Every effort has been made to trace all copyright holders, but if any have been inadvertently overlooked the publisher will be pleased to include any necessary credits in any subsequent reprint or edition.

For further information on Polity, visit our website: politybooks.com

Contents

Introduction
Religion as Structure and as Actor

A small book on so big a topic as "religion and politics" is no minor undertaking. I tackle it from a historical and institutional perspective, with a dual focus on Western Europe and North America, Christianity and Islam. This is still vast enough, but already less than everything. A historical-institutional perspective largely excludes behaviorism, such as the correlating of voting patterns or partisan identification with religious orientation, and so on, which has preoccupied much of the American political sociology of religion.[1] The regional focus on the West also excludes, now regrettably, the rest of the world, such as the Middle East or South-east Asia, where religious conflict may be far more dramatic and central to political life than in the temperate zones – this part of the world simply is beyond my competence (also linguistically).

I arrive at this topic as a long-standing student of the nation-state and its contemporary transformation in the West, especially if related to migration and multiculturalism. After the "challenge to the nation-state," to quote an earlier book of mine (Joppke 1998), now there is a "challenge to the secular state." One part of this story is academic, and it is astonishing to see how many fellow intellectual travelers of mine made similar moves.[2] But the other half of this story is in the real world, where even in the secularized West "public religion" has had a mighty come-back, to the degree that it had ever disappeared (the first to register this is Casanova 1994). Partially, but not exclusively, the revival of public religion is a result of international migration and the arrival of new religions into Western societies that challenge established arrangements between religion and the secular state.

A historical and institutional perspective takes "religion" both as structuring principle and as actor, as a structural force that has shaped the modern world like perhaps no other force and as a claims-maker within this world that religion helped bring about. On the structural side, religion (more precisely: Christianity) has shaped modern political life, including party systems, public institutions, and state structures and national identities, in the most profound yet often unacknowledged ways – Carl Schmitt (2005 [1922]) even argued famously that the lexicon of basic political concepts (such as "sovereignty") consists largely of secularized theological concepts. No one has articulated the unmatched structuring powers of religion in human history more succinctly than Tocqueville: "There is hardly any human action, however private it may be, which does not result from some very general conception men have of God, of His relations with the human race, of the nature of their soul, and of their duties to their fellows. Nothing can prevent such ideas from being the common spring from which all else originates" (1969 [1835–40]: 442–3).

Tocqueville, of course, was the unmatched theorist of liberal democracy, and he provocatively argued that in a democratic society religion was even more important than in feudalism for bringing about trust and cohesion in society: "[I]f [man] has no faith he must obey, and if he is free he must believe" (p. 444). Turning Tocqueville around, however, there is good reason to argue that liberal democracy itself, in which – pace Tocqueville – religion no longer is the central motive force and legitimizing principle and where society has become secularized (a key term thoroughly scrutinized in this book), could have arisen only in a Christian, and no other religious, context. At the same time, there is much variation in the relations between state and religion as the latter walked out of politics, being different in Europe (where church and state once were rival forces) and in America (where no such rivalry ever existed). Within Europe, religion–state relations differ in Protestant and Catholic or mixed countries, with a whole variety of church–state regimes, all compatible with the strictures of secularism, and with the peculiar presence of Christian Democratic parties in some countries but not in others. In short, religion (or rather Christianity) as structuring principle of even secular and secularizing societies needs to be acknowledged, and it will be done in this book in broad yet comparatively refined brushstrokes.

On the other side, religion is also an actor that appears in secular contexts with specific claims. Of particular interest here are *new* religions, which have entered Western societies by way of immigration – the standard bearer being, of course, Islam. These new religions stand to be integrated into existing church–state systems, which is a process with twists and frictions that are amply documented in an ever-expanding literature. Much of this literature is a lament over the discriminations and inequities inflicted on the newcomers by the powers that be. This obscures an astonishing and historically unprecedented fact: that nothing short of strict equality is the benchmark of including new religions, especially Islam. If one considers the power of religion (as "structuring principle") to make society and civilizations, which is always the power of a particular and not of any religion (in this case, of Christianity), the standard of equality is astonishing indeed. This is because the once dominant religion is reduced to just one among several religions, however extraneous to the respective culture and society these *other* religions might be. It is a specificity of the (Christian) West, exacted by the principles of secularism and neutrality that were born out of a specific history yet, once created, are imperative for liberal states and societies in general.

Chapter 1 provides a brief review of "Religion in Social and Political Theory." At its heart is a discussion of the two most imposing classical sociologies of religion that remain acute today, those of Émile Durkheim and Max Weber. Both espoused radically different concepts of religion that continue to be disputed and to inform scholarship today, functionalist (Durkheim) versus substantive (Weber). While each approach has its own virtues and deficiencies, a functionalist approach runs into the difficulty of saying what religion *is* and why and how it is no longer all-encompassing but one sphere or actor among many in a differentiated and secularized society.

Chapter 2, "Secularization and the Long Christian Exit," homes in on the central concept of the entire social science of religion, past and present, which is "secularization." While, following Casanova (1994: ch. 1), it has become canonical to consider only "differentiation" the heart of secularization, it is difficult to see how secularization could *not* imply the "decline" and "privatization" of religion, which for many (including Casanova) have been proved wrong by the return of "public religion." In particular, I argue in this chapter that secularism (as the result of secularization) is necessary for a liberal-democratic state, but that it was arrived at in a contingent historical process, in which Latin Christianity was pivotally involved. Take away Christianity, and we would not live in a secular age. This is hardly a new proposition, but it bears to be restated in all its simplicity.

In Chapters 3 and 4, I move away from religion as historical structuring principle or society-maker toward religion as actor and claims-maker in secularized settings. The underlying idea of these chapters is that the

Christian Right in America is what Islam is in Europe – the respective side of the Atlantic's major "challenge to the secular state" today.

Chapter 3, "Challenge to the Secular State (I): The Christian Right in America," argues that the main impact of the Christian Right has been not political but legal, partially moving America away from its strict separationist religion–state regime of the past toward a European-style soft establishment, in which state and religion cooperate in the fulfillment of important societal functions.

Chapter 4, "Challenge to the Secular State (II): Islam in Europe," starts by mapping out the principal frictions between Islam and thoroughly secularized Europe, yet moves on to stress the accommodating powers of liberal institutions, including the partial and indirect, yet no less effective, accommodation of Islamic sharia law within liberal state law. While "liberal Islam" is a chimera, Islam has nevertheless found its place as a constitutionally protected minority religion in secular Europe and the West. If there are undeniably problems surrounding Muslim integration in Europe, an insufficient integration of Islam, the religion, is not at the heart of them.

In a concluding chapter, "Islam and Christianity in the Secular State," I weave together the strands of the Christianity–Islam comparison in secular settings by contrasting how the key symbols of the two religions, the Christian crucifix and the Islamic veil, have been processed in the European and American legal orders. Both are instances of "public religion" (Casanova 1994) and have helped spark the renewed interest in the political role of religion. Two questions are central. First, how far can religion be included or excluded in the public sphere, and where is the line between legitimate inclusion and distortion of public functions by too much religion, particularly if religion violates the precepts of liberal states (like human rights and non-discrimination)? Secondly, can there be partiality in this respect, granting privileges to some religion(s) that are denied to others? To treat both religions, Christianity and Islam, symmetrically is what liberal neutrality and secularism seem to command. However, this would ignore the fact that one symbol, the Christian cross, is the central symbol of the majority religion, while the other, the Islamic veil, is the expression of a minority religion that owes its presence in the West only to international migration, most of it recent. To accommodate this difference, high courts in Europe and America alike have justified the secular state's identification with the cross, and thus partiality in this domain, by taking it as cultural, not as a religious symbol that stands for the history and tradition of a particular society. The religion–culture distinction, abstruse and problematic as it may appear to many, is the ultimate victory of secularism, as it allows privileging the majority religion only by denying its religious quality, transforming it into mere "culture."

1

Religion in Social and Political Theory

Religion, Politics, Secular State: An Introduction

In the secular state, religion and politics are separated, in the sense that religion does not control the political process and prejudice membership. The opposite is the case in a religious state, in which the official religion shapes the laws of the land and non-adherents are relegated to lesser status, if they are tolerated at all. The fusion of religion and politics has been the norm through much of human history, and it remains alive in the Islamic world today – in the "Islamic Republic of Iran," for instance, full membership is predicated on subscribing to the Islamic faith (more precisely, the Shi'ite variant of it), and the religious law of sharia (again, in the Shi'ite variant) functions as higher law that is enforced by the state. By contrast, the United Kingdom, even if Anglicanism is its established state religion, is still a "secular state," in the sense that membership as citizenship is not tied up with religious adherence and law and policy are controlled not by creed but by the legal-democratic process. In a secular state, such as Britain, the historical majority religion may be privileged and endowed with public status, but only as a matter of culture and identity, not as faith or doctrine imposed on people and institutions.[1]

As obvious and compelling as the distinction between the secular and the religious state appears, it still rests on a vocabulary that is historically particular and inescapably secularist even if an opposite, non-secular reality is to be denoted. This is a predicament from which there is no rescue. Indeed, the very notion of religion, understood as "a set of beliefs which is defined as personal conviction and which can exist separately from one's public loyalty to the state" (Cavanaugh 1995: 403), is the specific result of European history, in particular, the European Wars of Religion in the sixteenth and seventeenth centuries. Only since Thomas Hobbes established the "earthly God" of the Leviathan have we become accustomed to speak about "religion," which conveys the possibility of distance and of an observer's perspective, and no longer about "true faith," "the law," or the "revealed way," which are always experienced in the first person and to which there is no alternative (Lilla 2007: 88). "Religion," Martin Riesebrodt argues succinctly, is "an abstract concept through which concrete 'religions' become comparable" (2007: 17). But then the absolute truth claimed by any one of them is inescapably relativized. Moreover, the notion of "religion" takes the designated phenomenon as a sphere separate from politics, economics, or any other sphere. This is not a universal constellation but the result of secularization that is particular to Western modernity. On this is built a "postmodern" critique of the concept of "religion" as parochially Western and not applicable to other civilizations, such as Islam (Asad 2003) – which is vitiated by the fact that those who first denounce the concept of religion then "happily continue using it" (Riesebrodt 2007: 23), simply because "comparison requires general concepts" (p. 37).

In turn, religion thus understood is "correlative to the rise of the State" as an inherently secular force, whose purpose is "to keep peace among the warring religious factions" (Cavanaugh 1995: 398). In this sense, the notion of the secular state is a pleonasm, while the opposite notion of the religious state seeks to grasp with a secularist vocabulary a reality that denies its very premises and thus cannot but distort it.

Secularist assumptions also shape our modern understanding of "politics." Take Max Weber's classic definition of politics as "striving for power or influencing the distribution of power, be it between states or within a state between the social groups that it comprises" (1977 [1926]: 8). This is a thoroughly secular definition of politics, dominant in the Western tradition since Machiavelli and Hobbes. It does not travel well to other epochs and regions where the secularist premises are not in place or even are actively challenged. But even in the secularized West a mundane understanding of politics as struggle for power, or, more mundanely still, as "who gets what, when, how" (Lasswell 1936), excludes a dimension of serving the collectivity and pursuing the public good.

Hobbes had been the first to proclaim that there was no *finis ultimus* (utmost aim), no *summum bonum* (highest good), in politics, only a *summum malum* (highest bad), death, which results from the "perpetual and restless desire of power after power" that is the essence of the human condition. Statecraft thus could not be about realizing the good life, as had been the illusion since Aristotle. More modestly, all one could hope for through life in common was to "secure...life and liberty" (Hobbes 1996 [1651]: 67). This is indeed a "self-limited" concept of politics (Lilla 2007: 301). Under liberalism, it came to be formulated as the idea that the state should be "neutral" on questions of the good life.

The Hobbesian solution, which foreshadowed liberalism, was thenceforth critiqued by a Republican tradition that sought to bring back "highest goods" into politics, including a quasi-religious dimension that Paul Kahn (2011) has recently captured by evoking Carl Schmitt's notion of "political theology." "All significant concepts of the modern theory of the state," Carl Schmitt argued, "are secularized theological concepts" (Schmitt 2005 [1922]: 36). The most obvious example is "sovereignty." Like the Christian God, who is outside but also inside this world, the sovereign stands "outside the normally valid legal system...[but] nevertheless belongs to it, for it is he who must decide whether the constitution needs to be suspended in its entirety" (p. 7). This follows, of course, from Schmitt's famous definition, "Sovereign is he who decides on the exception" (*Ausnahmezustand*) (p. 5). Sovereignty is an extra-legal, extra-normative *decision* that cannot be derived from anything else but itself, much like God has created the world out of nothing, through his fiat: "Sovereignty is the highest, legally independent, underived power" (p. 17). Schmitt even draws an analogy between the "exception in jurisprudence" and the "miracle in theology" (p. 36).

Liberal theory, which grounds the political in a contract and the norm established by it, misses the element of sovereign decision that predates the contract and links the political with theology: "Liberal theory puts contract at the origins of the political community; political theology puts sacrifice at the point of origin" (Kahn 2011: 7). In fact, "citizens" are related to the "sovereign" not through "contract" but through "sacrifice" (p. 121). The proof for this is the state's legitimate imposition of killing and being killed in the case of war. As Kahn argues along Schmittian lines, "Sovereignty is constituted in the imagining of the sacrificial act: the willingness to kill and be killed establishes the temporal and geographic boundaries of the state" (p. 155). Kahn identifies a blind spot in liberal theory, which can't say anything about the moment of creating – and defending – the political community in which liberal principles are to be actualized. But he wavers with respect to the geographic scope of an argument that logically should bear no geographic restriction, making it a tractate about America with its peculiarity of "judicial review" being the site of popular sovereignty, and where sacrifice and state violence are never far from the surface. By contrast, Europe, especially the European Union, is said to "pursue politics without sovereignty: law without exception" (p. 16). This echoes Robert Kagan's notion of Americans as from "Mars" and Europeans from "Venus" (Kagan 2003). But is it true? For one, consider that America's "willingness to kill and be killed" is farmed out to professional soldiers (in fact, in a practice that the Roman Empire had already known, to immigrants lured by the promise of fast-track citizenship). And when talking beyond America, to call the ubiquitous threat of terrorism today's universal "moment of conscription" (Kahn 2011: 156) is helping oneself out with a metaphor when evidence is needed that *this* is political theology today. But Schmitt–Kahnian "political theology" does give a sense that there is something in politics that liberalism does not grasp, an element of "will" that cannot be collapsed into "reason" or "interest," and which links our secular politics of today with a past in which rulers were gods, or, rather, where the very distinction between politics and religion could not be made.

Religious Evolution

It is useful at this point to briefly reflect on the evolution of religion, from being coextensive with politics, society, the cosmos, to becoming merely private "belief," an option among others, in our secular age (for this *terminus ad quem* of religious evolution, see Taylor 2007). This reflection shows how presumptuous and historically unique the separation of religion and politics is, and their earlier fusion suggests that perhaps the two can never completely part ways.

In a classic article, expanded into a magisterial work half a century later (Bellah 2011), Robert Bellah (1964) distinguishes between five stages of religious evolution, each marked by an advance in the "freedom of personality and society" vis-à-vis their environment (p. 374). In the earliest stage, labeled "primitive" (later relabeled "tribal," Bellah 2011), a stateless society consists of egalitarian kinship units. Not only is there no distinction between religion and politics, but also the political is not differentiated from society. Ritual life is practiced in common, without priests or religious specialists, as a kind of "dreaming" that transforms the natural into a "mythical world." The purpose of this exercise is a latent instrumentalism, to get what one needs for life, "rain, harvest, children, health." But collective ritual also reinforces "the solidarity of the society" and thus is Durkheimian to the core (see below). Individual and society are "merged in a natural-divine cosmos" that is one without a transcendent reality, life being a "one possibility thing," a term Bellah borrowed from an anthropologist contemporary of his (1964: 364).

"Cosmological monism" persists in the second stage, that of "archaic religion." Examples are ancient Mesopotamia and the Egypt of the Pharaohs. The one difference here is the differentiation of political and military power, and thus the rise of hierarchy. Crucially, the higher-status group in these earliest state societies at the same time claims superior religious status. The new figure is the "divine king," that is, the "fusion of the divine and the human in the person of the king" (Bellah 2011: 232). In ancient Mesopotamia, the saying was that "kingship came down from heaven" (p. 217), and the Egyptian Pharaoh grew to be revered as the "son of god" and the "incarnation of god" (p. 232). Testimony to the god-like stature of the Pharaoh are the Great Pyramids, these most awe-inspiring of all human artifacts, in which the deceased rulers were buried along with their living servants or family (so-called "retainer burials"). Importantly, in the moment that "politics" came to be differentiated in these early civilizations, the emergent rulers immediately claimed superior religious or even divine status as well, being "priest-kings" in Mesopotamia or even "god-kings" in Egypt.

Accordingly, "politics" in its earliest incarnation had the hue of the "religious," or rather no distinction between the two could be made. This fact points to perhaps the oldest function of religion for politics, which is to legitimize power. "Nothing is ever lost" is Bellah's running theme (2011: 267), and kings "by divine right" and presidents acting in accordance with a "higher power" have persisted far beyond these earliest state societies, the latter right into the present time.

However, the third and most momentous stage in religious evolution has been the rise of "historic religions" (Bellah 1964: 366–8), later referred to as "axial-age religions" (Bellah 2011; see also the synopsis in Bellah 2005). The novelty is the differentiation of the religious from the political, so that power could not just be *legitimated* by claiming to be divine but could also be *challenged* by a new category of religious specialists who were *not* rulers, called "prophets" or "renouncers." The latter would find the existing world wanting in light of a "transcendent" world that was not here or was yet to come: "Political acts could be judged in terms of standards that the political authorities could not finally control" (Bellah 1964: 368).

The notion of "axial age" (*Achsenzeit*) stems from Karl Jaspers. He used it for the middle of the first millennium BC, in which almost simultaneously but without mutual influence the great world religions were born: Confucianism in China, Buddhism in India, Judaism in Palestine, but also philosophy in Greece (which was not a "religion" but which shared with it the new posture of rejecting or critiquing the existing in the light of transcendent or ideal possibilities).[2] This was the "age of criticism" (Bellah 2011: 268), or of "reflexivity" (Eisenstadt 1999: 8–9), marked by a "tension between political powers and intellectual movements" (Bellah 2011: 268). The new, previously inconceivable question was: "Who is the (true) king, the one who really reflects divine justice?" (p. 266).

Only in the axial age did "religion" as we know it come into being:

- It invoked a transcendental reality separate from this world, breaking up the old immanence of the one cosmos, to which there was no alternative.
- It was propagated by religious specialists who were not identical with political rulers, and who most of the time would be subservient to (and thus legitimize) rulers but who could also challenge them – the ancient prophets were also the first intellectuals and revolutionaries.
- It associated people apart and in abstraction from their ascribed family, kinship, even political ties, thus creating the universalism of "man as such" (Bellah 1964: 366) and the very idea of equality.
- Finally, it mobilized these people for "salvation," that is, rescue from the deficiencies of mundane life through their own action, which brought a dynamism and incentive for change into the world that had not previously existed.

The prime example for the associative, world-changing powers of axial-age religion is Judaism, whose central idea of the "covenant" is between God and the Israelites, thus bypassing their political rulers. This was "a new political form, a people in covenant with God, with no king as ruler. Moses is a teacher and a prophet, not a king" (Bellah 2011: 311).

With the rise of axial-age religions the two fundamental but inherently opposite religion–politics constellations, that of legitimating power and that of challenging power, have come fully into place. However, despite the notionally world-rejecting thrust of axial-age religions, their legitimating functions prevailed over their critical inclinations. As Bellah concludes, not without resignation, all axial-age utopias failed, while the religions lived on. Testament to this is the fate of Christianity, which quickly transmuted from a radical world-rejecting sect into the official religion of the late Roman Empire, and came to legitimize, at times to constitute, political rule in Europe for over fifteen hundred more years.

The door to the present age, in which the state distances itself from religion and becomes fully secular, was kicked open only in a fourth stage of religious evolution, which Bellah calls "early modern" (1964:

368–70). Alas, he fails to spell out its political implications. (In his later book, Bellah 2011, all post-axial-age developments are even left out altogether.) For Bellah, early modern religion is tantamount to Protestantism, that is, an offshoot of the Christian religion. The novelty of Protestantism is to "break through the whole mediated system of salvation" (Bellah 1964: 368), which Luther and other Protestant reformers had attacked in terms of an all-too-worldly, power-wielding and power-abusing Catholic Church. Instead, "immediate salvation" was now available to the believer facing God directly, through purity of belief or God-pleasing action in the world. Not mentioned by Bellah, Protestantism has in direct and indirect ways helped create modern liberalism, the idea that the state should stay outside the "care of souls," as John Locke phrased it in his *Letter Concerning Toleration* (1689). Thus the notions of state neutrality and secularism were born, which have framed the relationship between religion and politics ever since.

Bellah's early sketch of religious evolution remains the most compact and compelling in the sociological literature. It concludes with a fifth stage, which he calls "modern religion." It entails a "collapse of ...dualism" (Bellah 1964: 371). But this is no return to the cosmological monism of pre-axial times. Rather, the "double" world of axial religion is topped by an "infinitely multiplex world," with life turning from a "one possibility" into an "infinite possibility thing" (p. 371). This is a post-doctrinal (or postmodern?) situation in which "each individual must work out his own solution" (p. 373). Bellah illustrates the modern approach with Tom Paine's "My own mind is my own church" and Thomas Jefferson's "I am a sect by myself," which both flagged the possibility that not only the "social order" (as in early modern religion) but also "culture and personality" become "endlessly revisable", as Bellah put it in a Parsonian key (p. 373).

In a later work Bellah et al. (1985) immortalized the radical subjectivism of modern religion, which is a new *approach* to religion rather than new *religion* itself, as "Sheilaism" (p. 221). The label is derived from a young middle-class woman interviewed in *Habits of the Heart* (1985), called "Sheila Larson," who proved to Bellah and his team the transformation of American Protestantism from public and unified to private and fragmented religion: "I believe in God. I'm not a religious fanatic. I can't remember the last time I went to church. My faith has carried me a long way. It's Sheilaism. Just my own little voice....It's just try to love yourself and be gentle with yourself" (p. 221). For Bellah et al., this attitude entails the possibility of "over 222 million American religions, one for each of us," the "perfectly natural expression of current American religious life" (p. 221). However, if this is "modern religion," it falls outside the scope of an investigation of religion and politics, because its extreme individualism simply cannot be organized and rendered politically relevant.

The Great Debunking: Marx and Freud

Implicit in the notion of religious evolution is that, underneath its changing forms, religion persists as a universal form of human expression. Before we further lay out some classical sociological accounts of persistent religion, it is apposite to at least mention the alternative program of debunking religion as a kind of error or illusion, which stipulates the possibility of a society without religion. Only this program fully corresponds to the logic of secular modernity and the great Enlightenment narrative of exiting from "self-inflicted tutelage" (Kant), and not by accident was it formulated by the two most radical sons of the European Enlightenment, Marx and Freud. Still, the great debunking appears exotic today. This fact alone invites a look at it.

Religion as alienation: Marx

For Marx, religion is "false consciousness," a reflection of the "alienation" of humans under capitalism. While Marx grew up in the milieu of the "young Hegelians," for whom the critique of religion as a projection of human perfectibility was a central preoccupation,[3] he never bothered to pronounce much on the topic. He simply considered the critique of religion "accomplished business" (*im wesentlichen beendigt*). Or so he started his most extended reflection on religion, which is the first seven paragraphs in one of his earliest writings, the "Introduction to a Critique of Hegel's Philosophy of Law" (1964 [1843–4]). Religion, Marx argued there, is "the self-consciousness and self-feeling of man, who has not yet found himself or who has already lost himself again" (p. 378). However much in passing and by way of aphorism, Marx fully articulated religion's two main relationships to politics that remain acute today, to either legitimize or critique power. Accordingly, religion is at once an expression of a "false consciousness of the world" and a "protestation against the real poverty," the "sigh of the oppressed creature" (*Seufzer der bedrängten Kreatur*), the "opium of the people," as his famous verdict goes (p. 378). Like all of the expressions of "superstructure" (*Überbau*), as he would later call the non-economic realm of law, politics, culture, and ideology (Marx 1979 [1859]: 336), religion has "no content of its own" (Marx quoted in McLellan 1987: 11)[4] and is merely the "existence of a defect," whose source can be found "in the nature of the state itself" (Marx 1978

[1843]: 352). But then there was no point in dwelling long on it. One had to move quickly from the "critique of religion" to the "critique of politics" that made religion possible (Marx 1964 [1843–4]: 379), if not, even more urgently, from the "weapon of critique" to the "critique of weapons" (p. 385).

If religion had "no content of its own," it had to be explained by something outside of it. Accordingly, one might find in Marx's scattered remarks a stage model of religion as at first an expression of mystified nature to, later, an expression of mystified society (see McLellan 1987: ch. 1; Riesebrodt 2007: 85–8). With respect to the latter, in his famous chapter on the "fetish character of commodity" in *The Capital*, Marx (1975 [1867]) drew an "analogy" between the "religious world" and the "world of commodities," in both of which humanly made "products...appear as independent beings endowed with life" (p. 86). From this it follows that, once the sources of alienation and of the capitalist class rule that fosters and feeds on it have been abolished under communism, religion will cease to be. There is considerable optimism here about the finite sources of human suffering and of the nearing end of scarcity. It seems more plausible to argue that even if material goods were abundant and society was transparent, "absolute contingency" (Lübbe 2004: 156), grounded in the accident of birth and the certainty of death, would still plague human existence. But this is a condition that is "resistant to Enlightenment" (p. 156) and thus must generically spin forth "religion" as "recognition of the uncontrollable contingency of being" (p. 161).

The irony is that Marx, who is so overtly dismissive of religion, is covertly espousing a religious, more precisely, Christian, view of history as geared to salvation. Marx's is "a story of salvation told in the language of economics," as Martin Marty phrased it (1969: 53). The proletariat figures in it as "the "complete loss of humanity" that can only be redeemed by the "complete recovery of humanity" (Marx 1964 [1843–4]: 390); in a nutshell, the proletariat is "universal Christ" (McLellan 1987: 15, quoting E. Olssen).[5] Marx's view of history as a three-stage dialectic from the original bliss of communal property to the sin of private property and capitalism to redemption under communism, mediated by the "universal suffering" of the proletariat (Marx 1964 [1843–4]: 390), unmistakably echoes Old and New Testament motifs.

Religion as neurosis: Freud

To Freud, religion signals not "alienation" but "neurosis." But it amounts to the same great debunking, the message being that much like a patient can, even should, be healed of neurosis, society can and should be healed of religion (see Freud 1974 [1927]: 179). While a radical Enlightenment comrade with Marx in his wholesale dismissal of religion as "illusion" and in his view that a society without religion is not only possible but also desirable, Freud differs from Marx in going beyond mere anecdote to offer a full-fledged theory of religion, in fact perhaps the most provocative and daring theory of religion that has ever flowed from a human pen. The heart of it is the drawing of a close parallel between phylogenetic and ontogenetic psychological dynamics, with the "Oedipus complex," that "nucleus of all neuroses," as the point of origin where the "beginnings of religion, morality (*Sittlichkeit*), society, and art all flow together" (Freud 1974 [1912–13]: 439). For Freud, the "totemistic system," the earliest form of religion, with its twin precepts not to kill the totem animal and not to engage in sexual relations with females of the same clan, "has resulted from the conditions of the Oedipus complex" (p. 417), that is, patricide and marriage with the mother. In Freud's rather fantastic phylogenetic scenario,[6] in the beginning there is the Darwinian primary tribe (*Urhorde*), in which a jealous and violent "strong male" owns all females and castrates or expels his sons. In phase two, the expelled sons unite as "brother clan" to kill their father and "eat him raw" (Freud 1974 [1939]: 530). The sons' "guilt" over their heinous act then gives rise to "the two fundamental taboos of totemism" (Freud 1974 [1912–13]: 427).

However, as Freud subtly adds, the two core taboos of totemism are "not psychologically of equal value (*gleichwertig*)" (1974 [1912–13]: 427). Only the incest taboo has "practical meaning," as without it the new brother clan would disunite over the ongoing competition for females. By contrast, the prohibition on killing the totem animal (which for Freud represents the father figure) is "entirely based on sentiment," that is, devoid of a practical rationale (p. 428). Interestingly, only the latter counts as a "first attempt at religion." Religion proper thus denotes a purely psychic reality short of a practical function, so that it might be abandoned later. More precisely, the genuinely religious taboo figures as a "contract with the father," in which "security" and "protection," which humans have always sought in their fathers, is traded in against the obligation to "honor his life" and "not to repeat their act" (p. 428). Not just totemism, Freud concludes, but all religions are "identical reactions to this momentous event in which all culture is grounded" (p. 431). In short, the "root of all religion" is the "longing for the father" (*Vatersehnsucht*) (p. 431).

As fantastic as it sounds, Freud's scenario offers unparalleled insight into the deep psychology of religion in general, and of Christianity in particular. Of course, Freud is deliberately ambiguous about whether his phylogenetic scenario is fact or fiction. The mark of neurosis, after all, is to "posit the psychic reality over the factual one" (Freud 1974 [1912–13]: 442), so that thinking replaces the act. But then he insists, with Goethe's Faust: "*Im Anfang war die Tat*" (in the beginning, there was the act) (p. 444). Yet it is irrelevant whether Freud's murderous scenario of the transition from nature to culture is fact or fiction. What counts is his unraveling of the psychological mechanisms that undergird religion.

Of particular importance is Freud's picture of the human psyche as torn by "ambivalence." It provides a more complex and compelling view of the drivers of human action than one can find in the rational action theories that dominate the social sciences today (see Smelser 1998). Ambivalence is the simultaneous desire to overstep the taboos and the anxiety this prospect causes, with one of these taboos, that against incest, being qualified by Freud as "the most decisive mutilation of human sex life that had ever occurred over the course of time" (1974 [1930]: 233). This is because the "purpose of human life" is the "principle of lust" (p. 207), tilting toward "incest," "cannibalism," and "murder" (1974 [1927]: 144), which is exactly opposed to "culture" as based on "constraint and the renunciation of drives (*Triebverzicht*)" (p. 141). Again, one need not agree with this speculative, negative anthropology to find value in Freud's concept of ambivalence. The taboo, this identical origin of culture and religion, whereby human life rises above mere animal life, has the double quality of being both "holy" and "dangerous"/"frightening" (*unheimlich*)/"forbidden" – Freud accordingly translates taboo as "*heilige Scheu*" (holy fearfulness) (1974 [1912–13]: 311). Slightly modifying this theme in his later work *Moses and Monotheism* (1974 [1939]), Freud qualifies the "holy" itself, this "derived will of the primal father (*Urvater*)" that is the origin of all ethics, as marked by ambivalence, in that it is both "sacred" (*geweiht*) and "rotten" (*verrucht*) (as in the proverbial *auri sacra fames*) (p. 567). The holy, after all, is "also something that is frightening (*wovor man erschauerte*), as it required a painful renunciation of drives (*Triebverzicht*)" (p. 567).

This echoes Rudolf Otto's characterization of elementary religiosity as a kind of pre-moral combination of fear (*Tremendum*) and fascination (*Fascinans*) (Otto 1963 [1917]), except that Otto had no mechanism to hand to explain this strange combination (see my discussion below). Much like the child simultaneously loves and fears its father,[7] in totemism the totem animal is the object of cultic veneration but also ritually killed and eaten in the periodic "totem meal" (*Totemmahlzeit*). After all, there is a great pressure to overstep the taboo, which is "directed against the strongest desires of humans" (Freud 1974 [1912–13]: 326). The "feast" is always the "breaking of a taboo," and the totem meal, as "perhaps the first feast of humankind," is the ritual re-enactment of killing the "violent, jealous father" (p. 425). In this primal rite of sacrifice (*Opferritus*), which needs to be exercised in common, as Freud subtly speculates, there is the lingering "consciousness that one does something that is forbidden to the individual qua individual, and that may only be justified by the participation of everyone" (p. 425).

Some of the same psychodynamics that Freud detected in the earliest religion he naturally has to find in Judaism and Christianity also. In particular, the Holy Communion in Christian liturgy is "the totem meal repeated" (Freud 1939: 532). In fact, Freud sees in the simultaneous "guilt" and "defiance" of the sons the two "driving factors" of religious evolution (1974 [1912–13]: 432). The "guilt" element finds its most elaborate form in the Christian dogma of "original sin," which is, however, redeemed by the ultimate sacrifice of Jesus Christ, his death on the cross. In the Christian teachings, "humanity thus most openly admits its terrible deed at the beginning of time (*schuldvolle Tat der Urzeit*)" (p. 437), but it also implicitly repeats it. Here is the moment of "defiance," because by way of Christianity, in which God the Son rather than God the Father is central, "the religion of the son replaces the religion of the father." The Christian Communion, this repetition of the totem meal, is "in essence the renewed killing of the father" (p. 437).

Freud's theory of religion, by his own account, is "fantastic," as it approximates religion to a "psychiatric craze (*Wahnidee*)" (1974 [1927]: 165), an "illusion" that feeds on the "oldest, most powerful, most urgent desires of humankind" (p.164). But qua illusion, which requires the sacrifice of the intellect (*credo quia absurdum*), religion can also be shed in favor of the "primacy of the intellect" (p. 180). Accordingly, Freud concludes his core essay on religion, *The Future of an Illusion* (1974 [1927]), with a "plea for a rational foundation of the prescriptions of culture," in which the latter are the expression of "social necessity" only (p. 175).

The end of religion, however, this ultimate Enlightenment dream, is not plausible in the terms of Freud's own theory, which showed us the deep psychological grounding of religion. If, indeed, the Oedipus complex and the vicissitudes of "human helplessness" (Freud 1974 [1927]: 152) are the psychological source of religion, how could one expect it to ever go away? Therapy may cure the pathological extremes, but not the underlying psychic dynamics – the Oedipus complex, if it really exists, is going to be repeated in each individual life. If it is true that "morality is the true domain [of religion]" (p. 152), there seems to be a closer alliance between the two than the notion of a rationally grounded morality would have it. Must morality, that taming of nature by culture, not always be tainted by ambivalence, the simultaneity of awe and the desire to transgress, which underlies all religious expressions?

In fact, the relationship between morality and religion, which is of great importance for tackling the relationship between religion and politics, is not all that clear in Freud's work. In terms of the incest taboo, which serves the "practical" purpose of keeping the victorious "brother clan" away from strife (Freud 1974 [1912–13]: 428), religion and morality seem to be separate. By contrast, with respect to the second pillar of totemism, which is the "renunciation of the killing of the totem animal" (p. 428) and the related trading in, for security, of obedience, religion and morality are fused. Freud helps himself out with the compromise formula that *Triebverzicht* and ethics "don't belong to the essential content of religion" but are still "genetically most closely connected" with the latter (1939: 564). In his phylogenetic scenario of the transition from nature to culture, Freud mixes a stew of culture, morality, and religion as a joint "beyond" nature, so that one does not know what the added value of "religion" is. It is probably the element of craze that he wants to cure humanity of, but this craze is also too closely connected to his own depiction of what makes us human to be convincing.

Classical Sociology of Religion: Durkheim and Weber

If Freud offered profound insight into the psychology of religion, the classical sociology of religion, by Durkheim and Weber, homed in on the moral-ethical and political dimensions of religion, depicting it as a source of solidarity, meaning, and legitimacy (Riesebrodt 2007: 118).[8] In general, the relationship between religion and politics can be developed in two quite opposite directions. One is to ferret out the functions of religion for society, any society, abstracted from the concrete contents of religion, with religion fulfilling needs that have to be met, even under a different name if religion has faded away as a public force, as tends to be the case in secular settings. A second direction is to study and compare the society- and civilization-making powers of concrete religions as historical forces, which differ from case to case. These two options are exemplarily connected with the works of Durkheim and Weber, respectively, which – unlike Marx's aphorisms and Freud's speculations – continue to inform the social science literature today. It is therefore imperative to look at them more closely.

The function of religion: Durkheim

In his last and major work, *The Elementary Forms of Religious Life* (1960 [1912]), Durkheim tried to distill the universal function of religion, irrespective of time and place, which in his view is to create unity and cohesion in society. Durkheim's remains the model for the study of collective rituals and "civil religion" that make societies cohere, even in the contemporary United States, where there is a "wall of separation" between church and state (see Bellah 1967). In *The Elementary Forms of Religious Life*, Durkheim seeks nothing less than to "render comprehensible the religious nature of human beings" (p. 2) and thus to clarify "what religion is in general" (p. 593). This, he argues, could best be done by looking at "the most primitive and simple" known religion, which is the totemism of the Australian Aborigines. In Bellah's (2011) terms, Durkheim takes an instance of "tribal religion" to find out what religion is *überhaupt*. As religion is always a composite of beliefs and practices, the latter called "rituals," separate analyses are devoted to each.

With respect to belief, Durkheim famously holds that one defining element of religion is "the division of the world into two sectors, one of which comprises everything that is sacred, while the other comprises everything that is profane" (Durkheim 1960 [1912]: 50–1). The relationship between sacred and profane is one of "absolute otherness," and they are "always separated," "like two worlds that have nothing in common" (p. 53). The sacred–profane distinction is thus held to be different in kind from that between "good" and "evil" or "sick" and "healthy," which are opposed "genera" of the same "species", that is, of "morality" and "life," respectively. No such overarching concept is available, argues Durkheim, for the sacred–profane distinction.

Important in Durkheim's definition of religious belief is to take "God" out of it. This is a reasonable move as there is no god in primitive religion, not even in some of the developed religions, like Buddhism or Confucianism. Secondly, "dualism" obviously figures for Durkheim as inherent in religion as such, and not only as a feature of later axial-age religions, as claimed by Bellah. Thirdly, religion is distinguished in kind from morality: each is said to have a different logical structure, even if in reality they may be closely connected and aligned. This part of the analysis, while of pivotal importance for the very practical question whether there can be morality after and apart from religion, is not so convincing. Isn't "religion" the common denominator of sacred and profane much like "morality" is the common denominator of good and evil? There is a difference in content but not in form, as Durkheim claims. The quality of "absolute otherness" surely applies to good versus evil as well: isn't God, when looked at from a moral point of view, in a relation of "absolute otherness" to the Devil? Conversely, the notion of profane makes no sense apart from the context of "religion," which logically does the same for the sacred–profane distinction as "morality" does for the good–evil distinction.

However convincing one finds his way of keeping religion and morality (and other societal subsystems) apart, Durkheim's important move is to exorcize not just "God" but all creedal content from a formalistic definition of religion. This opens up the possibility of applying the sacred–profane distinction to extra-religious settings, which "Durkheimian" sociologists have done with relish. "Religion" can now be found in things that perhaps should not be called so if one wishes to avoid stretching the term.[9]

But Durkheim's definition of religion is not exhausted by the sacred–profane distinction. Instead, he adds as a second defining feature of religion that it always assembles a "church," which is "a society whose members are united because they imagine the sacred world...in the same way" (Durkheim 1960 [1912]: 60). This addition serves the purpose of excluding magic from the ambit of religion, because "there is no magical church" (p. 61).[10] In its broad scope, denoting any religious association, Durkheim's definition of church is certainly idiosyncratic, as it undercuts the church versus sect distinction that has been the trademark of the classic sociologies of religion of Max Weber or Ernst Troeltsch. But it is only a convenient gateway to the center of his analysis, which "abandoned the Gods and substituted ritual as the fundamental religious aspect," as Rodney Stark (2003: 367) put it, disapproving the move.

Combining the two elements of belief and practice, Durkheim thus arrives at this definition of religion: "A religion is a solidary system of beliefs and practices, which refer to sacred, that is, separated and forbidden things, beliefs and practices, and which unite in one and the same moral community, which we call church, all those who belong to it" (1960 [1912]: 65).

Durkheim's famous claim is that religion is a disguised form of society celebrating itself. The "typically sacred thing" for the Australian Aborigines is their totem, which is mostly an animal that symbolizes their clan. Accordingly, "god and society are one" (Durkheim 1960 [1912]: 295). Durkheim comes to this conclusion through analogy, namely, the similarity of the sentiments evoked by both, which is above all a "sentiment of permanent dependence" and a "moral power" that imposes itself irrespective of utility and cost–benefit calculations (pp. 295–6). "God" (in this context shorthand for the sacred totem) is like society, in that it is something that exists exterior to the individual and exerts a moral power that is to be followed for its own sake. Ergo, god must really be society. This is a typically Durkheimian sleight of hand, in which a causal proposition is proved more by logical twisting than by weighing the evidence. Importantly, however, the power of religion qua society is not crushing but enabling power: "At the root of totemism are feelings of friendly optimism rather than of fear and coercion" (pp. 320–1). Not only is religion not born of fear, as Thomas Hobbes had assumed, it also is not deception, which had been the line of the *critique* of religion by Feuerbach and Marx that preceded this first *sociology* of religion: "The believer is not deceived if he believes in the existence of a moral power on whom he depends and that constitutes what is best in him: this power exists; it is society" (p. 322). Certainly, the believer errs in the "letter of the symbol" but not in the "concrete and living reality" that is behind it (p. 322).

To identify religion with the moral power of society forces Durkheim to call "religion" even patently non-religious things: "The respect imposed by people that exercise a high social function is nothing other than religious respect" (1960 [1912]: 304). The invented cults of reason and the "Supreme Being" in the French Revolution also become indistinguishable from religion – this is simply a case of "society and its important ideals becoming the object of a veritable cult *directly and without any change*" (p. 306; emphasis added). Introducing an idea later elaborated by Edward Shils (1972: ch. 4), Durkheim finds that every society "sacralizes" its central ideas and principles, which are thus immunized from critique. This is the case even in societies that dwell in "free critique," where it happens to be this very "principle of free critique" that is "put above discussion and thus rendered untouchable, that is, sacred" (Durkheim 1960 [1912]: 305). This opens the door to a questionable relativism, in which there is no difference between a society of free critique and one in which monarchs are sacrosanct. On the other hand, one can now draw parallels between religious worship and the worship of "fatherland, freedom, reason" (p. 306), which might yield a sane distancing effect from the latter. However, this possibility is bought at the price of calling religion what perhaps should not be called thus. Take the example of worshiping the "fatherland," that is, nationalism. With Durkheimian tools we could not distinguish between religious nationalism, with its Old Testament motif of a "chosen people," which has energized the earliest European nationalisms and also American nationalism (see Gorski 2000b; Hastings 1997; Marx 2005), and "nationalism" proper, which in industrializing societies includes no explicitly religious themes (see Gellner 1978).

The same difficulty of distinguishing between the religious and the non-religious, or rather of an overtly abstract and content-free definition of the religious, is visible in Durkheim's treatment of ritual practice, which is the second fundamental dimension of religion, next to beliefs. It usefully distinguishes between negative and positive cults. Negative cults are prohibitions, taboos, and restrictions that produce the separation between sacred and profane and prevent their illicit combination. Being a "system of restrictions" (Durkheim 1960 [1912]: 441), the negative cult suggests that "systematic asceticism" (p. 445) is built into every religion qua religion, and thus is no privilege of the ascetic Protestantism that Max Weber famously connected to the rise of capitalism. In Freudian manner, asceticism as *Triebverzicht* is an "integral part of all human culture" (p. 452). But the negative cult is only preparation for the positive cult, in which the believer enters into contact with the sacred through feasts or sacrifices. As Durkheim puts it rather profanely, "[A] man of the kangaroo clan believes, he feels that he is a kangaroo, through this quality he defines himself. It determines his place in society. In order to retain this quality, he has to eat the flesh of this animal from time to time" (p. 482).

But the important point is that through the positive ritual society renews itself. In fact, Durkheim's insight is that without assembly society "cannot revitalize the sentiment that it has of itself" (1960 [1912]: 499). But such assembly cannot be permanent, because society's mundane needs have to be met. Hence the *periodic* nature of ritual. In the moment of assembly, a "kind of electricity" is discharged (p. 308), which Durkheim calls "collective effervescence," and which is the cement of renewal and of cohesion. Interestingly, Durkheim notes that "the pious life of the Australian" oscillates between the extremes of "complete ossification" and "nervous overreaction," and that it is exactly this contrast that may "evoke the sentiment of the sacred." The sacred is thus more difficult to produce among the "so-called civilized people," where this oscillation is less extreme and where the ties that bind must inevitably become weaker (p. 313). While the importance of ritual for society's renewal is indisputable, the problem is again that Durkheim provides no tools to distinguish the religious from the non-religious. Secular ceremonies of moral renewal cannot "by nature be distinguished from properly religious ceremonies." He asks rhetorically: "Is there any essential difference between the assembly of Christians who celebrate the waymarks of Christ's life, or of Jews who celebrate the exodus from Egypt or the pronouncement of the Ten Commandments, and an assembly of citizens who commemorate the passing of a new moral charter or a great event in their national life?" (p. 610). If there is no difference between a civic and a religious assembly, we have given away the possibility to identify *religion*.

Comparative religions: Weber

This charge could not be made against Weber, whose interest was not in a universal function of religion (which could then be differently met) but in the society- and civilization-making powers of distinct religions, with an eye on comparisons and historical variations. No wonder that Weber abstained from ever defining religion, arguing that what religion *is* could be ascertained only at the "end," not the beginning, of the "kind of investigation" that he set out to do (Weber 1976 [1921]: 245). While providing a comparative sociology of world religions of unmatched depth and complexity, Weber had as his primary ambition to explain the "occidental rationalism" that was specific to Europe and the West yet had global implications. As he wrote in the famous Introduction (*Vorbemerkung*) to his collected sociology of religion, "The son of modern European culture will treat universal-historical problems necessarily and justifiably in terms of this question: which unique circumstances have led to the fact that in the Occident, and only here, cultural phenomena have emerged that are – at least so we are inclined to believe – of *universal* importance and validity" (Weber 1978 [1920]: 1). There then follows an account of how the "rationalism" that he deems specific to the Occident could be found in all of its societal spheres, in science, law, the arts, state, but, above all, in capitalism, that "most fateful force of our modern life" (p. 4).

The role of Protestantism in the rise of modern capitalism is the topic of *The Protestant Ethic and the Spirit of Capitalism*, originally published in 1905, which is one of the most influential and heavily debated works in the history of sociology (republished in Weber 1978 [1920]). As this study attests, Weber directed his attention with respect to the society-shaping forces of religion more on economic than on political life. This is strange if one considers his own imposing sociology of the modern bureaucratic state, which surely required the same "disciplining" of people that modern capitalism did.[11] But probably Weber was under the spell of Marx, as a critical dialogue with whom the *Protestant Ethic* has been conceived. In this work, Weber shows an "elective affinity" between the ethics of ascetic Protestantism, especially Calvinism, which puts a premium on finding signs of salvation in the fruits of restless work, and the "spirit of capitalism," which is symbolized in Benjamin Franklin's proverb "consider that time is money" (Weber 1978 [1920]: 31). While the *Protestant Ethic* is sometimes simplified as a "culturalist" alternative to Marx, Weber's claim is rather more cautious and self-limited, in several ways. First, no claim is made that Protestantism has "caused" capitalism. "Elective affinity" suggests homology, but not causality; at best, it establishes a working hypothesis that awaits further empirical validation (as which in fact his later comparative-historical sociology of religion may be best understood; it shows why the East would *not* produce the capitalism and rationalism that is specific to the West). Secondly, Weber's is an argument at the level of mental dispositions, not of institutions, that is, of a particular *religious* disposition, Calvinism's "inner-worldly asceticism," showing a certain similarity with a particular *economic* disposition, to find meaning in the "restless chase" for money, which underlies modern capitalism but had to appear utterly "irrational" for "traditionalist" minds (p. 54). No argument is made of ideas spinning forth an institutional reality, which would invite the charge of "idealism" or "culturalism." This is entirely an analysis of ideas being homologous to other ideas – that is, of finding "elective affinities between certain forms of religious belief and professional ethics" (p. 83). It is an analysis of "ideas," furthermore, that may have been necessary for the *rise* but not the *functioning* of mature capitalism: "The Puritan *wanted* to be work-oriented (*Berufsmensch*), – we *have* to be it" (p. 203). Thirdly, Weber himself rejected the notion of "replacing a one-sided 'materialist' with an equally one-sided 'spiritualist' causal interpretation of culture and history: *Both* are *equally possible*" (p. 205). Neither does he claim that the "capitalist spirit" could have arisen "only" as a result of the Reformation (p. 83) – thus leaving open the possibility of other cultural fundaments of capitalism, of "multiple modernities," to use contemporary jargon (see Eisenstadt 2000); nor does he claim that "capitalism as an economic system is the product of the Reformation," which would discount the "immense complexity of mutual influences between the material bases, the social and political organizational forms, and the spiritual contents of the Reformist cultural epochs" (Weber 1978 [1920]: 83). In the end, Protestantism was only "one of several factors" (*mitbeteiligt*) in the making of modern capitalism (p. 83).

While the *Protestant Ethic* continues to shine for showing the importance of human motivation to an understanding of society and change (well observed by Greenfeld 2001: 16), its substantive findings are nevertheless questionable, and they have been torn apart by legions of historians. Perhaps the biggest problem is the claim of a sudden, radical rupture effectuated by the Reformation, which divided the "traditionalism" of the pre-capitalist era from the "rationalism" of ours. In reality, there was more of a gradual transition. Some historians pointed out that the Puritans remained rather "economic traditionalists" and thus were not the avant-gardists that Weber saw them as (see the brief summary in Greenfeld 2001: 15).

A particularly compelling critique of Weber's *Protestant Ethic* is by the British historian Hugh Trevor-Roper (1965), who confirms the importance of Calvinism for capitalism yet refutes the notion of a radical rupture with a "traditionalist" past during the Reformation period. True, Trevor-Roper argues that while Europe in 1500 was dominated by the Catholic south, by 1800 economic and intellectual leadership had moved to the Protestant north. And much like Weber would have it, he acknowledges that around the mid-1600s Calvinists were "the economic elite of Europe" (p. 22). However, rather than being beholden to "inner-worldly asceticism," "the great entrepreneurs lived magnificently" (p. 25). Moreover, their common bond was, yes, to be all based in Dutch lands, but also to be all "immigrants" from the European south. In fact, they were all "heirs of medieval capitalism" and the "large-scale industrial capitalism" that had *preceded* the Reformation (p. 29). These Calvinist entrepreneurs had been forced to move north because of their religion by the "Counter-Reformation state" taking hold in Spain, Italy, Flanders, and later also France. Accordingly, as Trevor-Roper concludes, with a critical eye on Weber's thesis of a radical rupture (which Weber shared in his own way with the other classics sociological thinkers, including Marx and Durkheim), "the novelty lay not in the entrepreneurs themselves, but in the circumstances which drove them to emigrate" (p. 32).

Weber's mature comparative sociology of world religions differs from his earlier *Protestant Ethic* in considering "both causal relationships" (Weber 1978 [1920]: 12), that is, considering both the social determination of religious beliefs and how these beliefs may change the world. However, the program remains the same, which is to examine the "economic ethic" (*Wirtschaftsethik*) of religions, and thus it retains an economic rather than political focus, for the sake of finding "points of comparison with the still to be analyzed occidental development" (p. 12). The meta-theoretical thrust of this enterprise is famously encapsulated in the notion, which also serves well as the motto of Weberian sociology in general, that "interests..., not ideas, directly rule human action," but that "'world views' created by ideas" have "very often laid the switches along which the dynamics of interests have driven forward human action" (p. 252).

With respect to "interests," that is, the social determinants of religious beliefs, Weber brings into focus the social strata that carry a religion and lend it its specific psychological temperature. Accordingly, Confucianism is the religion of "world-ordering bureaucrats," Hinduism of "world-ordering magicians," Buddhism of "world-roaming mendicant monks," Islam of "world-subjecting warriors," Judaism of "itinerant merchants," and Christianity of "itinerant craftsmen" (Weber 1976 [1921]: 311).

In this context, Weber offers some penetrating observations that make his a true "sociology" of religion that in this sense Durkheim's never was. Peasants, because of their nearness to nature, are the "originally non-pious," at best carriers of a magic-traditionalist religiosity (Weber 1976 [1921]: 285–7). Axial-age religiosity with its emphasis on transcendence is an urban phenomenon, as it requires distance from the circularity and immanence of nature. Here one must further distinguish whether the urban carrier groups are lower or upper class. The true salvation religions (*Erlösungsreligionen*), above all Judaism and Christianity, which reject this world in favor of one that is still to come, before or after death, are naturally "plebeian," carried by lower strata with an "interest" in utopia. Their psychological impetus is *Ressentiment*, as Weber says with Nietzsche, and a "theodicy of suffering." This entails a positive re-evaluation of suffering, which in archaic religion, by contrast, had been a symptom of "hatred by God" (*Gottverhasstsein*) and "secret guilt." Importantly, only a "theodicy of suffering" opens up the axial-age possibility of religion to criticize and challenge political power, whereas in archaic religion's "theodicy of happiness" religion had served purely to legitimize power (Weber 1976 [1921]: 242).

This reflection throws a paradoxical light on Islam, which Weber depicts as originally a *Herrenreligion* with a characteristically low emphasis on "asceticism" and "salvation" (Weber 1976 [1921]: 375). Through its upper-class crust, and an ensuing propensity more for static "being" than for a missionary "ought to" (Weber 1978 [1920]: 248), Islam is this-worldly to a point that its inclusion in the category of "salvation religion," about which, of course, Weber is not in doubt, appears questionable.

Apart from "lower-" versus "higher-status" carrier groups, Weber distinguishes between "practical"- versus "theoretical"-minded carrier groups of religion. "Practical"-minded carrier groups are more likely to see themselves as "tools" of God in active world intervention, while theoretical-minded carrier groups will make for a religion of "contemplative mysticism." This helps explain the difference between, on the one hand, the world-changing Abrahamic religions of the Near East, which were all driven by practically minded groups, from the Islamic "warriors" to the "bourgeois strata" constituting Judaism or Christianity, and, on the other, the world-fleeing Far East religions of Buddhism or Hinduism, which were carried by "intellectuals" (Weber 1978 [1920]: 253–7).

Logically prior to the distinction between carrier groups (see Schluchter 1991: 35) is that between religious "masses" and "virtuosi," which results from the "fact of the unequal religious qualification of human beings" (Weber 1978 [1920]: 259). In Weber's realist (if not cynical) view, religious "masses" always lean towards naïve affirmation of the world, and they remain stuck in a magical, pre-religious mode. Only "virtuosi" are capable of rejecting the world, and thus of becoming carriers of the great salvation religions (see Schluchter 1991: 97). Within the category of virtuosi, Weber has an eye for intra-religious struggle between "priests," who, as administrators of a religious apparatus, are naturally conservative, and "prophets," who rely not on organization but on their personal "charisma" only and whose revolutionary diction of "it is written but I say unto you" must bring them in conflict with the status quo oriented priests. Or rather, priests take over when the prophet's charisma becomes "routinized" and the problem of succession arises, a dynamic that shapes the internal history of all world religions.

Despite all significance attributed to "interests," Weber leaves no doubt that, in the end, "ideas" are primary: "Primarily [a religious ethic is] shaped by religious sources. Above all: by the content of their teaching (*Verkündigung*) and promise (*Verheissung*). Only secondarily do other spheres of interest enter, if often strongly and decisively" (Weber 1978 [1920]: 240). With respect to "ideas," one may distinguish in Weber's extraordinarily complex and dense elaborations between different *conceptions of god* and different *conceptions of salvation* underlying a religion (this distinction is explicit on p. 538). With respect to the conceptions of god, central to the Abrahamic religions is a transcendental creator God, which introduces a profound tension between religion and world, and an obligation on the part of the believer to transform the world or behavior according to His commands. By contrast, central to the Far Eastern religions, especially Confucianism, Taoism, Buddhism, and Hinduism, is a pantheistic conception of the divine, which stipulates living in harmony with the world, and contains no norm or command to change it. Distinguished from these different conceptions of god or the divine are the "type of religious promise (*Verheissung*) and of the paths of salvation determined by it" (p. 538). To talk about "salvation" requires a certain tension between the worldly order and religious values, which is weaker in the Far Eastern than in the Near Eastern religions, and which is entirely absent in Confucianism as an exceptional case of an axial-age but world-affirming rather than world-rejecting religion.

Following a proposal by Wolfgang Schluchter (1991: 89–104; also 2009: 305), one could break down the salvation component of religious ideas into different underlying notions of "human being" and "world." With respect to "human beings," they may either be a "tool" of God in terms of asceticism or a "vessel" of God in terms of mysticism; with respect to "world," it may either be a site of proving oneself or a source of danger, commanding "inner-worldly" versus "outer-worldly" stances in Weber's terms. While there is naturally an "elective affinity" (to use Weber's favorite methodological term) between certain conceptions of god, on the one hand, and conceptions of salvation (or, rather, of "human being" and "world" as its subcomponents), on the other, the two (or, rather, all three) may vary independently, which makes for a daunting number of possible combinations. Accordingly, Christianity, despite its conception of a personal creator god, which is conducive to a practical ethics of world intervention, still, of course, allows for the possibility of mysticism, and this in no small measure, including in Lutheran Protestantism, and such mysticism may, in turn, be either "inner-worldly," as in the life of the married Lutheran priest, or "outer-worldly," as in the life of the Franciscan monk.

While the thrust of Weber's comparative sociology of religion is to show variation in the behavior- and world-shaping powers of religions (in the plural) according to carrier groups and constitutive beliefs, on one remarkable occasion he engaged in a general reflection on how "religion" (in the singular) relates to the different spheres of the "world," including its economic, political, aesthetic, erotic, and theoretical knowledge spheres (Weber 1978 [1920]: 536–73). Because a central part of this famous reflection is how "religion" and "politics" relate to one another, it is necessary to look at it briefly. This so-called *Zwischenbetrachtung* (Intermediary Reflection) – which incidentally became the formal model for Habermas's equally celebrated *Zwischenbetrachtungen* in his *Theory of Communicative Action* (1980) – shows that for Weber the great world religions are all world-rejecting religions – with the one exception of Confucianism, discussion of which precedes the *Zwischenbetrachtung* in his collected sociology of religion. Hence this reflection is subtitled "Theory of the Stages and Directions of Religious World Rejection." This "contribution to a typology and sociology of rationalism" directs attention to the fact that "rationalism" for Weber is not to be narrowly identified with its means–end or instrumental variant, which has become dominant in the Occident. Instead, "rationalism" in this context refers to any attempt by religious virtuosi and intellectuals to bring religious views and ethical precepts into an "order of consequence" (*Gebot der Konsequenz*) (Weber 1978 [1920]: 537), and particularly to find meaning in a worldly existence that is permeated by suffering. While Weber, as noted above, refused to define what religion is, his answer for the great world religions (again, with the exception of Confucianism) is clear: they are a compensation for human suffering and a promise of salvation (and thus at heart a plebeian, lower-class phenomenon). This, however, brings these religions into a "permanent tension with the world and its orders" (p. 541), a tension that is all the more marked and extreme as not only religious beliefs but also the worldly orders (or "spheres") are "rationalized" on their part, in the sense that their "inner logics" are fully developed and differentiated.

In the *Zwischenbetrachtung*, Weber develops two insights of great import for gauging the relationship between religion and politics. First, the "prophecy of salvation" creates "communities on a purely religious basis," separate and apart from kinship-based and, by implication, any other kind of human association (Weber 1978 [1920]: 542). Secondly, the salvation religions are necessarily in conflict, if not incompatible, with the "political orders of the world," that is, with politics (p. 546). With respect to the first, the world-historical importance of salvation religion is to associate people apart from their "natural kinship community." It is the force to liberate people from the narrowness and circularity of clan and nature. *This*, and "only this," insists Weber (p. 542), is the meaning of the untypically ferocious New Testament verse "I did not come to bring peace, but a sword" (Matthew 10:34), because "who cannot be hostile to his housemate (*Hausgenosse*), father and mother, cannot be a follower of Jesus" (p. 542). The new religious association borrows from the old kinship association the principle of "simple reciprocity," but it differs from the latter in abandoning the old "dualism between internal and external morality," and moving toward a "universalistic brotherhood beyond all boundaries of social associations, often including the boundaries of the own faith" (pp. 543–4). This reads like a description of Christianity, but Weber sees in a "religious ethics of brotherhood," born out of "suffering" as its "constitutive principle," the essence of *all* salvation religions (p. 543). The more this "religious brotherliness" is developed, to the uttermost, of course, in Christianity, the "more severely" it has to "clash with the orders and values of the world," and more severely still to the degree that the latter *also* are "rationalized and sublimated according to their inner logics" (p. 544).

A peculiarity of Weber's depiction of the "political sphere," as one of the world's spheres with which the brotherly ethics of salvation religion must clash, is that it is thoroughly impersonal (and thus "unbrotherly") and formal-rational, much like the "economic sphere." This evidently reflects the logic of the rational bureaucratic state with its *sine ira et studio*, which in this form can be found only in the Occident. However, this is only one source of tension between religion and politics, specific to the Occident. On the part of religion, only the transition from "magic and functional-gods-religiosity," in which ethnic and religious boundaries overlapped, to "universalistic religions" with a "unified world-God" can set the religious and political collectivity on a collision course (Weber 1978 [1920]: 546). This is a question not only of particularism versus universalism, but also of the different operative principles in both spheres. Again unrelated to the specificity of the Occident, the state qua "political association" (*politischer Verband*) is based on the "naked violence of its coercive means," which is opposed to any "ethics," and to the Christian "Do not resist the one who is evil" (Matthew 5:39) at that.

These are all sources of tension that are based on *differences* between the political and religious spheres in various stages of their evolution. However, there are, in addition, subterranean *communalities* that may bring both spheres into "direct competition" with one another at *all* levels of political or religious development, but in modern times especially (Weber 1978 [1920]: 548–9). War, with its pathos of a "community unto death" (*Gemeinschaft bis zum Tode*), can lend meaning to death, conveying a sense of dying "for" something. War is redemption from the utter meaninglessness of death, particularly in "sublimated" cultures where "only a beginning" seems to be able to convey any "meaning" at all. But, in giving meaning to death, war, as a modality of politics, is in direct competition with religion: "Especially the exceptionality (*Ausser-alltäglichkeit*) of the brotherliness of war and of death in war, which is not unlike the holy charisma and the experience of the God community, drives the competition between the two to the utmost possible height" (p. 549). While this opens up a window into the common roots of religion and nationalism,[12] the notion of "direct competition" still suggests an essential difference between the two. This would notably be unthinkable for Durkheim, for whom nationalism could not be but a secularized form of religion, as both are only other ways of society celebrating itself. However, we would wish to retain the distinction because, clearly, the "brotherliness of war" has substantively little in common with the Christian gospel of "love your enemies" (Matthew 5:44).

If religion and politics are in a principled tension with one another, the question arises how this tension is resolved. "Consequent solutions" are *either* the Puritan asceticism of work, which adjusts to the "unbrotherliness" and "impersonality" of the political and economic spheres alike, and whose "particularism of grace," being available only to the preordained few and not to everyone, takes the sting of universalism, bothersome to the inherent particularism of the political, out of salvation religion; *or* the "radical anti-politism" of the mystic, who, in his search for salvation, renounces the "pragma of violence" that is intrinsic to all political action (Weber 1978 [1920]: 549). However, more common than these "consequent" solutions are some "compromise" solutions. The distinction between the two is not immediately clear – what Weber seems to call "compromise" is a kind of mutual accommodation (rather than one-sided adjustments or the lack of any adjustment) between political and religious spheres. In the Christian tradition, these compromises are above all the Lutheran "church religiosity" (*Anstaltsreligiosität*), which preaches "obedience to worldly authority," and the "organic social ethic" of medieval Thomism (pp. 550–1), which married worldly and religious inequality in a "state–church unitary culture" (Troeltsch 1994 [1912], Vol.1: 193).

To fully comprehend the distinctiveness of the religious, for which Weber has a sharper eye than Durkheim, it is helpful to refer briefly also to tensions between religion and other spheres of the world – in particular, aesthetics and eroticism – as "basically arational or anti-rational" forces (Weber 1978 [1920]: 554). More interesting than obvious differences are again hidden communalities, which Weber describes as a close "psychological nearness" (p. 556). Art, of course, differs from religion in pertaining to "form" where the latter pertains to "meaning," but in offering "inner-worldly salvation," art steps into a "direct competition" with salvation religion, and art therefore tends to be rejected by religion as blasphemy and deception.

But the most daring and extended reflection is devoted to the relationship between religion and eroticism, this "greatest irrational force of life" (Weber 1978 [1920]: 554), certainly reflecting Weber's own personal investment in this matter.[13] As in the orgiastic rites of pre-axial religion, the relationship between religion and eros was originally "very intimate" (p. 557). But even, or rather especially, in modern settings, eroticism offers "inner-worldly salvation from the rational," much like aestheticism, which brings to the fore the competitive aspect. The competitive aspect is particularly high for Christianity, because the erotic relationship offers the "insurmountable peak of fulfilling the gospel of love: the direct break-through of souls from human to human" (p. 560). The extraordinary "psychological nearness" (p. 561) between the Christian gospel of love and eros, Weber concludes in a Freudian key, has "naturally aggravated the inner enmity" of the former toward the latter.

However, the "greatest and the most principled" tension is between religiosity and the "realm of cognitive knowledge" (Weber 1978 [1920]: 564). This is ironic, if one considers Durkheim's second great insight in his sociology of religion, next to unraveling its integrative function: that in "combining what the senses had separated," religious mythology had *also* provided "a first explanation of the world" (Durkheim 1960 [1912]: 339).[14] Accordingly, there must be a hidden communality between religion and even this most patently a-religious sphere ("a-religious" at least within the ambit of modern society). Weber mentions in this respect the historical role of the priesthood as "regular carrier of learning" (1978 [1920]: 565). Not mentioned by Weber, but particularly strong, is the connection between "Christian doctrine" and the rise of modern science (Stark 2003: 147). This is because Christian doctrine "depicted God as a rational, responsive, dependable, and omnipotent being, and the universe as his personal creation, thus having a rational, lawful, stable structure, awaiting human comprehension" (p. 147). Weber is surprisingly deaf to this aspect of the matter. For him, as a result of the rise of empirical science, religion is increasingly "pushed from the realm of the rational into the irrational," and destined to be "*the* irrational and anti-rational...power par excellence" (Weber 1978 [1920]: 564). All common origins between the two spheres are finally wiped out in the "sacrifice of intellect" that religion must ask of the stubbornly religious in the age of Enlightenment – "*credo non quod, sed* quia *absurdum*" becomes the quintessentially religious attitude in the confrontation with scientific knowledge (p. 566). As the benchmark of science is not only to be rational (and thus to be impersonal) but also to be always replaced by better knowledge (and thus to be notoriously incomplete), the victory of science over religion culminates in an utterly pessimistic diagnosis of a "world domination of un-brotherliness," on the one hand, and a "devastating lack of meaning" (pp. 570–1), on the other, to which Weber sees life in modern society condemned.

After the Classics: "Secularization" and Problems of Defining and Demarcating the Religious

After Durkheim and Weber, religion disappeared from the radar of macrosociology, not to mention that it had never been central to the younger discipline of political science. With respect to political science, its "pervasive secularism in assumptions and methods" (Philpott 2009: 185) prevented "religion" from ever being taken seriously. After all, however "Protestant" its origins may have been (see Philpott 2000), the Westphalian state-system is exactly defined by subordinating religion to the state, and power and competitive self-interest have hence been the dominant categories for understanding international and domestic politics alike. With respect to sociology, its post-classical "inattention" to religion is more difficult to understand, particularly if one takes the view that "classical macrosociology was the offspring of comparative religion" (Gorski 2003: 164).

Two influential sociological works in the 1960s diagnosed an inevitable retreat of religion into the private sphere, and thus the penultimate decoupling of religion from political life (Berger 1967; Luckmann 1991 [1967]). In fact, the post-classical sociology of religion became tantamount to the study of "secularization," in a much more radical way than, of course, the classical sociology of religion had also always been about secularization. As Luckmann and Berger arrived at rather similar diagnoses of the fate of religion on the basis of very different definitions of religion, this points at unresolved conceptual issues in the sociology of religion. But it also suggests how irrelevant struggles over definition may be in the end.

Thomas Luckmann (1991 [1967]) still displays all the problems of an over-inclusive definition of religion in the wake of Durkheim, as he grounds religion not only socially (as did Durkheim) but anthropologically, in nothing less than human beings' "transcending" of nature through the construction of a world of symbolic meaning: "Religion is grounded in a basic anthropological fact: the transcending of biological nature through the human organism" (p. 108). Religion, in a nutshell, is symbolic self-transcendence. The commendable project of going beyond the narrowness of the "church sociology" of his time, and of reconnecting the sociology of religion to "general social theory" (*Gesellschaftstheorie*) (p. 61), yields a hyper-abstract view in which "everything genuinely human," that is, everything beyond mere animal life, becomes "ipso facto religious." As Peter Berger critiques this position: "It is one thing to point up the anthropological foundations of religion in the human capacity for self-transcendence, quite another to equate the two" (1967: 177). In an unclear conceptual move, Luckmann still parcels out from general "world views" (*Weltansicht*), which to him already constitute a "basic social form of religion" (1991 [1967]: 90), a more specific "holy cosmos," now in distinction from the "profane world" (p. 96), which obviously denotes the "religious" proper. However, under the contemporary conditions of "religious pluralism" and the "privatization" of religion, the "holy cosmos" becomes utterly profaned into a "warehouse of 'last meanings'" (p. 145), with an "autonomous individual" restlessly chasing the "self-realization" that is central to today's variant of the holy cosmos (pp. 153–4). If the "last meaning" for the individual now is "group sex" or any other "'ultimate' (*letztbedeutsame*) hobby," this, for all intents and purposes, is his or her "religion" (p. 150).

To escape the obvious impasse of an over-inclusive definition of religion, Peter Berger opts for a narrower, "substantive" definition of religion, as "the positing of a sacred cosmos" (1967: 177). While this sounds not unlike Luckmann's "holy cosmos," it has a rather different meaning, closer to the content of religious beliefs as elaborated by traditional German *Religionswissenschaft* (science of religion): "By sacred is meant...a quality of mysterious and awesome power, other than man and yet related to him, which is believed to reside in certain objects of experience" (p. 25). At the risk of simplifying: no religion without gods or transcendental powers. Religion is part of the larger human quest for "nomization" (p. 22), to build a shield against the "terror" and "chaos" of our random existence. In addition, and very Marxisant, Berger takes religion to be a form of "false consciousness," an (indeed, "the most powerful") "agency of alienation," by means of which the "humanly made world is explained in terms that deny its human production" (p. 89). Religion is thus, above all, a form of "legitimation," in fact, the "historically most widespread and effective" form of legitimation, because "the tenuous realities of the social world" are now grounded in a "sacred *realissimum*, which by definition is beyond the contingencies of human meanings and human activities" (p. 32). Indeed, this sounds Marxist, but for Berger this alienation via religion is no machination of the ruling class but grounded in a human condition that is desperate to tame cosmic randomness by symbolic order. His anthropological argument is obviously close to Luckmann's,[15] but the difference is that religion is never at risk of being dissolved into "'ultimate' hobbies" of the "group sex" type.

In its empirical respect, Berger's is perhaps sociology's classic statement of "secularization," which for him is above all Christianity's (more precisely, Protestantism's) self-induced retreat from religious monopoly into a "pluralistic situation" (Berger 1967: 145). Religion today is no longer a "sacred canopy," to quote the title of his classic work, that is, an "ultimate meaning binding on everybody" (p. 134), but merely "choice" or "preference" within a religious "market," or, less profanely, "a plurality of competing subworlds" (p. 152). A provocation at the time, Berger's choice of economic language to depict religion in the "pluralist situation" foreshadowed the language of rational-choice theory, which is today's dominant paradigm in the American sociology and political science of religion. However, the connotation is the opposite. For Berger, "pluralism" is a problem, because it must lead to a "crisis of credibility" (p. 127) – how can religion be "true" if there are various contenders all claiming, with equal legitimacy, to be "true"? By contrast, within the "newer paradigm" of rational choice (Warner 1993), "pluralism" is not a problem but a solution. Pluralism explains the unique vitality of American religions, which remain competitive and close to consumer preferences because they have to compete in a market. As one of the protagonists of rational-choice thinking on religion summarized the effects of "religious deregulation" in the United States, "[T]he sacred canopy was shattered, but the competing religious denominations of the free market were mobilizing people into the pew" (Finke 1990: 623–4).[16]

The rational-choice paradigm convenes with the functionalist paradigm in being agnostic about the gods or contents of religion, or rather leaving this question for the "market" to decide. But we still must dwell a bit further on the question of defining and demarcating the religious, which has never been satisfactorily resolved. As both the classical Durkheim–Weber and the more contemporary Luckmann–Berger contrasts suggested, a substantive understanding of religion has distinct advantages over a functionalist understanding, though it is not without its own pitfalls.

Berger (1967) was strongly influenced by Rudolf Otto's *The Idea of the Holy* (1963 [1917]), which is one of the most important texts of German classic *Religionswissenschaft*. Otto's work is of enduring significance for its substantive definition of religion, and for its proposition that religion and morality are separate phenomena. For Otto, the religious is at heart an experience, that of the "numinous." Otto defines it as "the sacred minus its ethical (*sittlich*) component," but also "minus its rational component" (p. 6). The original religious experience is that of "awe" (*Ergriffenheit*),[17] which Otto asks us not to mistake for "ethical elatedness" (*sittliche Erhobenheit*) (ch. 3). He specifies it as a combination of *Mysterium Tremendum* and *Mysterium Fascinans*, of simultaneous fear of and attraction to God. This echoes Martin Luther's "Small Catechism" with its running theme "We must fear and love God." Luther, indeed, had a sense for the rough-edged numinous core of the sacred, as he deemed God "more awesome (*schrecklicher*) and gruesome (*greulicher*) than the Devil," and as he raged against "Reason, the Whore" as the wrong way to get hold of Him (pp. 122 and 124). However, as Otto further argues, starting with the Old Testament, there has been a "rationalization" of the numinous. Its moment of *tremendum* took on the features of "morality," and that of *fascinans* was eventually rationalized into the "love" and "grace" of the New Testament (p. 169).[18] Only after this rationalization does the numinous become "sacred."

While, according to Otto (1963 [1917]), there *is* a moral dimension to religion, it is *not* constitutive of it. Otto even concedes that, if "demonic fear" is "at the origin of religious history," "the Devil must be older than God" (p. 160). This naturally changes in monotheist religions, where the notion of an all-powerful highest being has ethicized religion to an unprecedented degree. "Ethical" religion, argues Rodney Stark, "requires a particular conception of supernatural beings as deeply concerned about the behavior of humans toward one another," that is, a conception of God that one finds only in the "major world faiths," including Judaism, Christianity, Islam, and Hinduism (2003: 373). Conversely, "unconscious divine essences" are not sufficient for ethicizing behavior, because they are "unable to issue commandments or make moral judgments.... [O]nly beings can desire moral conformity" (p. 374). The baseline of this is that morality is only contingently attached to religion, to some religions more than to other religions, and to some religions perhaps not at all.

But the decoupling of religion and morality has worrisome consequences for the "privileging of religion," or, rather, the "exaggerated respect" that religion enjoys even in a secular and liberal state (Dawkins 2006: 44, 46). This privileging or respect tends to be grounded in the assumption that "morals and religion are inextricably joined," to quote from a famous defense of the notion that the state should legally enforce morality (Devlin 1963: 5). Even if one takes a distance from such a conservative view, religion is often presented as a "justificatory structure" (Scheffler 2007) or primordial "moral starting point" (Alasdair MacIntyre, quoted in Bedi 2007: 236), constituting the conscience of an individual that bears no compromise and stands to be protected, at least respected, in a liberal state.

Doubts about the fusion of religion and morality are warranted, not only from the vantage point of Otto's romantic *Religionswissenschaft*. Evolutionary biology suggests that morality predates religion, in terms of genetic altruism, and as a consequence has to be understood separately from religion (Dawkins 2006: ch. 6). Showing how "much of the Bible" is not only "systematically evil but just plain weird" (p. 268), at a minimum at a far distance from "modern morality" (p. 279), today's most famous religion smasher, evolutionary biologist Richard Dawkins, sharply concludes that even a "pick and choose" approach to the Holy Text requires an "independent criterion for deciding which are the moral bits" that thus "cannot come from scripture itself" (p. 275).

Overall, a substantive definition of religion helps avoid the problem of over-inclusiveness that plagues a functional definition (see Pollack 1995: 179). But it generates its own problems. Most damningly, it exposes the religious to the fundamental attack by the intellect, which of course is as old as the European Enlightenment. No one has done this with more venom than Dawkins (2006), who inherits the mantle of great debunkers of religion from Feuerbach to Marx and Freud. A substantive definition of religion inevitably leads to a "God Hypothesis," as Dawkins calls it. The problem is that it may be plain wrong. After the demise of the scholastic proofs for the existence of God, the one proof left that is commensurate with the sensitivity of modern empirical science is the sheer improbability of life on earth – a chance as high (or low) as "a hurricane sweeping through a scrapyard...[assembling] a Boeing 747" (British mathematician and astronomer Fred Hoyle, quoted by Dawkins on pp. 137–8). Its improbability allegedly suggests that life cannot but be by design. However, as Dawkins turns the tables against the "argument from improbability," the "ultimate Boeing 747" is the assumption of an intelligent designer, which is more improbable still. Instead, he argues, "We need a 'crane', not a 'skyhook', for only a crane can do the business of working up gradually and plausibly from simplicity to otherwise improbable complexity" (p. 188). This "crane" Dawkins finds in the Darwinian theory of natural selection, according to which the most complex thing of all, "creative intelligence," can only be the "end product of an extended process of gradual evolution" (p. 52).

"Religion" in this sobered perspective is explained as a "misfiring" of the brain, the "hypertrophy" of our "causal instinct," as Georg Simmel (1912: 17) once put it. Religion is the false imputation of intentionality and design that may have been useful in other (more primitive) settings. In a way, religion is the solemn version of Basil Fawlty's immortal thrashing of his defunct Austin Morris in *Gourmet Night*. Paradoxically, the impasses of a substantive definition of religion lead us back to a functional definition, which had been found wanting for other reasons.

Conclusion: Religion and Politics, Historical and Phenomenological

Discussing the problem of how to define and demarcate religion, Karel Dobbelaere and Jan Lauwers (1973/4: 546) usefully suggest that "sociologists should not look for the essence of religion," as this is a "philosophical" question. Instead, definitions of religion should be taken as "part of the social reality to be studied" (p. 550). Then these definitions vary with the "actors" promoting them and with their "position" and "situational context" (p. 446). Definitional abstinence also resonates with the practice of liberal states, which, within limits, leaves the question of how to define religion for its believers to decide. (For the reluctance of liberal courts to define religion, see Walter 2006: 204–17.)

As attractive and realistic as such agnosticism appears, the shortcomings of a functionalist definition of religion (and conversely: preference for a substantial definition) still stand out, at least when tackling the relationship between religion and politics. Martin Riesebrodt correctly pointed out (2007: 98) that with Durkheimian means it is impossible to:

- distinguish between "religious" and "political" community;
- acknowledge the fact of religious pluralism in a single society;
- keep apart "orthodoxy" and "heterodoxy" in intra-religious discourse;
- and, in general, grasp the entire dimension of power and interest in religion.

This catalogue is even short of the one deficit that, as we saw, plagues functionalist definitions at large: their comprising of things that should not be called "religious," thus stretching the term. Accordingly, any account of the relationship between religion and politics, including the one to be conducted in the following chapters, is automatically geared toward a substantive, Weberian understanding of religion, with an eye for religion's varying features over time and across places.

The best available current analysis of the role of religion in "global politics" spends barely two pages on the question of "What is religion?" and swiftly settles for a substantive definition that includes, as one of several elements, "belief in a supernatural being (or beings)" (Toft et al. 2011: 21). Without necessarily endorsing *this* definition, without a narrower, substantive definition of this *kind* one just would not be able to distinguish between "religious actors" and "political authorities" (p. 21) as distinct entities and one would miss the requisite level of concreteness for relating the two.

Monica Duffy Toft et al. (2011: ch. 3) also offer a succinct overview of the changing relationship between religious actors and political authorities over the centuries, which may provide us with a reference point, both positive and (sometimes) negative, for the chapters to follow. In their account, the earliest, *pre-modern* stage, to be found in all axial-age civilizations, is that of a "friendly merger" between religious and political actors. While there is a sense that "different people" perform "separate tasks," "mutual deference" marks the relationship between spiritual and earthly powers. Both constitute "organic, holistic systems of authority" (p. 57) in which none of them rules supreme. In the next, *early modern* stage, the friendly merger gives way to a "friendly takeover" of religious actors by the emergent sovereign state. In this period, ca. 1450 to 1750, the evolving religion–politics relationship becomes centered on Europe. Exemplified by the teachings of Machiavelli, the possibility arises for princes "not to be good" but to pursue only *raison d'état*. Still, this was a "friendly" takeover by the nascent European state. Examples are the "Gallican church" system in Catholic France or the "Erastianism" of Protestant lands, in both of which "modern religious actors were increasingly incorporated into the structures of government, and were called on to serve...as spiritual departments of the state" (p. 64).

After the French Revolution of 1789, the self-aggrandizement of the European state reaches new heights in moving from a "friendly" to a "hostile takeover" of religion (Toft et al. 2011: 65–70). The novelty is that the state no longer draws on the ideological support of religious actors and justifications but itself seeks to provide meaning and shape souls through the secular construct of nation and nationalism. The state becomes an "ideological self-provider," as Wolfgang Reinhard (1992: 254) put it. In fact a whole family of "radical secularisms," Republican, Marxist, Positivist, Nationalist, among others, now reduces religion to a merely private matter. Even though the French revolutionary hubris of a new calendar and the Cult of the Supreme Being quickly subsided, the church lastingly lost the right to perform marriages, educate the young, or own land on a large scale. Well beyond merely "separating" state and church, the new ambition was for "Caesar to decide the place of God

– and, if necessary, eliminate God's place in politics and society altogether" (Toft et al. 2011: 70). In the course of twentieth-century Communism and postwar decolonization, which were driven by secularist (Marxist or nationalist) doctrines, the "hostile takeover" expanded beyond Europe, so that between 1917 and 1967 an estimated half of the world population lived under political regimes that restricted religious liberties (p. 72).

The gist of Toft et al.'s analysis, however, is that more recently we are witnessing the rise of "politically assertive religions" (2011: 74–9), or what José Casanova (1994) called the return of "public religion." The examples abound: the Catholic Solidarity movement that brought down Communism in Poland; the revival of right-wing Evangelicalism in the United States; and, most enigmatic of all, the Islamic Revolution in Iran, which galvanized a global Islamic movement. What accounts for this revival of politically assertive or public religion, which can be observed across all the world's major religions, and which arguably is responsible for the renewed interest in religion across the social sciences? Toft et al. (2011) intriguingly point to the global spread of democracy. According to the Freedom House Index, the number of "free" or "partly free" countries expanded from 93 in 1975 to 147 in 2005 (p. 77). But the growing "independence" of religious actors from state institutions that accompanies democratization creates the space for more political assertiveness on the part of religious actors. The combination of "greater independence" from state institutions with "activist political theologies"[19] then explains why the twenty-first century will be "God's Century," not just in the Christian West, but across all axial-age civilizations (p. 82).

Underlying the bold announcement of God's Century (Toft et al. 2011) is the argument that modernization and democratization, far from causing the decline of religion, may actually effect the exact opposite. Note that of 78 "substantial democratizations" between 1972 and 2009, religious actors have played a "democratizing" role in no fewer than 48 cases (p. 93). Moreover, in 36 of these 48 cases of religious involvement at least one of the pro-democratic actors was Catholic, reflecting the Catholic Church's new enthusiasm for human rights and democracy after its momentous Second Vatican Council in the early 1960s.

But this interesting finding also creates problems for Toft et al.'s analysis (2011), because religion's "independence" from state institutions is circularly deployed as both cause and effect in religion's reappearance in global politics. Moreover, the ideational factor of "political theology," that is, of creed as it relates to politics, receives all too short shrift. To call both the Catholic Church's current human rights thinking and Salafist Jihadism's deadly ideology "activist" to denote their joint political ambition may be formally correct but it is low in information, even substantially misleading.

As political scientists and experts in international politics, Toft et al. (2011) have a keen sense of the importance of religious actors' institutional positioning, which at times yields original cross-civilizational insights.[20] Yet they lack the sociologist's eye for motivation and creed, which requires a closer attention to the "cultural stuff" of religious action (see Brubaker 2013a: 5). For a start, an institutional approach that simply lists varying religion–politics constellations over time or across places remains bland and factual if not framed by a phenomenology of religion. Only the latter shows how religion is different from other forms of human expression and claims-making, and thus is sensitive to the fact that religion generates specific problems or conflicts that other activities or forms of group formation do not. Weber (1978 [1920]) had accomplished this in his famous *Zwischenbetrachtung*, comparing the logic of "salvation religion" with the logics of other social spheres, such as economics, politics, aesthetics, and so on.

Weber's most-different-sphere comparison may be fruitfully complemented with a most-similar-sphere comparison. This would compare religion with kindred sources of cultural difference that have recently become politicized across Western societies, most notably language. Despite a mushrooming literature on multiculturalism, something as elementary as comparing religion and language with respect to their import for politics has hardly been tried (the two exceptions are Brubaker 2013a and Zolberg and Long 1998). But such a comparison bears interesting insights.

First, religion and language are similar in being "principles of vision and division" of the social world (Bourdieu, quoted in Brubaker 2013a), both having the potential to provide people with identities and sorting them into groups. In this respect, religion and language are akin to ethnicity and nationhood. However, underneath these similarities, there are important differences between religion and language that matter with respect to their potential to become politicized. Aristide Zolberg and Long Litt Woon (1998) noticed that language is "additive" while religion is "substitutive," that is, exclusive. This implies that to learn several languages is a routine expectation in developed societies, while – in monotheist contexts – one can adhere to only one religion at a time. This feature makes religion a potentially stronger identity-maker than language. Zolberg and Long further note that contemporary liberal states tend to take "assimilationist" positions on language, but "pluralist" positions on religion. That is, states expect immigrants to adopt the language(s) of host societies, simply as a matter of practical necessity because no state could operate without a specific language as the medium of communication. But no such expectation can be held with respect to immigrants adopting another religion. The "liberal" state has learned to take distance from religion over the past few centuries, with any other posture negating what "liberalism" is.

Pushing the comparison of language and religion as potential group- and conflict-makers an important step further, Rogers Brubaker (2013a) argues that religious divisions are more "robust" and "deeper" than linguistic ones, religion actually "displac[ing] language as the cutting edge of contestation over the political accommodation of cultural differ- ence in Western liberal democracies" (p. 16). Adding fuel to the drama, this diagnosis is counterintuitive if one considers the inevitable partiality of the state on language, which *should* make language "chronically politicized" (p. 5), at least under conditions of linguistic heterogeneity. And it is doubly counterintuitive if one considers the separation between religion and state and the privatization of religion that, to a degree, inevitably follow from secularization. Why, then, is religious division more "robust" and "deeper" than linguistic division? It is more *robust*, among other factors, because religion can be more easily transmitted by the family, while linguistic reproduction requires "exo-socialization," generally by state-provided institutions like schools. The differential robustness of language and religion is confirmed by the fact that second- and third-generation immigrants tend to exclusively use their host- society language and become incompetent in their origin language, while no such change is observable with respect to religious adherence (p. 9). Secondly, religious division is *deeper* than linguistic division because religion, in contrast to language, is a "structure of authority" with "intrinsic normative content" that must challenge the state in its own domain. Language, by contrast, is just a "medium of communication" that is neutral in this respect – no "conflicts of principle or world view" can arise here (p. 15). Brubaker evocatively says, with Ernest Gellner (1978) (who famously demonstrated the centrality of language in the rise of nations and nationalism), that in the case of linguistic conflict the contending parties "'speak the same language,' as it were, even when they do not speak the same language" (Brubaker 2013a: 15), which makes for less conflict than with respect to religion.

Note that this phenomenological analysis remained strictly formal, distinguishing "religion" as such from "language" as a cultural source of group identity and conflict. It abstained from drawing any distinction *within* the religious umbrella. Brubaker (2013a: 13) notices at one point that "public Islam pose[s] a particularly difficult challenge to liberal states," but does not provide the tools to understand why. Even within his chosen focus on religion and language "more generally" (p. 13), it is not clear why and how the stated shift from language to religion as "cutting edge of contestation" in contemporary liberal democracies could have occurred (p. 16). This reversal is particularly puzzling if one considers Brubaker's own (Gellnerian) exit observation that language "*should* be more deeply and chronically politicised than religion under modern conditions" (p. 5; emphasis added), and that apparently it once *was*. This is not to load a conceptual analysis with the undue expectation that it will explain historical fact. Brubaker's is an important first stab at a complex matter that awaits more complete explication, some of it to be provided in the chapters that follow.

2

Secularization and the Long Christian Exit

"Secularization" as Contested Concept

"Secularization"[1] can mean many things – if there ever was an "essentially contested concept" (Gallie 1956), here is one. In a classic discussion, José Casanova (1994: ch. 1) distinguished between three different understandings: the "decline," "privatization," or "differentiation" of religion. But he deemed only one of them, "differentiation," the uncontestable core of the "theory of secularization." Accordingly, Casanova defines secularization as the "process of functional differentiation and emancipation of the secular spheres – primarily the state, the economy, and science – from the religious sphere and the concomitant differentiation and specialization of religion within its own newly found religious sphere" (p. 19). However, as a critic of the "secularization thesis" retorted, "if this were all that secularization means, there would be nothing to argue about" (Stark 1999: 252). If not nothing, there may certainly be less to argue about than commonly thought. Indeed, Stark's response, which otherwise claimed to "carry the secularization doctrine to the graveyard of failed theories" (p. 270), throws an unwittingly critical light on the entire "debate" surrounding secularization (which, ironically, his polemical intervention helped shift to a higher gear).

42

The "secularization debate" (Gorski 2000a), it should be said, is conducted between advocates of a "rational-choice" or "supply-side" approach to religion, who argue for its unbroken vitality, and proponents of "secularization theory," who tend to argue for the opposite: the inevitable decline of religion. (For an overview from a rational-choice perspective, see Warner 1993.) But, as Philip Gorski (2000a: 143) pointed out, this oppositional line-up is misleading. Both paradigms are in reality "complementary," the supply siders arguing at the individual level of belief, but also the meso level of religious organization (and intra-religious competition), while secularization theorists argue one floor up, at the macro level of institutional differentiation, where religion is set apart from other social spheres.

Interestingly, decades before there was a "secularization debate," which was spurred by the fact that religion was not going to disappear from the modern world, Talcott Parsons had argued that the "differentiation" of the Christian religion could be accompanied by a further "institutionalization" of its values, so that as a result society could become "more Christianized than before" (1963: 57). This was more by way of a theoretical reflection on the implications of Protestant Reformation and American denominationalism than based on empirical survey evidence (which could, however, be easily procured, even half a century later; see Chaves 2011). But it is intuitively plausible that the retreat of religion into its own "religious sphere" (Casanova 1994: 19) need not imply that people are any less intensely committed to it. On the contrary, if the logic of functional differentiation holds, which stipulates the improved performance of specialized functions (see Parsons 1964), the exact opposite should be expected, as the refining of religious products and services should make them more attractive for their users, to use a bit of supply-side jargon here.

On the other hand, there *are* incompatible assumptions between the warring paradigms on secularization. Note that the main representative of classic secularization theory loudly recanted his earlier view, now declaring that "'secularization theory' is essentially mistaken" because "the world today...is as furiously religious as it ever was, and in some places more so than ever" (Berger 1999: 2). Indeed, in his classic theory, Peter Berger had complemented an institutional account of secularization, as "the process by which sectors of society and culture are removed from the domination of religious institutions and symbols" (1967: 107), with the individual-level assumption of a "secularization of consciousness." According to the latter, an "increasing number" of people in the "modern West" would live their lives "without the benefit of religious interpretations" (p. 108). This is the part of the secularization theory that the rational-choice critique has homed in on, so that there seems to be some reason for "debate" after all (Stark 1999: 252–3). But it also appears panicky, on Berger's part, to invalidate a theory that had mostly aimed at the "modern West" (Berger 1967: 108) by citing Islamic and Evangelical "counter-secularizations" mostly in other parts of the world (Berger 1999: 7).

With respect to the "modern West," recent surveys, while confirming the exceptional vitality of religious beliefs in the United States, *also* point to a growing number of "nones," that is, non-believers, though more as an internal reaction to resurgent post-1980s Evangelicalism than driven by a general secularizing logic (Putnam and Campbell 2010: 121–2). Surely, there are dubious aspects of Berger's secularization theory, such as the assumption that the "rise of science" would spread an atheist outlook (Berger 1967: 107), that *canard* of the Enlightenment critique of religion,[2] which rational-choice adepts and others have demolished with joy and, one must say, good evidence (see Stark 2003: ch. 2).[3] But Berger's main argument of a "sacred canopy," in which religion is a world-making imperative (and thus not even visible *as such*), having given way to a "pluralist situation" (Berger 1967: 135), in which religion is "choice" (p. 152), seems incontrovertible. Who would doubt *that*? In fact, Berger anticipated, in so many fewer pages, Charles Taylor's monumental account of our "secular age," as the "move from a society where belief in God is unchallenged...to one in which it is understood to be one option among others" (Taylor 2007: 3). Berger also depicted the coming of the secular age as the predominantly "Christian" story that Taylor would tell later.

If one is well advised to be less readily revisionist with respect to classic secularization theory, one must also cast doubt on Casanova's (1994: ch. 1) reduction of the "secularization" concept to a hard "differentialist" core and his discarding of the further "decline of religion" and "privatization" assumptions. This revisionist move is one with which hardly anyone disagrees today and that has made Casanova's the canonical statement on the subject. However, it does not entirely convince. How can the retreat of religion into a narrowly "religious sphere" not be considered its "decline"? Once religion was everything, now it is just something and nothing for many as well. This is surely what common sense would call "decline." Moreover, "privatization," the second "moment" of secularization theory that is thrown out by Casanova, which claims that religion becomes "subjective" and "depoliticized," seems to be logically connected to differentiation. Privatization is just another word for religion's withdrawing into its proper sphere and no longer constituting a "sacred canopy" for society as a whole. Religion is now being looked to only if people choose it, and in the sense of being choice it is "private." Rather than acknowledge the fact, Casanova fashionably demolishes the "liberal" private–public distinction, with the help of a feminist-cum-republican-style "redrawing of the boundaries" (p. 43). This is conceptually necessary for his grand return of "public religion," at the level not of the "state" but of "civil society," that "amorphously complex, yet autonomous sphere...between public and private proper" (p. 42). Having pushed the door open and made "public religion" the default option in contemporary scholarship, Casanova (2006) would later consider this move as still too cautious – why "restrict...public religion to the public sphere of civil society" (p. 21), if a "complete separation" between state and religions has proved to be not necessary for democracy?[4]

There may be good reasons to argue thus, but it does not require throwing out the privatization thesis. On the contrary, a variant of it is necessary to grasp the modality of the religious in a "secular age," as described by Charles Taylor (2007). For Taylor, the secular is not about a first-order "falling off of religious belief and practice" (p. 2) but about the second-order "conditions of belief" (p. 3). If belief, however strongly one may adhere to it, cannot be anything more than an "option" (p. 3), with the "presumption of unbelief" now being "dominant," private religion is the necessary starting point (as well as endpoint for most) for any further "public" claim raised in religion's name. In a nutshell, the assumptions of differentiation, decline, and privatization underlying or entailed by the process of secularization come as a package that cannot be slickly sliced for the sake of rendering "public religion" plausible.

Reconnecting to our discussion of "religion" in Chapter 1, it is important to note that the concept of secularization logically requires a substantive definition of religion – otherwise there would be nothing to "subtract" or no "grounding" for the process to unfold, as one could put it with Taylor (2007). Accordingly, Steven Bruce intuitively starts off his recent "defense" of secularization theory with a "substantive" definition of religion (2011: 1), and Karel Dobbelaere explicitly argues that, for understanding secularization, "we need, indeed, a substantive, exclusive, and real definition of religion as a baseline" (2009: 600). Talal Asad's (2003) critical genealogy of the secular also has no patience with a functionalist understanding of religion, according to which, say, the "gravity of high politics" is equivalent to the "solemnity of high worship"[5] (though his real intention is the opposite, to debunk "secularism" as a Christian doctrine that does not travel well to other religious contexts).

While the Christian origins of secularization are incontrovertible, even to the degree that it can be argued that the concepts of "secular" and "religion" logically imply one another (Asad 2003: 200), it does not follow that its provincial genesis vitiates the validity of the secular as a necessary feature of a democratic society. Charles Taylor argued plausibly that secularism "has Christian roots, but it is wrong to think that this limits the application of its formulae to post-Christian societies" (1998: 31). Taylor grounds the necessity of the secular in the nature of the modern democratic state, in which citizenship constitutes a direct link between individual and state, short of the intermediations that had marked a feudal "society of orders." Modern society, to introduce Taylor's catchy term, is a "horizontal, direct access society" (pp. 38–40). This society requires, first, a "certain degree of commitment on the part of its citizens," a "patriotism" or "citizen identity" that takes precedence over other identities (p. 43); and, secondly, a non-sectarian idiom for public debate that is shared by all, above religious lines. In sum, "both the sense of mutual bonding and the crucial reference points of the political debate that flow from it have to be accessible to citizens of different confessional allegiances, or of none" (p. 46). In this sense, Taylor insists, "secularism is not optional in the modern age" (p. 48).

However, as if struck by guilt over so blunt a line, Taylor (1998) steps back with respect to the question of how to arrive at secularism. Surely, a "common ground strategy" of building a "deist" consensus, which had guided the early American republic and is echoed in the idea of "civil religion" (Bellah 1967), is vitiated by increasing pluralism that must reckon with non-believers (and non-deist believers), who would be excluded this way. However, Taylor also finds fault with an "independent political ethic" strategy, pioneered in Grotius's famous diction *etsi deus non daretur* ("and if there were no God"), which forces people to abstract from their religious beliefs, or rather to limit them to private life. In a context of pluralism, argues Taylor (1998: 37), this second strategy would entail the "imposition of one metaphysical view over others," this time the atheists pushing aside the religionists, as in the founding of the French republic and its ongoing doctrine of *laïcité*. Instead, Taylor proposes a third strategy of "overlapping consensus," which he borrows from John Rawls (1993). It "lifts the requirement of a commonly held foundation" (Taylor 1998: 38) and allows people to agree on shared political principles *from within* their religious beliefs. This way of arriving at secularism precisely mirrors, and affirms, Rawls' evolution from "metaphysical" to "political" liberalism. But it also inherits its problems, particularly the charge of incoherence.[6] To proclaim this third strategy as not optional but as the way that "must be followed" (p. 38) is a touch too strong. It confounds the necessity for secularism with one (ideal, perhaps idealistic) way of getting there, unduly narrowing the range of historical possibilities and being hopeful about the civic-ness of whatever may pass as "religion."

The Christian Origins of Secularization[7]

This is not to distract from Taylor's (1998) powerful assertion of the necessity of secularism, however parochial and historically specific its origins may be. But what exactly are these origins? It is apposite to trace in very broad brushstrokes the ways in which Christianity, and only it (corroborated by occasional asides to Islam), has propelled secularization, which entailed not just its but *all* religions' exit from the political stage. Christianity was, as Marcel Gauchet put it pointedly, "a religion for departing from all religion" (1997 [1985]: 4). Only against this backdrop does one realize the provocation of "public religion," which has so much become the default assumption today that not it but its opposite, "secularism," has acquired the touch of the exotic, if not the rigid and fanatic that more often than not the religionists had excelled in.

A depiction of the long Christian exit, as I shall attempt in the following, must be equally attentive to the religious ideas that limit the range of possibilities and to their contingent realization in historical time – following the dialectic of ideas and interests that had been the lodestar of Weber's sociology of religion.

Etymology

The easiest way to catch the Christian origins of the concept of secularization is to scrutinize the roots of the word itself.[8] The Latin word *saeculum* is "one term of a dyad" (Taylor 2011: 32), literally meaning "century," the other term of the dyad being eternal, sacred time. The original formulation is by Augustine, for whom the *saeculum* was profane time in distinction from *eschaton* as sacred time, marking the period between the fall into sin and the second coming of Christ (Gorski and Altinordu 2008: 60).

A second moment in the evolution of the concept is in early medieval church law (canon law), where secularization referred to the return of monks from their secluded life in a monastery to living as parish priests in lay society. A *saecularis* or *canonicus* was a *Weltgeistlicher* (worldly cleric), still subject to the rules of the church, but no longer a *regularis*, who is subject to the stricter though "regular" (that is, generally expected) condition of a cleric living as member of a fraternal order (Conze et al. 1984: 795–8).

A third moment in the evolution of "secularization" occurred during the Reformation, where it referred to the expropriation of Catholic Church property by worldly rulers in Protestant lands, or, legally speaking, the transformation of *bona ecclesiastica* into *bona saecularia* (Conze et al. 1984: 799). Into the early modern period the Catholic Church was Europe's biggest property holder, owning a third of the land within the Holy Roman Empire of the German Nation, including a quarter of the property in the cities (Philpott 2000: 210). More than that, bishops acted as sovereign rulers in so-called "spiritual principalities" (*geistliche Fürstentümer*) within the Empire. These religious mini-states were abolished in the last legal act of the outgoing Empire, imposed by Napoleonic France, the so-called *Reichsdeputations-hauptschluss* (RDH) of February 1803, which also transferred all church properties into the hands of worldly rulers. While a neutral term within canon law, in this period the notion of "secularization" took on a pejorative hue, which it already had had for Augustine, but now connoting "legal dubiousness" and "loss of cultural patrimony" (Conze et al. 1984: 806).

Only in a fourth moment of its evolution did the concept of secularization become uncoupled from church law and take on properly "secular" meanings. At first, it referred to a teleological understanding of history within the post-Enlightenment philosophy of history. For Hegel, *Verwelt-lichung* (secularization) meant the realization of the Christian idea of freedom in the principle of the modern state. In his effusive conception, Christianity was no longer merely "religion" but had become "principle of the world and the state" (Conze et al. 1984: 813). While Marx had only bad things to say about religion and Christianity (as we showed in Chapter 1), he inherits the crypto-theological tradition of "world history as salvation history" (Löwith 1953), in which "progress" steps in for the biblical hope of "salvation."

But to inject a higher meaning into history, and thus to sacralize it, obscures the true novelty, which Charles Taylor dates as early as the seventeenth century: this novelty is to conceive of the secular as "all there was," "profane time without any reference to higher time" (2011: 32). Now, "mutual benefit" and "humanism" advance as exclusive goals of human association, without any reference to a transcendent order. The novel way of understanding the "secular" is, as it were, to discard the other part of the dyad, and to stipulate an "immanent frame" (Taylor 2007: ch. 15).

Commenting on the changing meaning of secularization, Talal Asad sharply observed its transition from a traditional context, in which religion was dominant, to a modern context, in which the secular dominates, as the "ground from which theological discourse was generated" (2003: 192). If once religion produced the secular, in the "discourse of modernity" it is the other way around, the secular generates religion. At worst, religion now figures as "false consciousness" from which the "secular" had luckily emancipated itself. At best, religion is "enlightened and toler-ant," giving in to be reduced to a merely "religious" sphere, on *this* side of the private–public divide and separate from politics, economics, and so on, as the only form in which religion is accepted today. In Asad's radical, postmodern view, "religion" has no essence; it dissipates into "discourse" and in its irremediably Christian, self-limiting tilt cannot be extended to other religions, above all not to Islam. But what, then, *is* Islam (and any non-Christian religion), if not "religion"? While Asad forcefully anticipates Charles Taylor's critique of the "subtraction story" of secularization,[9] he boxes himself into an untenable relativism. If he depicts Islam and Christianity as categorically "alter" (p. 169), he natur-ally attributes this to the exclusive and identity-building needs of "Europe." But the radical "alterity" between the two springs more from his own approach than from any underlying reality.

The gospel of Jesus

When turning from the etymology to the history of secularization, the first step is to identify certain elements of the Christian religion that mark it as different from other world religions and, in delimiting the realm of the possible, have functioned as "tracklayers of history" (Mann 1986: 341, borrowing the term from Weber).

Ernst Troeltsch identified as the "content of the gospel of Jesus" a "religious communism of love" (1994 [1912], Vol. 1: 41), which is other-worldly oriented. "Nowhere is there mention of the state," observes Troeltsch (p. 45), and there is a "complete lack of a program of social renewal" (p. 48). Jesus had not founded a "social movement"; instead, the salvation he promised was a "purely inward, ethical, and spiritual" matter (pp. 16–17). In a nutshell, the "sociological structure" of the Christian gospel is "individualism" and "universalism" (p. 41). Few would argue with this characterization, which sets Christianity apart from the collectivistic and particularistic, and thus more directly politi-cal, logic of its direct ancestor, Judaism: "The realm of God (*Gottesreich*) announced by Jesus is the reign (*Herrschaft*) of God and not of the Jewish people" (p. 45).

At the same time, the Christian gospel contains "few prescriptions" for the "formation of the religious community" (Troeltsch 1994 [1912], Vol. 2: 967). This community formed only after Christ, through the "belief in Jesus" (p. 967). Ingeniously combining an emphasis on ideas with one on social organization, Troeltsch distinguishes between three types of Christian organization, church, sect, and mysticism, which have generated rather different, if not radically opposite, interpretations of the gospel and of the believer's relation to the world (pp. 965–86). From a church point of view, Christ is "savior"; for the sect, he is "master"; for the mystic, he is "pious sentiment." The "idea of salvation" differs accordingly: for the church, salvation has already been accomplished for all in the death of Christ, and it is now routinely administered and passed on through the church sacraments; for the sect, salvation is yet to come in the return of Christ and the erection of his realm; for the mystic, salvation is the recurrent union of his soul with God. But most importantly, for our purposes, the relationship to the "state" and attitudes toward "tolerance" differ according to type of organization and community: the church claims "absolute truth" to which all have to be converted, which entails conformity to the state as the necessary instrument for implementing this truth; the sect exists "besides" state and society, demanding "freedom from" the state and "toleration" rather than collaboration with the state in the spreading of the truth, as the church would; the mystic likewise relates negatively to the state, demanding tolerance and the freedom of conscience. This echoes Georg Jellinek's (1904: 90) notion of the "religious origins" of the idea of human rights, which Troeltsch dates back long before the democratic revolutions in France and America, to the "Reformation and its struggles."

So there is a bewildering variety of belief, practice, and relating to the world that all go under the "Christian" name. Troeltsch still identifies a core "Christian ethos": that of "rising above the world without negating the world" – *this* he deems the source of Christianity's "pan-historical, universal value" (1994 [1912], Vol. 2: 979).

Dualism

With a sharper sense of paradox, and a loftier imagination, Marcel Gauchet characterized as "axiomized ambiguity" the Christian's simultaneous being in the world and out of the world. Gauchet locates the doctrine of Incarnation at the source of this ambiguity. God's becoming human in Christ "made the Christian into a being torn between a duty of belonging and one of distancing, between forming an alliance with the world and being estranged from it" (1997 [1985]: 131). The Incarnation created a "split" between two realities: God became "wholly other" in no longer being accessible to humans except through his son (and the institution built in his name, the church), while the "terrestrial sphere" was upgraded in that it "gain[ed] enough dignity for the Word to become flesh" (p. 77).

Gauchet (1997 [1985]) calls this condition "dualism," in a rather more specific but also more radical sense than *all* axial-age religions may be called "philosophically dual" (Mann 1986: 365). Through the Incarnation, both spheres, the godly and the terrestrial, could not be rendered into a hierarchy and thus a unity. Jesus' God, after all, was "not the totally superior being, but the absolute other." This makes for "two coexisting systems of requirement" (p. 133). The Incarnation entailed a "de-hierarchization" of godly and worldly spheres, and henceforth "Christianity always kept the two spheres separate" (p. 134). The most momentous implication is for the legitimation of political rule. "After Christ," Gauchet brilliantly argues, "no one could simultaneously be both priest and king," that oldest condition where religion and politics were one. This is because "the place of the perfect mediator had been occupied" (p. 139). In principle, power now had to be differently legitimized, eventually as "representation." To reduce somewhat the audacity (more bluntly: the empirical incorrectness) of this claim, Gauchet concedes that this fact "remained concealed for a long time" (p. 140). Prevented from occupying the place of Christ, the king could only try to be "*like* Christ," with the new and very concrete risk that what "sustained" the Christian monarch was also likely to "dislodge" him, an unthinkable possibility as long as the king was god (pp. 140–1).

Dualism allowed the Christian to handle multiple affiliations and requirements flexibly, foreshadowing the modern condition. In one of his most valuable writings, Talcott Parsons noted that conversion to Judaism "meant accepting full membership in the total Jewish community," while a converted Christian "could remain a Roman, a Corinthian, or whatever" (1963: 42). This contrast could also be drawn with Islam, which makes the oneness of God (*Tawhid*) its badge of distinction from Christianity.[10] Christianity is the only monotheism where there is no "absorption of the secular society into the religious community," but instead "acceptance of the fundamental differentiation between church and state" (pp. 42–3).

"Dualism" is a first stab at delineating the specificity of Christianity that would make it conducive to secularization. As we saw, any such reflection immediately leads us to contrast Christianity with other religions, most notably Islam, which took rather different directions. This comparison is not inopportune because Islam is often at the forefront of concerns that "public religion" may be difficult to reconcile with liberal principles, while Christianity is much less mentioned in this context (e.g., Brubaker 2013a: 13). One rightly wants to know whether there are good reasons for this. In tackling this delicate question, however, one is well advised to start at the opposite end, by mapping the similarities rather than the differences between the two religions. In his monumental comparison of the world's axial-age civilizations, which goes under the understated title *The Sociology of Philosophies*, Randall Collins remarkably finds that Islam and Christianity are "equally West" (1998: 451). This springs to the eye when comparing the two with the *really* different Far Eastern "philosophies" of Buddhism and Brahmanism. According to Collins, both Islam and Christianity merged the same two traditions of the "politicized, socially activist monotheism" of Yahweh and the "sophisticated abstractions" of the Greeks (p. 451). More concretely, one finds in both religions the same four strands of rational theology, scriptural literalism, Greek philosophy, and mysticism. What differed were not so much these ingredients and conflicts surrounding them, but their long-term *outcomes*. In this plausible, contingency-affirming optic, the trajectory of Islam still appears as the "bad dream of the West," showing what Christendom would look like if the "theological conservatives" had won the fight (p. 451).

In the spirit of not reifying their differences, let us lay out some further elements that help explain why only Christianity would engender secularization, with some references to why Islam would not.

The church

Next to "dualism," the "church" is the second key factor that makes Christianity distinct. The church, of course, is only another, institutional, name for dualism. While just one of three types of Christian organization and community according to Troeltsch (1994 [1912]), the church is still that "absolutely original creation" (Gauchet 1997 [1985]: 79) that no other religion has brought forward. It is described by Gauchet as a "systematic project for recruiting and training souls by bureaucratizing interpretation" (p. 80) and a "first administration of ultimate meaning" (p. 135). In monopolizing dogma, the church made "heresy" a permanent possibility: "No clergy, no Reformation," as Gauchet says, with a nod to Islam (p. 80). The church is an expression of Christian dualism, in that it divides *this* world into two spheres ruled by two authorities, religious and political. In stipulating that a relation to God could only be had through mediation of the church, the church accomplished the "differentiation of Christianity as a religious system (a cultural system) from the conception of a 'people' as a social system" (Parsons 1963: 40). This is the Parsonian reformulation of the famous New Testament formula, "Render unto Caesar the things that are Caesar's." In the medieval period institutional dualism was enshrined in fifth-century Pope Gelasius' famous doctrine of the "two swords" with which God ruled the world, the *auctoritas* of the church and the *potestas* of the king. While the line between the two powers was notoriously contested, the church even having the upper hand over the king from the eleventh to the thirteenth centuries (see below), the important matter is the very existence of a line. Even at the height of its powers, the church never claimed to replace the king. In monopolizing religious authority within society, the church "ipso facto defines the rest of society as 'the world,' as a profane realm at least relatively removed from the jurisdiction of the sacred" (Berger 1967: 123).

In his classic study of the medieval origins of the modern state, Joseph Strayer similarly argued that the church's victory over the question of who had the right to appoint the pope, in the so-called "Investiture Struggle" of the eleventh and twelfth centuries, "unwittingly sharpened concepts about the nature of secular authority," and that the "Gregorian concept of the Church almost demanded the invention of the concept of the state" (1970: 22). More than that, the medieval church in many ways looked like a state itself, providing a template for the emergent state, with its involuntary membership, bureaucracy, system of rationalized laws and courts, and taxation; the pope at times even had an army (Strayer 1958: 39). While this made for a uniquely "long and complicated process" of settling the relations with political authority, which "no other religion" had known in this extremity, the important thing, again, is that the church "never took over all the functions of the State" (p. 39). The primordial coexistence of church and state forced both of them back on themselves from early on, namely, to define clearly what only it and not the other was, and to nervously guard the boundaries that guaranteed their separate existence.

By contrast, Islam, not having a church, needed the state in a much more direct and elementary way to implement and police the creed. In Islam, political rulers had to do the job that in Christianity was the church's: uphold religious law, appoint religious judges, and so on (see Collins 1998: 460). The lack of a church, of course, reflected the political history of Islam, its Prophet being "simultaneously a military and a political ruler," and a most successful one at that (p. 460). Islam's intrinsic "political connection" (p. 460) obliterated the need for a separate bureaucratic organization. As a result, there could not be conflict between religious and political institutions, simply because religion did not have independent institutional substance – in Parsonian terms, it was not "differentiated" as a cultural system from the social system but remained identical with society at large. On the other hand, "the state had to be a Mohammedan state; neutrality or hostility to the established religion was unthinkable" (Strayer 1958: 43). Here is one explanation why today we no longer have "Christian states" in Christian-majority societies, not even where Christianity is an officially "established" religion, while the majority of states in Muslim-majority societies are either "Islamic states" or, when secular, more closely and protectively aligned with Islam than any Western state would ever dare to be aligned with Christianity.

In his punchy comparison of Christianity, Islam, and the political state religions of classical Greece and Rome, Joseph Strayer (1958) identifies the Islamic as the "most common pattern in history." This is a pattern in which religion is neither "state-controlled," as in classic Greece or Rome, nor "a state in itself," as in medieval Christianity, but where religion "harmonizes with its society without being entirely dominated by it, which is a moral force..., but which becomes a political force only in exceptional circumstances" (p. 43). In this mellow description Islam is not the primary candidate for "public religion" that it appears to be today. This is simply because in its indigenous setting, Islam's public status goes without question; there is no need to raise it as a claim.

One last feature of the Catholic Church that appears anachronistic today should be mentioned for its autonomy-generating but also self-limiting effects: celibacy. Through celibacy the church could not be a counter-society within society, a quasi-"people," because it remained dependent for its reproduction on secular society – it always had to be "of" society but could never become "society" itself. Positively formulated, celibacy allowed the church to become differentiated from family, kinship, and community ties, making it universalistic in orientation and potentially open to all, a "model of social organization" for secular society, as Talcott Parsons put it evocatively (1963: 46). In a society of heritage, clerical celibacy constituted a harbinger of things to come, "a universalistic basis of role allocation manifested in careers open to talent" (p. 46). The stupendous wealth- and knowledge-producing wonders of the Catholic Church, which are without parallel, probably cannot be separated from the peculiar prohibition of its personnel from getting married and procreating. By contrast, the Islamic *ulama* but also the Jewish rabbis, for whom no celibacy rule existed, would retain organic ties with their respective communities. This potentially allowed them to become religious, legal, and political leaders all in one, but through being close to their communities, *ulama* and rabbis could only support "particularism" and "traditionalism" (Collins 1998: 460).

Natural law

Next to dualism and church organization, a third element that made Christianity prone to a secularizing logic was its early embracing of natural law as a second source of law, alongside revealed law or religious law proper. This is a case where, initially, Islam and Christianity had similar potentiality, which, however, only the latter managed to exploit. In early Islam, there was a momentous confrontation between the adherents of rational theology, the so-called "Mu'tazilites," the earliest school of Islamic thinking, and the scriptural literalism of hadith scholars, who emerged in critical reaction to the Mu'tazilites. The Mu'tazilites, inspired by Greek philosophy, took positions that are strikingly progressive and modern: they defended free will, held that God does no evil, that "good" and "bad" are not arbitrary categories and thus accessible to human reason, and that God is rational (Collins 1998: 397). To this the literalist hadith scholars retorted that human free will would limit the will of God, and that calling Him "loving" or "rational" and considering "good" and "bad" objective categories would unduly restrict His power. God is so powerful that He could have wanted everything to be the opposite, quite literally, "good" to be "bad." Accordingly, revelation, the study of God's word as it was dictated by Him to the Prophet in the Qur'an, is the only access to truth. Crucial for the success of the traditionalists, in the early 900s there was a split within the rationalist Mu'tazilites, with the great Islamic scholar al-Ash'ari denouncing his old friends and affirming, with the traditionalists, that the Qur'an was not created. Henceforth the conservative Ash'aris would constitute the Islamic mainstream. Their position was canonized by the influential eleventh-century Islamic scholar al-Ghazali, in a work tellingly titled "The Incoherence of Philosophy." Paradoxically, with the means of acute logical reasoning al-Ghazali established that "possibility" must be prior to "necessity" (the latter being a purely logical relation), and that the world could only have come into existence through a "voluntary" cause, God's will (Collins 1998: 422). With al-Ghazali's final nail in the coffin of rationalist theology, Collins observes, the "innovative struggle" between competing schools in Islam was finished. "Voluntarism" came to constitute the "orthodox culture of Islam" that is still with us today (p. 452).[11]

Interestingly, in Christian thought the thirteenth- to fourteenth-century scholars Duns Scotus and William of Occam formulated "voluntarist" positions that were very similar to that of the Islamic Ash'aris. However, they remained marginal to a Christian mainstream that was dominated by Thomas Aquinas. Aquinas incorporated Aristotle into the Roman Catholic legal tradition, to the effect that there were two systems of divine law, with divine *natural* law in addition to divine *revealed* law (see Ferrari 2012a). Aquinas' momentous achievement was to marry Greek philosophy, with its idea that the world is eternal, infinite, and in its existence necessary, with the Jewish-Christian view of the world as a historical entity created by God. The latter is not a philosophy, as Alan

Ryan correctly observed, but "a historical, particularistic creed [that] rests on revelation" (2012: 231). *Gratia naturam non tollit sed perfecit* (grace does not destroy nature but perfects it): this was Aquinas' synthesis of metaphysics and faith. Armed with Aristotle, Aquinas could argue that good and evil, right and wrong are objective categories that can be apprehended by human reason, even without any intervention by divine revelation. Divine natural law is given by God through His creation, and it is accessible through the rational faculties that every human being is endowed with qua having been created in the image of God. While divine revealed law is limited in its application to the faithful, divine natural law extends to the lives of all human beings, believers and non-believers. As the *Catechism of the Catholic Church* (no. 1956) formulated it, "[T]he natural law, present in the heart of each man and established by reason, is universal in its precepts and its authority extends to all men. It expresses the dignity of the person and determines the basis for his fundamental rights and duties" (quoted in Ferrari 2012a: 5, fn. 10). Certainly, "natural sin" clouded human rationality and necessitated the intervention of Church authority to define its contents *erga omnes* (that is, as valid for all), but this definition still had to meet the test of human reason.

As Silvio Ferrari argues, the Roman Catholic recognition of natural law as a second source of divine law made the development toward a secular state possible. This is because it allowed non-believers to be treated on a basis of equality, anticipating the possibility of attributing equal civil and political rights to citizens independently of their religion, which is the hallmark of the secular state (Ferrari 2012a: 12). Note, for instance, that in the Jewish legal tradition, which, like Islam, acknowledges only divinely revealed but not natural law, the prohibition of usury only applied to intra-Jewish relations, while non-Jews could be charged interest. By contrast, in Christianity this prohibition from the start was understood as a principle of divine natural law, and therefore extended to all people, including non-believers (p. 7, fn. 15). Not having a source of law or moral principles to treat non-believers on a par with believers, the Islamic legal tradition could treat the "other" not in terms of equality but only in terms of "diversity and separateness" (p. 13). This is expressed in the notions of *dhimmi* and *millet*. They allow a modicum of religious freedom and self-determination for non-believers but only attribute to them a second-class membership in the political community. Even the refusal of today's European states to still define themselves in Christian terms, and the opposite propensity of contemporary states in Muslim-majority societies to define themselves as nonchalantly Islamic, may be attributed to the presence or absence, respectively, of a natural law tradition.[12]

Legal pluralism

Finally, "legal pluralism" is a fourth important element for understanding how Christianity was conducive to secularization. The "legal" part matters as much as the "pluralism" part in this composite term. With respect to the first, law seems at first a most unlikely idiom to be advanced by Christianity, whose ethic of "melting all divisions in the fire of God's love...does not know law (*Recht*) and the struggle for rights (*Kampf ums Recht*)" (Troeltsch 1994 [1912], Vol. 1: 331). Indeed, it is not Christianity at large but a distinct segment of it, the Catholic Church, in a distinct moment of its development, which matters here. Concretely, only the eleventh-century "Papal Revolution," which Harold Berman importantly established as the "first of the great revolutions of Western history" (1983: 520), made "Christianity into a political and legal program" (p. 528). Not only did the church in this moment pioneer the ideas of rule *by* law, of policy-making in the medium of law, and of rule *of* law, the idea that rulers are bound by law, it also pioneered the idea that law's reign was to be divided into a plurality of jurisdictions, whereby we arrive at the second element of the composite term "legal pluralism." As Berman argues in his seminal work, "[P]erhaps the most distinctive characteristic of the Western legal tradition is the coexistence and competition within the same community of diverse jurisdictions and diverse legal systems. It is this plurality of jurisdictions and legal systems that makes the supremacy of law both necessary and possible" (p. 10). Legal pluralism is a "source of freedom" (p. 10), as the same individual can escape the grip of one regime through resorting to the other, and as these legal regimes control one another. The origin of legal pluralism is the differentiation of the church as an autonomous institution ruled by its own law, canon law, during the Papal Revolution. Only this differentiation created the possibility of a purely secular order. Berman likens the event to an "atomic explosion that split Germanic Christendom into two parts: the church and the secular order" (p. 531).

With its canon law, which incorporated and systematized the tradition of Roman law, the early medieval church developed a model of law that could be applied to other spheres and that in fact anticipated the modern legal state (*Rechtsstaat*). Constitutive of this model of law is the idea of "legal" as a separate and autonomous institution administered by its own special corps, "lawyers," who are educated in legal science; that law is an integrated system (*corpus juris*) with an ongoing character and a history; that law binds politics and the state (constitutionalism); and, as mentioned, that law is embedded in a plurality of jurisdictions and legal systems (Berman 1983: 9–10). Of particular importance are constitutionalism and pluralism, which are interlocking principles. Constitutionalism is, most generally, a check on absolutism. As Berman argues, "[T]he very separation of ecclesiastical and secular authority was a constitutional principle of the first magnitude, which permeated the entire system of canon law" (p. 214). Constitutionalism as self-limitation naturally engenders pluralism, in which "none of the coexisting legal systems claimed to be all inclusive or omnicompetent" (p. 225).

The church's canon law claimed jurisdiction only over specially designated areas, never social life as a whole, and the church in turn expected the state to accept these prerogatives as lawful limitations of its own power. Concretely, in the twelfth century, church courts claimed jurisdiction over all civil and criminal cases involving clerics; all matrimonial cases, which derived from the church sacrament of marriage; all testamentary and inheritance cases, as the making of a will was considered a religious act; certain criminal cases, that is, those involving "sinful" behavior (heresy, sacrilege, usury, homosexuality, adultery, etc.); and certain contract and property cases, that is, those involving breach of a pledge of faith (perjury) (see Berman 1983: 260–1). These claimed jurisdictions were certainly not always accepted by secular rulers and often subject to acrimonious conflict (ch. 7). But one sees the self-limiting reach of church law, which never claimed to be about everything.

At the same time, canon law, with its systemic and rationalized character, provided a model for the rise of parallel secular legal systems: feudal law (within the upper class), manorial law (between peasants and lords), mercantile, urban, and royal law – all of which derived important inputs, even personnel, from the church because most lawyers at the time were clerics. Of particular interest in this respect is urban and royal law.

Since Max Weber (1976 [1921]: 727–814), we have known of the importance of the occidental city for the rise of freedom – *Stadtluft macht frei* (city air liberates). Berman (1983: 361–3) goes beyond Weber in linking the rise of cities to the Papal Revolution with its twin factors of "religion" and "law." Cities, argues Berman, were inspired by the religious zest of reforming and redeeming the world that was set free in the medieval reform of the church, yet in a secular space of plural jurisdictions that was *also* created by it, by means of rational law (for which the Roman-law-inspired canon law provided the model). The rise of cities is thus intrinsically linked to the religious, political, and legal dimensions of the Papal Revolution (pp. 400–1).

Royal law, the law of the emergent territorial state, is even more directly implicated with the Papal Revolution, in that the king now "was no longer the supreme head of the church" but set to be a purely secular figure (Berman 1983: 404). Yet he learned to compensate for this loss of function through increasing his power over other secular polities, feudal, urban, and even imperial. The close connection between the Papal Revolution and state-making is brought home in the peculiar story of the Norman Kingdom of Sicily, Europe's first territorial state, which, of course, has long since disappeared. This kingdom resulted from Pope Gregory VII's calling the Normans for help against Henry IV, ruler of the Holy Roman Empire of the German Nation, Europe's most important political structure at the time. Accordingly, "by recognizing each other's legitimacy, the pope and the Norman ruler of Sicily established the first two modern states in Europe; the one an ecclesiastical state, the other a secular state" (p. 412). The rise of the sovereign state would obviously moderate, but could not eradicate, what Berman considers "the unique feature of the law of Western Christendom": the fact that "the individual person lived under a plurality of legal systems, each of which governed one of the overlapping subcommunities of which he was a member" (p. 395).

Dualism, church organization, natural law, and legal pluralism are elements of Christianity that made it conducive to secularization, the retreat of religion into a properly religious sphere that is entailed by societal differentiation. This is certainly a partial view, which focuses only on the institutional dimension of linking – or rather separating – religion and state. We have left out all non-religious factors that mattered in this process, not to mention the historical detail. A more complete understanding of the – often ironical and backtracking – dynamics of secularization requires, at a minimum, the singling out of two crucial phases in the evolving relationship between Christianity and state: medieval Christian civilization and the Protestant Reformation.

No Dark Age: Medieval Christian Civilization

In their global historical synopsis of the religion–state relationship, Toft et al. (2011: 53) characterized its pre-modern phase as a "friendly merger," where religious actors provide "ideological" support for political rulers, while rulers reciprocate with "material" support for religion. This account, which draws a sweeping continuity from the axial-age civilizations to the rise of the sovereign territorial state ca. 1450, obscures the "radical discontinuity" (Berman 1983: 23) that was brought about by the Papal Revolution. The latter prepared the secularization of political rule, radically dividing the religio-political world into a Before and an After, and it enabled a medieval Christian civilization of "reason," "logic," and "law" (Strayer 1955: 144) – attributes that are *not* usually associated with the proverbial Dark Ages. Indeed, the achievements of medieval Christian civilization defy the tradition–modernity duality that we have grown accustomed to since Émile Durkheim.

Having moved closer to politics since its days as official religion of the late Roman Empire, the Christian church has seen its political ambition classically formulated in Pope Gelasius' "two swords" or "two coordinate powers" theory. While it did reserve separate domains to secular and spiritual authority, it *also* stipulated that both powers were not equal, the religious being the truly universal one trumping the political (Strayer 1958: 40). This asymmetry was grounded in the church's monopolization of the sacraments, on which "salvation" was based, that highest good that dwarfed all worldly strivings (p. 40).

However, from the onset of the post-Roman Middle Ages, in the fifth century, to the eve of the Papal Revolution, six centuries later, the reality was the reverse: the king ruled the church. The break-up of the Roman Empire had left "Western Europe" as the "weakest and poorest" region of the territory it once occupied (the new Arab-Islamic Empire to the south and west actually being the most developed!) (Strayer 1955: 43). While the Christian church was, in principle, "the only stable institution among the ruins [of Rome]" (p. 21), which would eventually provide the unity of an emergent Christian civilization in Europe, it was initially weak. The early medieval church lacked central administration and a rural infrastructure, as its traditional site during the days of Rome was urban. When Charlemagne was crowned emperor in 800, thus inaugurating the Holy Roman Empire of the German Nation, which would last a millennium, he was "the absolute master of the Church; the pope depended on him for protection" (p. 49). More than investing him with the highest political authority on that giant stretch of land from the two Nordic seas to the northern Adriatic, his coronation in Aachen gave Charlemagne the spiritual authority as head of Western Christendom, making him the "deputy of Christ" (note that the Bishop of Rome then was only the "deputy of St. Peter," the founder of the church of Jesus).

In the early medieval period, which Ernst Troeltsch (1994 [1912], Vol. 1: part II) described as the period of Germano-Romanic "state churches" (*Landeskirchen*), political rulers had entirely subdued the churches as their feudal masters, and they even came to own most church properties. In turn, the young Germanic state was "poor in culture," and thus was readily Christianized, making for a "Christian State" presiding over a nominally "Christian society" (pp. 202–3). Importantly, the collapse of the Roman money economy had caused an acute shortage of money and the civil servants of political rulers had to be paid with natural goods, that is, land. This fact made the employment of clerics doubly attractive. Not only were they alone able to read and write, but clerics also could not hand on property to a succeeding generation. Employing clerics warded off the risk of the fragmentation of the Reich into small inheritable principalities. As a result, clerics became the "key civil servants (*Beamtenschaft*) of the Reich" and "essential basis of kingly power" (p. 205).

This was a constellation where political and religious authority were "thoroughly intermingled" (Strayer 1970: 20), kings appointing abbots, bishops, often popes, even formulating church doctrine, and clerics in turn advising kings or ruling ecclesiastical principalities. However, the important point is that there was no symmetry. Until the eleventh century, the clergy in Western Christendom was under the authority of emperors, kings, and feudal lords, *not* of the pope. The religion–politics nexus was a "Caesaropapist" fusion of religious and political spheres, kings being "sacral figures" and "religious leaders of their people" (Berman 1983: 88).

This changed with the Papal Revolution, whose importance for the rule of law and legal pluralism we have already discussed. In 1075, Pope Gregory VII, under the motto "Freedom of the Church," declared the independence of the church from worldly authority. Article 18 of his *Dictatus Papae* stunningly commanded "that no judgment of his [the pope] may be revised by anyone, and that he alone may revise [the judgments] of all" (in Berman 1983: 96). Strictly speaking, this amounted to the subordination of worldly to religious power, that is, "theocracy" (Troeltsch 1994 [1912], Vol. 1: 226). This at least was the bold claim of the Catholic Church in its most heroic period, between the eleventh and thirteenth centuries. Only now, *both* swords were wielded by the pope, though one still indirectly through secular rulers. The concrete bone of contention during this "Investiture Struggle," which would end only 100 years later,[13] was Gregory's denial of the king's traditional power to appoint the successors to deceased abbots or bishops, in a sacral ring-and staff-bestowing ceremony that included the king's solemn words *Accipe ecclesiam!* (Accept this church!). In one stroke, the Papal Revolution proclaimed the right of the pope to depose emperors, the independence of clergy from secular control, and papal sovereignty over the church, thus establishing the office of the pope as we know it today. This was also one of the church's busiest internal reform periods, including the prohibition of simony (the selling of the sacraments) and of marriage among clerics (celibacy).

The Papal Revolution had two unintended consequences. First, and most importantly, it secularized state power: thereafter emperors and kings were "laymen," they could no longer claim "competence in spiritual matters" (Berman 1983: 114). Positively turned, this gave impetus to the formation of the early modern state in Europe. Note that the idea of the territorial state had to win against the dominant political structure at the time, the Holy Roman Empire of the German Nation, whose quasi-sacredness is flagged by the "holy" in its name, but which was critically weakened in the Investiture Struggle (Strayer 1970: 22).

The second unintended consequence was the fact, already mentioned, that the church itself took on the insignia of a state, with a legal and bureaucratic infrastructure that came to provide a blueprint for secular institutions. Looking like a state, it is no wonder that the papal church would also *act* like a state, being drawn into a persistent power struggle that deflected it from its main function, to administer salvation. As Joseph Strayer observes, "[T]hrough playing politics the popes...[became] politicians" (1955: 162). To twelfth-century Hohenstaufen emperor Friedrich Barbarossa, whose armies repeatedly faced armies enlisted by Roman popes for the control of Germany and Italy, "the Church was a political force, to be treated in exactly the same way as other political forces" (p. 158). The profaning and spending of the Catholic Church as a worldly force would keep the wheel of internal reform moving, sowing the seeds of the Reformation. "Martin Luther in 1517," year of the posting of his famous 95 theses for church reform on the door of Wittenberg's *Schlosskirche*, "may be considered the final result of more than 200 years of attempted regeneration of theology and piety" (Reinhard 1989: 385).

But at the height of its power, between the late eleventh and thirteenth centuries, "the Church set the goals and fixed the standards for Western European society" (Strayer 1955: 82). Ever since the fall of Rome, Christianity had been central to the making of "Europe." As Michael Mann argues for the post-Roman period, "if Europe was a 'society,' it was a society defined by the boundaries of ideological power, Christianity" (1986: 338). Evidently, the boundaries of that society could not be those of a state, which did not exist at the time. Instead, Christianity filled a "civilization," defined by Randall Collins (2004: 132) as a "zone of prestige" kept together by "social identification" and "networks of attraction at a long distance." But only after the unification of the papal church can we witness the rise of an "integrated Christian culture" (*christliche Einheitskultur*) (Troeltsch 1994 [1912], Vol. 1: 330). Not coincidentally, the first European universities were founded only after the Papal Revolution, notably under the auspices of the church, but increasingly independent of the latter. As Talcott Parsons observes, "Catholic Christianity made a place for an independent intellectual culture which is unique among all the great religions of the medieval phase" (1963: 47). To pick up our running thread of comparing Christianity and Islam, this is in marked contrast to the Islamic *madrasas*, which would never escape from religious tutelage and turn into autonomous, peer-controlled institutions, and in which there was no similar differentiation between theology, law, and ever more branches of specialized knowledge (Collins 1998: 461).

In the "medieval summer" (Strayer 1955: ch. 4), whose heaven-bound yet earthly energies are symbolized in the magnificent Gothic spires that still today adorn European cityscapes, "Europe" was more of a lived and unified space than it would ever be again, even linguistically (Latin being the shared language of the scholarly and religious elite). Between 1050 and 1350, writes Howard Berman, the "whole of Europe formed a single and undifferentiated unit" (1983: 161), united by Latin, canon and Roman law as "disciplines without national boundaries" (p. 162), and – of course – the Christian faith. Philip Gorski vividly describes this reality: "Because the territories of (Western and Central) Europe shared a common religion, an English prince could marry a Spanish bride, a monk from Leipzig could study in Padua, and a poor traveler from Lisbon could receive public alms in Antwerp" (2000a: 157). Indeed, this never-matched level of European union was made possible by "Christendom as a general civilizational frame" (Meyer 1989: 402).

The Protestant Reformation

The Protestant Reformation is a "historically decisive prelude to secularization" (Berger 1967: 112), in two respects. Institutionally, it broke the power of the universal church and spurred the rise of the sovereign state and the modern state system – "no Reformation, no Westphalia" (Philpott 2000: 206). In the realm of ideas and mentalities, it pushed the "autonomy," "individualism," and "this-worldliness" that Ernst Troeltsch found constitutive of "modern culture" (1906: 9). However, these results were achieved only indirectly and as unintended consequences. The immediate effect of the Reformation was the exact opposite: *institutionally*, religion and politics became "more tightly intertwined" than ever before in European history (Gorski 2003: 3); *culturally*, far from being emptied of religion, everyday life was revalued and upgraded as a site of religious belief and practice, in a disposition that Helmut Plessner called *Weltfrömmigkeit* (worldly piety) (quoted in Graf 2007: 92), and which made society more Christian than it had ever been before.

In the following, I will address each side of this paradox in turn, beginning with the cultural and then moving to the institutional one.

Cultural impact: "modern religiosity"

In his influential account of secularization, José Casanova (1994) astutely observed that secularization's point of departure was the existence of three, not two, realms: not only was the "other world" (heaven) divided from "this world" (earth), but "this world" was itself divided into a religious (or church) and a secular realm (Augustine's sinful "City of Man"). "Secularization" proper is the collapse of the dualism of "this world," so that there was only *one* "this world," in which religion had to find its place (p. 15). Catholicism, with its sacraments and strong emphasis on liturgy and rite, had attributed a constitutive place to the sacred in "this world"; the church as "temple of the Holy Spirit" was quite literally a "holy" institution (Lehmann 2007: 50). The world of Catholicism is not radically disenchanted; it contains elements of mystery, miracle, and magic – the most important being the sacrament of confession, which endows the priest with the power to relieve believers of their sins, and which not by accident became the first target of Luther's reforms.[14] Catholicism, one could argue with Peter Berger (1967: ch. 5), reversed the "transcendentalization" of God and the "rationalization of ethics" that had already been achieved in Judaism, and as the recovery of which Protestantism may be interpreted.

In stipulating the "priesthood of all believers" (Graf 2007: 79), Protestantism does away with the necessity for the church to mediate between believer and God. It amounts to the "religious 'enfranchisement' of the individual" (Parsons 1963: 50), as the believers "in their secular roles" were charged with the realization of Christian values (p. 58). The old medieval "church culture" was aptly described by Ernst Troeltsch (1994 [1912], Vol. 2: 973) as marked by a "double-graded morality" (*Moral der Doppelstufigkeit*). According to it, world-renouncing asceticism was reserved to religious virtuosi, while the "masses" were subjected to a less exacting *lex naturae* (natural law) that allowed them to go about their social functions. In this graded morality, there is a division between an "average morality of the worldly" and a "strict morality of the holy," tied together in an organic "ascension from nature to grace" (p. 973). "Catholicism," argues Troeltsch in his earlier Protestantism essay, "is characterized by a most elastic unity of authoritative-ascetic and natural-inner-worldly life" (1906: 6), under the leadership of the church.

In Protestantism, this graded morality is replaced by a unitary asceticism for all, an "inner-worldly asceticism," as Troeltsch borrows Max Weber's famous formula. This is an ethic of "internally renouncing the world without externally leaving it" (Troeltsch 1906: 26). The important matter is the upgrading of the world as a site of religious duty – Luther expressed it in his famous notion of "calling" (*Beruf*) (see the classic discussion by Weber 1978 [1920]: 63–83). However, this inner-worldly asceticism takes rather opposite directions in Lutheranism, which favors the "passive endurance" of the world, and in Calvinism, which tends toward its "active mastery," the two being driven by rather opposite visions of a "loving" and "graceful" versus "honor"-exacting and "punishing" God, respectively.

The important matter, emphasized by Troeltsch (1906), is that both variants of Protestantism *remain* within the ambit of traditional "church culture" – not abolition but reform of the church has been their joint program. Anticipating later theories of "confessionalization" (see below), Troeltsch even interprets the "old" Protestantism as "renewal and strengthening of the ideal of a churchly culture of coercion (*kirchliche Zwangskultur*)," leading to a two-centuries-long "full reaction of medieval thinking" in Europe (p. 28). The old "idea of theocracy" is still virulent, only the "Bible" has taken the place of "hierarchy" and sacrament (p. 22). However, this change of fundament has important implications. Because the Bible as God's word is directly accessible to each believer, the position of the church is fatally weakened: it can at best "teach" but no longer dispense grace through sacraments (Parsons 1963: 59). Having lost the privileged access to God, the church can no longer claim to be superior to worldly authority: "Rather, both, worldly and spiritual power, are jointly subordinate to the Bible" (Troeltsch 1906: 22). This is a significant departure from the "ethical predominance of the church over state and society" in Catholicism (Graf 2007: 161). In the Protestant order, the state is still "a religious institution," obliged to the "furthering of the Christian community and the moral law," state and church being parts of a *Corpus Christianum*. But the state is no longer subordinate to the church hierarchy, having greatly gained in "sovereignty and autarchy" (Troeltsch 1906: 34).

Stressing the continuity rather than the discontinuity of the Protestant Reformation is methodologically significant. Troeltsch (1906: 28) was surprisingly explicit about the causal aspect of his argument, making his study also an exemplary work of historical sociology (not unlike Weber's famous Protestantism study). If the task is to explain the transition from "church culture" to "modern culture," Protestantism necessarily must grow out of the first and thus share many of its features; otherwise the argument would be circular. Troeltsch distinguishes in this respect between "old" (church) and "new" (sectarian) Protestantism, arguing that only the former could be "causally" involved in the making of "modern culture" because the latter is "itself a part of modern culture" (p. 17). However, if the old Protestantism is still part of "church culture," its causal contribution to the making of "modern culture" can logically be only "unintended" or "indirect" (p. 18). Troeltsch (p. 56) thus emphasizes the "hindrances" as much as the "decisively contributory" elements of Protestantism in the making of the "modern world." At heart, Protestantism returns to the individualism and apolitical quietism of the early Christian church of Paulus, the one apostle who had never seen Christ but, after his myth-making conversion from Christian-persecuting "Saul" into Christ-loving "Paul," the first Christian theologian and one of the most influential of all time (see Troeltsch 1994 [1912], Vol. 1: ch. 2). Calvinism developed the individualist prong of Pauline theology, now relying on the Bible rather than the priesthood; Lutherism recovered Paulus' conservative spirit of "patience and submission," abandoning the high-medieval ambition of "bettering the world" that had energized the "hierarchical world church" (Troeltsch 1906: 47).

Paradoxically, if one considers the world-changing effect of Protestantism, the "Protestant principle," as formulated by Paul Tillich, is that "in relationship to God, God alone acts" (quoted in Graf 2007: 89). All contribution by sinful humans in the achieving of salvation is rejected as *Werkgerechtigkeit*, a hubris that falsely attributes to humans what can only come from God, *sola gratia* (from grace alone). The idea of "natural equality," to name one of the "modern world's" most fundamental principles, is equally foreign to Luther and Calvin, as this had been a reality only in the "primeval condition before sin" (Troeltsch 1906: 47). Equally foreign to both champions of Protestantism is the modern idea of freedom of conscience and of human rights, which originated instead in the spirit of the Baptist sects, which were ruthlessly persecuted by church Protestantism as heresy (see Jellinek 1904). Finally, neither Lutheranism nor Calvinism may be considered as furthering the idea of democracy. Lutheranism greatly supported the absolutist state, endowing it with additional power over the church, and Luther himself became infamous for rejecting any right to oppose *Obrigkeit* (worldly authority) and for favoring capital punishment and even the most brutal medieval methods of torture, such as quartering and dismemberment, with "utmost severity" (Troeltsch 1994 [1912], Vol. 2: 538). Calvinism did introduce the right to resist godless authority and it recovered the biblical idea of covenant as the basis for a contract theory of the state; however, as a community of the "chosen" hovering above the rest of the "condemned," it is "aristocratic" not "democratic" in spirit (Troeltsch 1906: 47).

Accordingly, in political, social and other respects the role of Protestantism in the making of "modern culture" was only indirect and unintended. Most fundamentally, through the very fact of breaking the old universal church into three competing parts, Protestantism undermined "the power of church culture" (Troeltsch 1906: 29), bringing about a relativism and necessity for permanent theological reflection that had to nag at old certainties and spur the wheel of reform. Not by accident, the only "direct and immediate" effect of Protestantism in the making of modern culture was to generate a "specifically modern religiosity" (Troeltsch 1906: 57). In a way, Troeltsch anticipates Niklas

Luhmann's idea that, like any "autopoietic system," religion can only influence and change religion itself. His argument goes like this. At first Protestantism is little more than a "reformulation (*Umbildung*) of Catholicism" (p. 19). It started off by following the old goal of establishing the certitude of salvation (*Heilsgewissheit)*, though relocating it from the external authority of the church into the inner sphere of belief. However, this new way of finding *Heilsgewissheit* eventually created a new "religion of conscience and conviction without dogmatic constraint" (p. 61). "Modern religiosity" as pioneered by Protestantism is a "preference for seeking truth over possessing ultimate truth," as Troeltsch put it with reference to Enlightenment icon Lessing (p. 62). In other words, faith itself (*fides qua creditur*) takes precedence over the contents of faith (*fides quae creditur*). But in prioritizing the search for truth over the possession of truth, modern religiosity is "intrinsically and electively related" (*bluts- und wahlverwandt*) to the idea of modern science (p. 64). Here is the window for exiting from religion as set by religion itself, which was prepared by Christianity but perfected by Protestantism as the "consummate" religion (Lilla 2007: 187).

Institutional impact: the "Confessional Age"

The release of religious energies into a morally upgraded everyday life was one, the cultural, half, of the ironic and indirect ways in which the Protestant Reformation furthered the process of secularization. The other half was *institutional*, by bringing about a closer fusion between state and religion than Europe had ever experienced before, with the state, however, now gaining the undisputed upper hand. The Reformation, as Toft et al. (2011: 64) correctly described it, amounted to a "friendly takeover" of religion by the state. From being the "senior partner" of the state in the High Middle Ages, the church was demoted to the state's "junior partner" (Reinhard 1999: 264). In the process, "Christian universalism" gave way to "confessional particularism" (Gorski 2000a: 157), as religion had to align itself with the boundaries of consolidating territorial states. Within these boundaries, the reality was that of a "de-differentiation among church, state, and society" (p. 143), setting a counter-point to the differentiation of functional subsystems as which the story of modernizing societies has been told from Durkheim to Luhmann. However, what might look like a regression, the "blurring" of the line between political and religious authority (p. 157), was the first round in the creation of the cultural homogeneity that is the central feature of the modern nation-state. What historians refer to as the Confessional Age planted the seeds of modern nationalism, which may incorporate religious motives but must ultimately be understood as a secular phenomenon.

Traditionally, historians of early modern Europe had sharply demarcated a "progressive" Reformation (1517–55) from a "reactionary" Counter-Reformation (1555–1648), until the Age of Absolutism (1648–1789) brought about the victory of the religiously neutral state that is still with us (see Reinhard 1989: 384). Today, historians prefer to view the period as one of "confessionalization," marked by the very opposite of advancing state neutrality, namely, an "overtly intolerant" stance on religious affairs (p. 384). The Confessional Age was one of religious expulsions, generating the novel category of "refugee" (Zolberg et al. 1989: 5–7). It was the age of the Catholic Inquisition, which in the Spanish extreme screened subjects for *limpieza de sangre* (purity of blood); the age of *Kirchenpolizei* (church police) to control religious participation in parishes; the age of "visitations" of local parishes by mixed church–state bodies to enforce religious correctness; and the age of witch hunts, which may be understood as release valves for the "latent aggressiveness" that built up in the process (Reinhard 1989: 397).

Already Ernst Troeltsch had noted that the sixteenth and seventeenth centuries were not "modernity" (*Neuzeit*) but a "confessional age" (*konfessionelles Zeitalter*) (1906: 29). As his wording suggests, Troeltsch sees this as a retrograde phenomenon, a return to "medieval thinking" and the "churchly culture of coercion" (*kirchliche Zwangskultur*) (p. 28). He thus underrates the novel edges that came with confessionalization, above all its "most intimate" connection with the "differentiation of territorial states or nation-states" (Reinhard 1981: 177). Wolfgang Reinhard, who pioneered the confessionalization paradigm (Reinhard 1981), describes the two centuries that followed upon Luther's 95 Wittenberg Theses as follows: "'Church' and 'State' collaborated everywhere to cut autonomous parts out of the body of one single Christian community (*Kristenheit*) by establishing a particular group conformity of religious doctrine and practice among their members" (Reinhard 1989: 390).

However, the *differences* that were thus introduced into Western Christianity, particularly the Protestant versus Catholic divide, mattered less than certain *similarities* across confessions. Philip Gorski, who built on the confessionalization paradigm to highlight the hitherto ignored role of religion as "disciplinary" force in modern state formation (2003), described these similarities in terms of a "close alliance between church and state...and the efforts of religious and political elites to discipline and control the populace" (2000a: 150). The key word is "discipline." Even before religion, in particular Calvinism, caught their attention, historians of early modern Europe had homed in on the "non-absolutist in Absolutism," a shift in statecraft from crude force to "social disciplining" – *non crudelitas, sed disciplina* being the new motto of an era that saw the rise of *Polizei* (police) and workhouses (Oestreich 1969: 193). The missing link in this Foucauldian scenario[15] is religion. In particular, Calvinist Protestantism provided the idea and rationale of the early modern state's disciplining efforts (see Reinhard 1997).

As Philip Gorski (2003: 59) observes for the case of the Netherlands, local magistrates and Calvinist consistories "saw eye to eye on matters of social discipline," cooperating closely in the provision of poor relief (with a new distinction made between the "deserving" and "undeserving" poor), education, and the regulation of sexuality and marriage – the Calvinist obsession was interestingly more with controlling "social" than narrowly "religious" matters (p. 58). There were important variations in this process. It was top-down in Brandenburg-Prussia, where the Calvinist Hohenzollern court staffed bureaucracy and military with foreign co-religionists to gain "state autonomy" from the Lutheran territorial estates (*Stände*). And it was bottom-up in the Low Countries, where a strong local state with high-paid officials helped build an impressively orderly society with low crime rates, low illegitimacy, and large citizen militias. Overall, the Calvinist "disciplinary revolution" explains how some of the "least centralized" and "most backward" monarchies of Europe could develop into some of Europe's most powerful states at the time (Gorski 2003: xvii).

The cooperation between churches and state in the Confessional Age was of mutual benefit. The churches needed the "support of secular powers" for their internal reform efforts: "Saxony" for the Lutherans, "Geneva" for the Calvinists, "Milan" for the Catholics (Reinhard 1989: 396–7). Conversely, fledgling states, which still lacked a developed bureaucracy, could "utilize the clergy to get hold of even their remotest subjects at the edges of society" (Reinhard 1997: 47). However, states everywhere had the better of this cooperation. The constellation corresponded exactly to Hobbes' vision of how to govern the "Christian Commonwealth," in which religious power should be subordinate to the political sovereign (Hobbes 1996 [1651]: part 3; see Reinhard 1989: 400). In Germany, the churches became *Landeskirchen* (regional state churches), in which the princes did not just take over church property but also, in the context of so-called "Episcopalism," exercised the formal role of bishops (if only by circumstance, as Catholic bishops did not accept the Reformation and the role of Evangelical bishops had to be filled by the princes) (Reinhard 1999: 271). This was a complex regime that had to juggle the formal sovereignty of the prince over church affairs with the Lutheran principle of freedom of conscience and internal church autonomy. However, as a result, princely power was "re-sacralized," the mundane *Landesherr* (state leader) spiritually upgraded into *Landesvater* (state father) (p. 267). This foreshadowed the modern ideology of nationalism, which deserves separate treatment.

Nationalism

An important effect of confessionalization is the aligning of confessional with "political identities," so that the two become "nearly identical" (Reinhard 1981: 188). In the second half of the sixteenth century, there was even a linking between "confessional allegiance and citizenship rights" (Gorski 2000a: 158), in that political office-holding was made contingent on being a member of the state church; the same proviso applied to membership in trade guilds. The Confessional Age was an age of proto-nationalism. As Philip Gorski draws the connection, "'confessionalization' helped to create the cultural homogeneities that nationalism would later mythologize and extoll" (2003: 163). At one level, the linking of confession and loyalty and the cultural homogenization that results from policing the creed is independent of the content of the creed, that is, its Protestant or Catholic character. For Catholic Bavaria, ca. 1615, it was said, *tota regio nil nisi religio* (the whole region is nothing but for religion). Spain during the Inquisition likewise became identified with Catholicism, as did the France of Catholic martyr Joan of Arc. Invading England, in turn, identified itself with Protestantism as a "symbol of national integration" (Reinhard 1981: 188). Ireland and Poland espoused Catholicism in the distinct context of minority nations being threatened by much larger (other-religious) powers. Sweden officially accepted the Confessio Augustana (the Lutheran confession as codified in Augsburg 1530) against the threat of Catholic Poland in 1593 (p. 188). And so on. Catholic or Protestant, religion defined the content of emergent national identity.

One scholar of nationalism and religion argued intriguingly that nation and nationalism "are both characteristically Christian things" (Hastings 1997: 186). And he contrasted in this respect Christianity with Islam as "profoundly anti-national." In support of this thesis is the fact that Islam has a holy language, Arabic, making it resistant to vernacularization. By contrast, Christianity does not know a holy language but has "the use of the world's vernaculars inscribed in its origins" (p. 194). Jesus spoke Aramaic, while Muhammad – most Muslims believe – received the word of God in classical Arabic, which made Arabic a sacred language in which to conduct all prayer and ritual. Consequently, vernacular-friendly Christian culture is one of "translation," whereas vernacular-unfriendly Islamic culture is one of "assimilation," drawing "peoples into a single world community of language and government"

(p. 201). The *ummah* conflicts with the nation-state in a way that the universal Christian church does not. A contemporary Muslim activist expresses what even the most Catholic integrist would not dare to say: "The path of the *ummah*... is blocked by nation-states.... All nation-states must of necessity be dismantled" (Kalim Siddiqui, founder of the British Muslim Parliament, quoted in Hastings, p. 202). While Siddiqui certainly is an extremist, this is no extreme position within Islam. Liberal reformer Abdullahi An-Na'im confirms that the "nation-state" is a concept "difficult to assimilate and implement" for "Muslim peoples" (1990: 7).

At the same time, the propensity to embrace the national principle is differently strong among the Catholic and Protestant branches of Christianity. While stipulating an affinity between the Christian and the national fact, Hastings (1997: 198) also observes that Christianity could go either way, "nation-state" or "empire," and that "empire" was actually more germane to the New Testament universalism of "neither Jew nor Greek... but all are one in Christ" (1997: 198). It is not to be forgotten that Christians acquired even the behaviorally less exacting political form, empire, only in an "accidental" way, because a "self-distancing from politics" has been "somewhere in the DNA of all Christian political theology" (Lilla 2007: 42).

In an insightful reflection on religion and nationalism, Conor Cruise O'Brien contrasts in this respect the overt (Hebrew) nationalism of the Old Testament, in which "God chose a particular people and promised them a particular land," with the very different, apolitical spirit of the New Testament, which "runs away from this whole conception of any earthly Promised Land" (1998: 3). If any place is to be named in the New Testament, it is a non-earthly "New Jerusalem" (p. 9). Having said this, Christianity's imperial streak found expression in the Holy Roman Empire of the German Nation, which lasted from 962 to 1806. From the age of confessionalization on, this empire was embraced above all in Catholic quarters in the middle zone of the European continent, from Germany to Italy. In fact, the "European Saints" who advocated a federated Europe after World War II, like Monnet, Adenauer, Schuman, de Gasperi, and Spaak, were not by accident all Catholics (Milward 1992: ch. 6).

By contrast, nationalism, while powerfully prefigured in the Hebrew Bible, became the distinct inclination of Protestantism. Ernest Gellner, who associated nation and nationalism more closely with secular modernity than most other scholars, still drew a close link between Reformation and nationalism: "The stress of the Reformation on literacy and scripturalism, its onslaught on a monopolistic priesthood (or, as Weber clearly saw, its universalization rather than abolition of priesthood), its individualism and links with mobile urban populations, all made it a kind of harbinger of social features and attitudes which...produce the nationalist age" (Gellner 1978: 40–1). In short, what nationalism and Protestantism have in common is "abstract faith, presiding over an anonymous community of equal believers" (p. 41).

Vernacular, individualism, and the rejection of hierarchy are obvious affinities between Protestantism and nationalism. Conor Cruise O'Brien mentions a further element: the Reformers' hostility to "medieval allegorization" and "new emphasis on the literal meaning of the Old Testament" (1988: 25). In this way, the nationalism of the Old Testament, with its topoi of "Israel" and a "chosen people," could be reactivated and brought to bear on new cases, in the plural. Accordingly, we find a "Mosaic moment" or "Hebraic nationalism" (Gorski 2000b) in several, mostly Calvinist, early modern peoples, particularly the Dutch and the English, and by way of Puritan dissent and North American colonization this has come to shape American nationalism as well, in terms of a deist "civil religion," up to the present day (Bellah 1967).

The relationship between nationalism and religion, Protestantism in particular, is vastly more complex and variegated than can be conveyed here. (For a succinct conceptual overview, see Brubaker 2012.) But ultimately the dividing line between the two is that nationalism is a "distinctively secular phenomenon," which may be deeply "intertwined" with religious thinking and mobilization but does not thereby become identical with religion (p. 15). Providing a shell for nation and nationalism, which is the most potent, universal legitimation of the modern state, has not been Protestantism's smallest contribution to the process of secularization.

Varieties of Secularization

The process of secularization has occurred in great historical variety, with widely different conflict dynamics and institutional outcomes. But only recently has it become de rigueur to talk about "secularisms" and "secularizations," in the plural, influenced by S.N. Eisenstadt's (2000) evocative notion of "multiple modernities" (e.g., Casanova 2011; Stepan 2011; Warner et al. 2010). Much as in Eisenstadt's insistence that there are "modernities" outside and distinct from the West, with their own particular patterns, the gist of the plural is to "provincialize" the European and Western experience, and to reject the claim that the latter is of "general or universal" import and applicable elsewhere (Casanova 2011: 64). In this mode, Rajeev Bhargava (2010; see also his classic 1998) argued crisply that the "Indian model of secularism," with its constitutive focus on accommodating *several* religions from the start, is better suited to accommodating "deep religious diversity" than all Western models. This is because the Western models grew out of a context of a "single-religion society" and thus encountered religious plurality only belatedly, now facing obvious difficulties in dealing with other than Christian religions, especially Islam.

However, the intra-Western varieties of secularism are complex enough to warrant further attention, and I can depict some of this variety here in only a highly abridged way. While the gist of such comparison cannot but be empirical, it is useful to start it normatively, by pointing out that from a liberal point of view there is not just one but two equally legitimate solutions to relate religion and state. Cécile Laborde (2013) called them "modest separation" and "modest establishment." Both regimes provide "adequate protection of religious freedom" – hence the "modest" in their name. However, a "separation" regime keeps religion at bay, refusing to support, acknowledge, or fund religion in any way. By contrast, an "establishment" regime officially recognizes and supports religion, although under the "modesty" proviso this must occur in an even-handed way, not to unduly privilege the citizens of one religion over those of other religions. According to Laborde, "orthodox political liberalism," with its focus on "basic justice" in matters subject to coercive state power, such as income and education, is "inconclusive" about the question of the "modest separation" or "modest establishment" of religion – both are equally possible under its umbrella. Only a loftier "Republican" version of political liberalism, which is concerned about the power of symbols and "intangible forms of social recognition," favors "separation" and rejects "establishment," because the latter "send[s] a message to non-adherents that they are outsiders" (US Supreme Court Judge O'Connor, cited in Laborde, p. 86). From such a maximalist view, which is not shared by all liberals, only the "strict separation" regime of the United States meets the test of liberalism, while all European regimes, which tend to be variants of "establishment," are ruled out (e.g., Nussbaum 2008).

Laborde's (2013) important message is that for a less exacting, nuts-and-bolts liberalism there is not just one (idealized American) way of placing religion in a liberal state, but two ways, "separation" *and* "establishment." This reasonably situates most European regimes within the ambit of liberalism, even if they do not distance themselves from religion, American-style, but align themselves with it in one form or another.

Having said this, the reality of European secularisms is a good deal messier. The traditional legal view distinguishes between three church–state regimes in Europe, "separation," "concordatarian," and "national church" (Ferrari 1995).[16] An obvious example of "separation" is France with its *laïcité*, which expels religion from a broadly conceived state sphere, including public schools. "Concordatarian"[17] regimes are Germany, Austria, and Italy, which grant privileged public status to the main religions in society, and cooperate with them on important public functions (like welfare and education). Finally, "national church" regimes can be found in England, whose head of state is also head of the Anglican Church, and in Scandinavia (with the exception of Sweden), where the Lutheran Church is the official state church.

However, as Ferrari (1995; also 2002) argues, this conventional typology is out of touch with reality – it "overemphasizes the formal aspects of church–state relations and…does not pay enough attention to their content, that is, the legal powers given to churches and the protections afforded to individual believers" (1995: 421).[18] Instead, he identifies a "common pattern of church–state relations in Western Europe." It converges on:

- first, at the individual level, state neutrality and strong religious liberties;
- secondly, at the collective level, the "demarcation within the 'public' sector of a 'religious' sub-sector…where the different religious subjects can enjoy a preferential treatment in comparison with nonreligious subjects" (p. 421);[19]
- thirdly, at both individual and collective levels, state intervention being limited to "setting the ground rules" and "seeing that the 'playing field' is level and its boundaries are respected" (p. 421).

While it is difficult to integrate France into the "common pattern" thus conceived (as granting "preferential treatment" to religion),[20] Ferrari (1995) usefully homes in on the actual workings, rather than the formal appearance, of European church–state regimes, which mostly seem to meet the liberal "modest establishment" criterion as devised by Laborde (2013).[21] At the same time, Ferrari's account allows us to see that "Europe" combined differs in this respect from the United States, whose constitutional "non-Establishment" clause, as traditionally understood,[22] rules out any such development.

America versus Europe

A helpful way to contrast Europe with the United States is to point to a paradox, set out by James Whitman (2008). While in the United States there is a strict institutional separation between church and state, there is *no* clear separation between religion and politics, as demonstrated in the routine references to "God" in American political language (which famously motivated Bellah's [1967] notion of "civil religion in America"). Europe, conversely, is cavalier about the church–state separation, while painstakingly seeking to keep religion out of politics – the unease about a US president (George W. Bush) who apparently talked to God before breakfast led two secular European intellectuals to the conclusion that there was, after all, a "European identity" (Habermas and Derrida 2005: 296). Whitman reasonably sees both, the European and the American regimes, as expressions of the "Western Christian tradition," which "has always demanded that church and state be separated in some way" (2008: 90).

However, he identifies as the specificity of Europe that "the state, over many centuries, has gradually assumed many of the historic functions performed by the medieval Church" (Whitman 2008: 91), from regulating marriage and providing education and welfare to "creation of a common culture" (p. 93). As a result, the European state, most drastically perhaps the piously secular French, came "to constitute itself as a kind of updated, secularized Church" (p. 95), a provider of meaning. In the process, the church was robbed of its "moral force and much of its political energy," losing its "charismatic" character. This is the exact opposite constellation to that in the United States, where, owing to the absence of a church, there could not be a self-aggrandizing state, but where in turn religion could remain a vital force in society.

In his sweeping overview of how Christianity has shaped Western society, Talcott Parsons (1963) argued that, following upon the "medieval synthesis" and the "Reformation," the United States, and only it, has ushered in a third phase in the evolution of Christianity, one where the "institutionalization of Christian ethics" has gone further than ever. He dubbed it the phase of "denominational pluralism" (pp. 60–70). The "denomination," that distinctly American innovation, is neither "church" nor "sect," thus requiring us to enlarge the Weber–Troeltsch typology of religious organization. The denomination shares with the church the "differentiation between religious and secular spheres of interest," and thus the idea of multiple allegiances and legitimations, but also the drive to bring the secular sphere into "better conformity with Christian values" (p. 61). Both of these are *not* the usual inclination of the sect. On the other hand, the denomination shares with the sect the principle of voluntarism, which Parsons sees as "logically...associated with the constitutional separation of church and state" (p. 61). Combining both elements, of church-like differentiation and sect-like voluntarism, the denomination "accept[s] secular society as a legitimate field of action for the Christian individual in which he acts on his own responsibility without organizational control by religious authority" (p. 61).

The denominational constellation allows for a "path to the secular" that Martin Marty (1969), in one of the earliest comparative studies of secularization, has called "controlled secularization." It denotes a peculiar mutual permeation of the religious and the secular, whereby religion loses its "sense of transcendence or of otherworldliness" (p. 108), while a "Christian glow" (p. 105) is thrown upon all secular strivings, including "enterprise and nationalism" (p. 109). Max Weber (1979 [1919/20]) immortalized the ensuing religio-secular habitus in his travel encounter with an American trading in "undertakers' hardware," who would not do business with anyone who "does not belong to a church," whatever the creed might be: "why pay me if he does not believe in anything?" (pp. 281–2).

A further important element of the denomination, which it shares with the sect, is its definitional coexistence with other denominations, none of which can claim to encompass all believers in society – hence "denominational pluralism" (Parsons 1963: 62). Parsons finds it "implicit in the voluntary principle," which bears a disposition to "toleration." The denomination accepts the principle of religious freedom, not just as factual necessity but as "religiously legitimate," that is, required by the creed itself. This principle thus provides a "common matrix of value-commitment which is broadly shared between denominations, and which forms the basis of the sense in which the society as a whole forms a religiously based moral community" (p. 62). Importantly, not just Protestants but all religious groups, including the Catholic and Jewish, partake in the structure of denominational pluralism, which thus constitutes an "underlying consensus" in society (p. 62). It is the secret of the unique compatibility of religion in America with democracy and nationhood, which already Tocqueville had marveled at. Moreover, in institutionalizing a "principle of mutual trust," where the adherents of other denominations are not perceived as less "good" than the "members of our camp," denominational pluralism implies "a great further extension of the institutionalization of Christian values" (p. 66). In Parsons' optic, the United States can thus simultaneously appear as the most "modern" and the most "Christian" of all societies, which turns on its head the traditional assumptions of secularization theory.

Intra-European varieties

When turning to intra-European varieties of secularization, three of their features are especially noteworthy. First, secularization has everywhere been a protracted, conflict-generating process, which has only rarely ended in a clear disestablishment, or separation between religion and state – a fact already conceptually encountered but yet to be historically concretized. Secondly, amongst a great variety of national conflict patterns and outcomes, one may distinguish between two broad paths, one of polarizing "laicization" in Catholic countries, and another of joint "secularization" of state *and* religion in Protestant or mixed countries. Thirdly, a particularly important factor in mending the non-negligible risk of an anti-secular, Catholic counter-modernity has been the rise of Christian Democracy. In the remainder of this chapter, I will address each of these features of European secularization in turn.

A Second Confessional Age?

Throughout the nineteenth century, commonly viewed as the "Age of Secularization," religion remained an "ontic power of the highest importance" (*Daseinsmacht ersten Ranges*) (Osterhammel 2009: 1239). Religion was not only an institutional force resisting the state but also "the most important form of creating meaning in the everyday life of people" (p. 1239). Accordingly, "rarely" did religion consign itself to its theoretically allotted place of one "functionally differentiated subsystem amongst others" (p. 1239). Particularly virulent causes of conflict were the introduction of civil marriage and public schooling. For the peak years 1860–70, Jürgen Osterhammel speaks of an "almost pan-European struggle between church and state" (p. 1254).

In a widely noted reflection on the "unexpected renaissance" of religion in the nineteenth century, the German historian Olaf Blaschke (2000) wonders whether this period should not be considered a "second confessional age." Only now did the Catholic Church succeed in a "thorough organization of religious life" (p. 50), top-down, boldly pronouncing the "infallibility of the Pope" at its First Vatican Council (1869), while engaging in unprecedented moves of "re-Christianization," "clericalization," "centralization," "social disciplining" (p. 53). One observer spoke similarly of a "New Catholicism" in late nineteenth-century Europe, which was "more uniform, more centralized, and more 'Roman' than the eighteenth-century church had been" (Christopher Clark, quoted in Tyrell 2008: 161). Only now, as it were, did "Confessionalization" seem to come into its own. However, as Blaschke (2000) concedes, in contrast to the first-round confessionalization, in its second round the confession no longer was the "lead sector" in society. Instead, "other forces are dominant" (p. 71), such as "industrialization" or "democratization," to name only the "double revolution" that marked the nineteenth century (see Nisbet 1966: ch. 2). Rather than being the "fundamental process," second-round confessionalization was merely a "countermovement" to state and modernity (Blaschke 2000: 71), a rearguard battle in the Long Christian Exit.

A major comparative study of nineteenth-century "secularization in Western Europe" (McLeod 2000) nevertheless confirms the tenacity of institutionalized religion. The exception, of course, is France, which pursued a state-level "systematic secularization," particularly under the Third Republic (post-1870), ramming through religious "neutrality" in the public sphere with a vengeance. This was naturally resisted in the provinces. In the Pyrenees, local opponents of the 1905 Law on the Separation of Churches and State (which deprived the clergy of their state salaries and transferred all church buildings into municipal property) chained bears to church porches and emptied chamber pots over gendarmes. Catholics were subjected to severe discrimination, such as disallowing them from becoming prefects (in force for six decades, between the 1880s and the 1940s) or, as the even harsher 1903 Law on Associations prescribed (among other things), excluding from civil service anyone not educated in a non-religious public school for at least three years (p. 64).

If in France the "secularization of the state ran ahead of the secularization of everyday life," in England and Germany the "reverse was true" (McLeod 2000: 83). England witnessed at best "very gradual and unsystematic institutional secularization," its focus being more the equality of religious dissenters than the cleansing of the public sphere of things religious, Saint-Just style. The Education Act 1870 established a compromise "dual system" of religious and public schools, and elite education even remained religious through the ages – compulsory chapel attendance in some Oxford colleges ended only in the 1950s. How far, apart from the (largely symbolic) Anglican monarchy, public bodies remained religious is epitomized in England's long-standing "sabbatarian legislation," whose last remnants (restrictions on Sunday trading and pub openings) were not lifted until the 1990s (p. 84). Protestantism constituted a cornerstone of English, later British, national identity through the centuries, in demarcation from "foreign Catholic despotism" (p. 235; see also Colley 1994). The Empire, while from the 1890s justified more in terms of "race," was strongly associated with Protestantism, or rather "Christianity" at large (see van der Veer 2001), as a "God-given mission to spread true religion and good government around the world" (McLeod 2000: 237). Eventually, however, as Martin Marty phrased it in his vivid description of the move toward "mere secularity" in "everydayish" England, God and the church were just found to be "superfluous" (1969: 92). Life went on without them, with no French-type rupture.

Germany, to complete a review of Europe's Big Three, was similar to England in retaining a "privileged and powerful public role of churches" (McLeod 2000: 29), though with important nuances. Germany, after all, was the site of the vitriolic *Kulturkampf* between the Lutheran Prussian core of the *Kaiserreich* and a recalcitrant Catholic minority, allied with the "Ultramontane" Papacy, which resisted the pending separation between church and state and, in particular, the imposition of civil marriage. In Germany, close ties between church and state were retained until the official abolition of a state church in the Weimar Republic in 1918, and "systematic secularization" would occur only under the Nazi regime (confirming Ralf Dahrendorf's [1968] famous diagnosis of Nazism as Germany's unacknowledged modernizer). Note that the state-implemented "church tax" was introduced in Prussia in 1875 (McLeod 2000: 58), at the height of the *Kulturkampf*. Despite the latter, the state continued to farm out the provision of welfare to the churches, and confessional schooling remained the norm – religion and reading being the two principal subjects taught in the *Volksschulen*. Quite similar to England, "nationalism and religion were often so intermingled that the two cannot always be easily separated" (p. 80). The German Empire was a Protestant state, in which the joint "reverence for God and love for the fatherland"[23] was proverbial. In 1883, the year of Luther's 400th birthday, there was a state-engineered cult of Luther, the "German man," and his portrait adorned German school walls, along with those of the Emperor, Bismarck, Blücher, and Moltke. "Luther oaks" were planted all around the Reich, and Wilhelm I ordered church bells to be rung on November 9 (Luther's actual birthday) (Blaschke 2000: 53). At the same time, the confessional division between Lutherans and Catholics forfeited any "genuine churchly participation in the nation," so that there never was a "Christian Germany" akin to "Catholic France" or "Anglican England" (Tyrell 2008: 171). Perhaps for this reason, there was from the start a tilt toward "exalted nationalism" as "new religion" itself (McLeod 2000: 241), making "a God of the State" rather than using God for the state (Marty 1969: 57). *This* framed Germany's tortured entry to modernity. Symptomatic of exalted nationalism is the infamous "Deutschland über alles" (Germany above everything) incanted in the second verse of the "Lied der Deutschen," the German national anthem (though ironically only since 1922, under the first German Republic). The mid-eighteenth-to mid-nineteenth-century writer and parliamentarian Ernst Moritz Arndt expressed the *Höchstrelevanz* of the nation: "This is the highest religion, to love the Fatherland more than all masters and princes, fathers and mothers, wives and children" (quoted in Tyrell 2008: 167, fn. 250). Interestingly, the Catholic minority always boycotted the Wilhelminian national holiday, the *Sedantag* (commemorating the victory of German over French troops in 1870), as the "cult of Satan" or "St. Sedan," thus attacking a sacralization of the state that was devoid of religious roots (McLeod 2000: 68).

This short review of some European paths of secularization still suggests, among other things, that a global interpretation of Europe post-1789 in terms of a "hostile takeover" of religion by a self-aggrandizing state (Toft et al. 2011: 65–70) misses the degree of cooperation and collusion that persisted between the two well into our secular age (see Madeley 2009).

"Laicization" versus "secularization"

But isn't it possible to simplify the twisted and often contradictory ways in which European societies turned secular? A helpful starting point is to distinguish between a Protestant and a Catholic path. On the Protestant path, there is no clear boundary between the religious and the secular; instead there is a double movement of making "the religious secular and the secular religious through mutual reciprocal infusion" (Casanova 2011: 57). This movement continues a long-standing attempt to overcome the dualism of medieval Christendom, by making the *saeculum* religious. It has the ironic result of keeping the state religious to a degree, as in the North-Western European fusion of monarchy and Establishment, while religion loses its other-worldly, cultic edges, and, by dissolving into individual belief, allows a thorough secularization of society. By contrast, in the Catholic path, the boundary between the religious and the secular is "rigidly maintained" (p. 57). Here, largely in the "French-Latin-Catholic cultural area," it comes to a polarization between religious and secular forces, the latter seeking to marginalize the former and "emancipate all secular spheres from clerical-ecclesiastical control" (p. 57). On both paths, "monastery walls" have to be crushed, but with the opposite intentions of either letting the religious float everywhere or wiping it from the secular landscape.

Françoise Champion (1993) has usefully contrasted the two paths in terms of Catholic *laïcisation* versus Protestant *sécularisation*. Protestant secularization is marked by a "conjoint and progressive transformation of religion and of the different spheres of social activity" (p. 47). This occurred without much conflict between state and church, simply because the latter, in the form of "national churches," always existed within, not outside, the state. To the degree that the state democratized, the church could not adopt an anti-democratic posture, and the state in turn would not feel challenged by the church and take on the garb of militant secularizer. By contrast, the logic of Catholic laicization is that the church, qua universal church existing outside the state, competes with the state, and there is virulent conflict between "clericals" and "anti-clericals." Eventually, the state disempowers religion, which is reduced to a "private" residue. Interestingly, however, Champion *also* takes the distinction between "laicization" and "secularization" as an analytical one. Accordingly, Catholic societies like Italy or Spain, to the degree that they could relax their stance toward a disempowered church and more recently have moved toward a "recognition" of society's major religions, are now shifting from a logic of "laicization" to one of "secularization."

Building on the distinction between Catholic and Protestant paths to secularism, David Martin (1978) has developed a "general theory of secularization" that adds complexity and variation to the matter; but also identifies so many "patterns" that the case for a "general theory" is undermined (reasonably so, one must say). His distinct contribution is to spell out the larger impact of the confessional mix (or absence thereof) on the severity of social and political conflict in a given country. "Catholic monopoly," to begin with, is the most difficult to accommodate, because society threatens to break apart into two "rival societies," without "cumulative legitimation" to the rescue, that is, overlapping group memberships. In this most dangerous of secularization patterns, there is a tight symbiosis of Catholicism with the political right, whereas on the leftist side stand secular "intellectuals" who act as inverted "Catholics," the two sides becoming locked into a "vicious spiral" of militant polarization. The only exception is where "Catholicism" becomes a symbol of "repressed culture," as in Ireland or Poland; here "internal conflict over religion is muted" (p. 42). Most benign, by contrast, is a "mixed" or "pluralist" constellation, with a Protestant majority, in which Catholicism leans to the left and the religious groups spread evenly over the political spectrum, so that the "issue of religion *as such* [is removed] from the arena of political confrontation" (p. 32). And so on. The message is that religion's "social location" (p. 24) and monopoly or plurality status matters greatly for the logic and severity of political conflict at large.[24]

The irony of Christian Democracy

At the height of its powers, during the Second Confessional Age, the Catholic Church constituted an "adversarial counter-culture" not unlike Islam in the West today, as some believe (Caldwell 2009: 329). The Vatican's *Syllabus Errorum* (1864) denounced liberalism and democracy in a breathtaking sweep: freedom of speech, freedom of press, freedom of conscience and religion, legal equality of cults, sovereignty of the people, the doctrine of progress, separation of church and state, liberalism – *all* were denounced as of the Devil. Indeed, this was "ultramontane fundamentalism" (German historian Christoph Weber, quoted in Kalyvas 2003: 298). Representative of parallel movements in the Netherlands, Germany, Austria, Italy, and France, the Belgian Catholic movement deemed itself a "crusade against Liberalism" (p. 299), whose objective was to use liberal representative institutions only to destroy them. One of its leaders declared: "What should subjects do if the law is indifferent and places error and truth on the same level, as it does in Belgium?... [T]hey will use freedom to do good: to redress the ideas, expose the true principles, and spread the understanding of how much God abhors these general freedoms (of speech, press, conscience and religion, etc.)" (p. 299).

David Martin noted that Christianity had always been marked by a tension between being "an aspect of social differentiation," distinguishing an earthly from a heavenly kingdom, *and* being prone to a "vigorous Durkheimian pull toward a total unity of church and state" (1978: 278). This "Durkheimian pull" reached new heights in the Catholic Church's "ultramontane" moment. At the First Vatican Council in 1869, the church emboldened itself as a *societas perfecta*, not just pronouncing the infallibility of the pope but also degrading the national bishops to "civil servants of a foreign sovereign" (Tyrell 2008: 162). Under the battle cry "Christ must also reign upon earth" (Kalyvas 1996: 172), the Catholic Church entered into its last-ditch battle against the secularizing state.

The Catholic Church's radicalism triggered a liberal attack on the looming *Pfaffenherrschaft* (reign of priests). The two key issues, as noted, were marriage and education. In 1865, one year after the *Syllabus Errorum*, the recently united Italian state (which was not recognized by the Vatican) passed anti-clerical laws for civil marriage and the suppression of religious bodies (Kalyvas 1996: 216). In the 1870s, the state monopoly over public education was imposed in Belgium, the Netherlands, Austria, and France (p. 173).

This was the moment of "Christian Democracy," whose story has been told in a classic work of political science (Kalyvas 1996).[25] Unlike conventional explanations, which depict the new parties as agents of the Catholic Church or the result of traditional conservative elites appropriating "religion," Stathis Kalyvas explains the religious parties' rise as "the unplanned, unintended, and unwanted by-product of the strategic steps taken by the Catholic Church in response to liberal anticlerical attacks" (p. 6). In the beginning, the Catholic hierarchy responded to the liberal attacks by supporting Catholic mass organizations, outside the electoral process, with the intention of building a "counter-society" that would "swallow the liberal state" (p. 23). This "organizational strategy" could rely on an established subculture of Catholic schools, newspapers, youth clubs, sport clubs, and other associations. Discussing the case of Germany, Olaf Blaschke (2000) speaks of nothing less than "Catholic Apartheid": still by 1910 only 10 percent of marriages in Germany were mixed marriages, and around 1900 every second Catholic was a member of a Catholic association. When the "organizational strategy" proved insufficient, having "no effect on policy" (Kalyvas 1996: 74) and being unable to fend off a "new wave of anticlericalism" (p. 75), the church moved toward an electoral alliance with the old conservative elite parties. This was to be a temporary alliance only, and the church entered it with strong aversion, because political participation amounted to "implicit acceptance of democracy and modernity" (p. 48).

When the "participation strategy" reaped surprising electoral successes (1871 in Germany, mid- to late 1880s in Belgium, the Netherlands, and Austria, and 1913 and 1919 in Italy), this fueled the process of building Christian Democratic parties. But it brought to prominence a new political leadership of lower clergy and Catholic lay activists, which had already driven the Catholic mass organizations. In turn, among the losers of the process were the old elite of *Honoratioren*, who originally had tried to co-opt the Catholic cause; and, of course, the church, which lost the monopoly over representing Catholics and was forever diminished as a political force.

Importantly, the confessional parties "detached the Catholic political identity from the church and eventually even from religion" (Kalyvas 1996: 222), thus removing perhaps the biggest remaining obstacle in the European process of secularization. Once the logic of the vote-maximizing electoral process kicked in, it could not but "declericalize" the confessional parties, wrecking their initial project of "rechristianization and the building of a Christian society" (p. 245). The irony of Christian Democracy is that the force that was meant to derail European secularization brought it to completion.

Conclusion

The irony of Christian Democracy, which is that it furthered secularization by way of religious party formation, bears important lessons for today's Muslim-majority societies of the Middle East – societies that, not unlike Europe in the late nineteenth century, struggle to become democracies, yet where religious (Islamic) parties are often the strongest political force. The European experience suggests a clear "No" to the question whether there needs to be theological reform (in a liberalizing direction) before Islamic parties can embrace democratic values and help stabilize budding democracies. The reason for optimism is the logic of vote maximization, which is likely to temper the ideological edges of Islamists, much as it once did for the Christian Democrats. In a nutshell, the European lesson is that "political change will precede religious change" (Nasr 2005: 16).

This chapter has shown the many twists and ironies, even partial reversals, which marked the European path of secularization – this has been a crooked path or many paths indeed. I have tried to strike a balance between conceptual clarification and historical illustration, between surveying a field and making a contestable argument, and thus to contribute to the current debate over secularism and secularization – a debate that has exploded recently (above all with the publication of Charles Taylor's *A Secular Age* in 2007), but which has *always* been at the center of the sociology and political science of religion.

What has been said can be summarized in two and a half propositions. First, secularism is necessary for a liberal-democratic state, wherever it may be. Secondly, secularism was arrived at in a contingent historical process, in which (Latin) Christianity was pivotally involved – take away Christianity, and we would not live in a secular age. Thirdly, and this is the half-proposition as it has often remained implicit and could not be systematically developed, Islam (to take only the most developed and pristine monotheism as a reference point) did not or could not launch a similar "exit" from religion – Islam is destined always to be religion, and in a more encompassing but secularization-arresting way than Christianity. The other side of the same coin is that Islam is destined always to be political also, as it cannot be as easily compartmentalized (or "privatized") as the Christian faith allowed itself to become.

These propositions are obvious and there is nothing novel about them. But they bear to be repeated in this simplicity, to cut to the essence of the vexed concepts of secularism and secularization. This exercise required breathtaking simplification, and many will refute the possibility of talking about "Christianity" and "Islam" as such. But as the words exist, it should be permitted to try to fill them with meaning, much as Ernst Troeltsch or Marcel Gauchet did with respect to "Christianity," and I have done little more than report what I learned from them. The new orthodoxy, of course, is the "multivocality" of world religions (Stepan 2001), Islam in particular, as if everything is possible under their roof. But not everything *is* possible, as the very story of secularization as the "long Christian exit" suggests. And then it should be permitted or even deemed necessary to identify a core of the creed that limits variation and, while not explaining the full outcome (secularization), at least may render it plausible. This I have tried to do in the section on the "Christian origins of secularization," which is very much the heart of this chapter.

With respect to the ongoing debate on secularism and secularization, there are two smaller take-away messages. First, the dominant trend, following Casanova (1994: ch. 1), to limit secularization to the dimension of "differentiation" is unconvincing – "privatization" and "decline" are a logically necessary part of secularization. The many exceptions to the rule, from America's Evangelicals to Europe's Muslims, to mention only the two examples that receive further attention in this book, require a specific explanation. At least for the West, the return of public religion has been rather exaggerated, and a private and diminished mode of religion is still the reality for most. In the parts of the world where this is *not* the case, there is reason to worry because liberal democracy is either at risk or out of reach.

Secondly, the "multiple secularisms," very much the fashion of the day, are interesting for the historian and the comparativist, but they add little to the core of the concept, which requires a retreat of religion from politics. This retreat does not have to be as extreme as in a separationist regime. The "modest establishments" of Europe, in which religion is only symbolic and does not control the political process, are fully compatible with the requirements of liberalism (Laborde 2013). As I once argued with respect to the legal integration of Islam, there is "no best practice" to handle religion in a liberal state (Joppke and Torpey 2013: 158–61). If that is the punchline of "multiple secularisms," it is confirmed here, though for the admittedly small range of intra-Western cases that are *not* the gist of the concept.

3

Challenge to the Secular State (I)
The Christian Right in America

Tocqueville observed that America's settlers "brought to the New World a Christianity which I can only describe as democratic and republican.... From the start politics and religion agreed, and they have not since ceased to do so" (1969 [1835–40]: 288). Do they still agree? Before tackling this chapter's central question, one must recall Tocqueville's paradox, which is the due beginning of all reflection on religion in America: "[T]he most free and enlightened people in the world zealously perform all the natural duties of religion" (p. 295). Indeed, the same country that the French aristocrat had turned to for figuring out the nature of democracy and the modern condition at large *also* impressed him through its "religious atmosphere" – this was "the first thing that struck me on arrival in the United States" (p. 295). Tocqueville's explanation for the "quiet sway" of religion over America is counterintuitive, even though it could be from the pages of today's rational-choice or "supply-side" theory of religion: "the complete separation of church and state," about which he found "nobody, lay or cleric," in disagreement (p. 295). In contrast to Europe's established churches at the time, which were controlled by states within "Erastian" church–state regimes, the radical separation between church and state constitutes what Thomas Jefferson called a "fair" and "novel experiment" in human history, and it is certainly the novelty of the "American constitutional experiment" with respect to religion (Witte and Nichols 2011: xix).

Unwittingly throwing a critical light on the contemporary Christian Right's[1] lament about a "naked public sphere" and the alleged demise of "Christian America" (Neuhaus 1984), Tocqueville grounds the vitality and strength of American religion, paradoxically, in its political abstinence and self-limitation. "In America," Tocqueville observes, "religion...restricts itself to its own resources, of which no one can deprive it; it functions in one sphere only, but it pervades it and dominates there without effort" (1969 [1835–40]: 299). This was, again, in contrast to Europe, where not only liberty and religion parted ways, but also Christianity's "[intimate unity] with the powers of this world," according to Tocqueville, was destined to "bury" religion under the monarchy's "ruins" (p. 301).

If Tocqueville's diagnosis is correct, today's Christian Right, whose project is precisely to roll back the separation of religion and state, would not just fundamentally alter the parameters of the American system but also bring about religion's own demise. Pat Robertson, TV Evangelical, one-time presidential candidate, and founder of the influential Christian Coalition, finds it "amazing that the Constitution of the United States says nothing about the separation of church and state." And he adds maliciously, "That phrase *does* appear, however, in the Soviet Constitution" (quoted in Daniel Williams 2010: 218). Indeed, Tocqueville would be surprised to learn about, and condemn as profoundly un-American, the Christian Right's political theology, as expressed by Robertson: "Government was instituted by God to bring His law to people and to carry out His will and purposes" (p. 218). As Jean Cohen pointed out in alarm, though substantially correct, in the American context of a religiously vital society, any rapprochement between state and religion would, in contrast to Europe, lead "toward the theocratic rather than the Erastian end of the spectrum" (2013a: 460).

Before looking closer at the Christian Right's challenge to the secular state in America, it is necessary to first lay out the elements, both ideational and institutional, of the American religion–state regime[2] that is put to the test. John Witte and Joel Nichols (2011) have usefully described the American regime as a confluence of "Puritan," "Evangelical," "Enlightenment," and "Republican" currents. Despite their differences, these currents convene on repudiating the Anglican establishment that they all fled, and on a minimal commitment to Lockean "liberty of conscience" as grounding religion in society and state. However, the emergent religion–state regime was marked by a tension between a

Puritan–Republican pole, on the one hand, and an Evangelical–Enlightenment pole, on the other.

America's proverbial founders, of course, were Puritan, that is, Calvinist dissenters from England. However, they did not bring freedom of religion to America. If Tocqueville was impressed by their "spirit of liberty," it was their political not religious liberty, in terms of a voluntary and self-governing "covenant" that at the same time ruthlessly repressed religious dissent (Quakers were flogged, had "their ears cropped," and were hanged; MacCulloch 2010: 723). The Puritans' Massachusetts Bay Colony was, as nineteenth-century historian and statesman George Bancroft put it, a "sort of theocracy" (quote in Lacorne 2011: 32). Technically this is not correct because the church's government was separate from, if complementary to, secular government, "as in Geneva" (MacCulloch 2010: 721). The "elect" in charge of the Commonwealth, after all, were only a minority of the population, so that, short of dictatorship, religious and civic government could not overlap (p. 720). But the Puritans imposed a European-style established church nevertheless, forcing everyone, the dissenters included, as turned out to be explosive, to support it through taxation.[3] Only later did it mellow into a "mild and equitable establishment of a public religion," as eulogized by John Adams (Witte and Nicols 2011: 36), respecting a modicum of minority rights, yet only for fellow Protestants.

Witte and Nichols (2011: 34–6) interestingly argue that the Puritan ideology went hand in hand with the views of Republicans, whose interest in religion was only instrumental, as a tool of "good" government. In this Republican vein, George Washington found that "religion and morality" were "essential pillars of civil society," and Benjamin Franklin, like Washington no religionist, still advocated "Publick Religion" (p. 34), in anticipation of Robert Bellah's "civil religion" (1967). The 1787 Northwest Ordinance of the Continental Congress is obviously at odds with the separationist First Amendment passed in the same year: "Religion, morality and knowledge, being necessary to good government and the happiness of mankind, schools and the means of education shall forever be encouraged" (quoted in Witte and Nichols 2011: 35).

Indeed, the religion–state regime that became constitutionalized in terms of the First Amendment is *not* of Puritan–Republican but of "Evangelical" and "Enlightenment" cloth. With respect to the first element, the quintessential American Protestantism turned out to be not Puritan but Evangelical, rocking the United States in a series of "Great Awakenings" from the early 1700s, and by the early 1800s this was the dominant religion of the land. Evangelicalism traces its roots to the sixteenth-century Anabaptism of the Swiss and German Amish,

Hutterites, Mennonites, and Baptists, with adult baptism and a purely voluntary and non-statist idea of religious community at the center. Its American hero is Roger Williams, a dissident Puritan who was expelled in 1636 from the Massachusetts Bay Colony for his heretical rejection of a politico-religious "Christian commonwealth," and who championed the principles of "liberty of conscience" and of "no establishment" upon which the American religion–state regime came to be built (see Kramnick and Moore 2005: ch. 3). Williams would also provide the American system's central metaphor, some 160 years before Jefferson, to whom it has mainly been attributed, which prevailed until its recent challenge by the Christian Right: "a wall of separation" had to shield the "garden of the Church" from the "wilderness of the world." To associate the "garden" with the "Church" says everything necessary about the pro-, not anti-religious foundations of American secularism (Witte and Nichols 2011: 27). Born in the first Great Awakening of the 1730s, American Evangelicalism was a "religion of the heart" (Casanova 1994: 137), in departure from the scriptural and theological penchant of the Puritans, and it countered Calvin's harsh and elitist Predestination teachings with the friendlier notion that "saving grace had universal reach" (Lacorne 2011: 43), available to everybody. In its instinctive and experiential blending of the religious and the secular, to the point that the "very distinction religion–secularism loses its meaning" (Herberg 1960: 270), American Evangelicalism, at least in its earliest incarnation, provided the template for American religiosity at large.

Last but not least, the Founders of the American Republic espoused at best "cool versions of Christianity, or virtually no Christianity at all" (MacCulloch 2010: 763). In Witte and Nichols' terminology, the Founders held "enlightenment views," which is the fourth – and in the moment of constitution-crafting, decisive – current that undergirds the American religion–state regime. If a contemporary leader of the Christian Right claims that "what Christians have got to do is to take back this country," to "make it a country once again governed by Christians" (Christian Coalition leader Ralph Reed, quoted in Kramnick and Moore 2005: 22), one must respond: it has never been that way. There is no reference to God in the American Constitution (see Kramnick and Moore 2005). If there was a prevailing religious sentiment among the Founders, it was Deist, with a distinct sympathy for Evangelical and other religious dissenters who toiled under Puritan or Episcopalian (the US variant of Anglican) establishments. In his famous letter to the Danbury Baptists, which canonized the "wall of separation" justification of the First Amendment's religion clauses (the latter stipulating that Congress was to "make no law respecting an establishment of religion, or prohibiting the free exercise thereof"), Thomas Jefferson (1802) left no doubt that the whole point was to assure that "religion is a matter which lies solely between Man and his God," that is, no matter for either church or state. At the same time, the thrust of separating religion and state was not *only* to protect religion (more precisely: the religionist's liberty of conscience), but *also* to protect the integrity of the state. Separation was meant to be a *double* protection, and thus an instance of Alfred Stepan's global principle of "twin toleration" (2001). Note that in seven of the original 13 states, clerics were formally barred from political office, which is the institutional backdrop to Tocqueville's observation of American religionists' political abstinence. In his famous Federalist Letter no. 10, James Madison, the author of the First Amendment, pointed to religion as one of the causes of the "mischiefs of faction" that stood to be controlled by intelligent institutional design.[4] But then it would be wrong to deny, as does Stephen Carter (1994: 105),[5] that the integrity of the state was a major concern. Note that Madison advocated a "perfect separation between ecclesiastical and civil matters," assuming "religion and Government will both exist in greater purity, the less they are mixed together" (quoted in Witte and Nichols 2011: 31). This obviously cuts both ways, as government *also* was deemed better off if left alone.

If not by institutional design, America was still sociologically a Christian society, as observed by Tocqueville, but from the start with a strong non-doctrinal, secular bent that is obscured in the Christian Right's theocratic rhetoric. It is again apposite to approach this fact with Tocqueville. He observed that religion has different functions in democratic and aristocratic societies. In the latter, people are unequal but there are strong ties between them, linking them in a hierarchical order and also across generations. In a democracy, these ties dissolve and under the reign of "individualism" people turn inwards and withdraw into their own small circles. But then, why trust the other, what is the minimal agreement between strangers that is required for social exchange? For Tocqueville, the function of religion is to fill the social vacuum that arises with the dissolution of hierarchy: "Despotism may be able to do without faith, but freedom cannot. Religion is much more needed in the republic...than in the monarchy..., and in democratic republics most of all. How could society escape destruction if, when political ties are relaxed, moral ties are not tightened?" (1969 [1835–40]: 294). This is why Tocqueville's American interlocutors, without exception, and surprisingly to the untrained eye, would tell the French visitor that religion is "necessary" – it was necessary because Americans were free (p. 293).

But for purposes of "social control" (Johnson 1978: 136) the content of faith is less relevant than the possession of "faith" as such – "faith in faith" is the quintessentially American religiosity (Herberg 1960: 89). This peculiar American meta-religiosity is captured in many a European's travel notices, from Tocqueville to Max Weber. In a footnote of *Democracy in America*, Tocqueville mentions a New York judge who refused to swear in a witness who was an atheist: according to this judge, belief in God "constituted the sanction of all testimony in a court of justice."[6] As Hugh Heclo argued, under the impact of democracy American Christianity leaned "toward a simple fideism with scant regard for doctrinal reasoning" (2007: 61). At the political level, President Eisenhower has immortalized this fact: "Our government makes no sense unless it is founded in a deeply felt religious faith – and I don't care what it is" (quoted by Herberg 1960: 84).

In this respect, it is more accurate to call the American exit position "religious" rather than "Christian" society, and it explains the unique elasticity to include other than Christian faiths. In the late 1950s, Will Herberg famously observed that "to be an American today means to be either a Protestant, a Catholic, or a Jew"; more than that, that it was "mandatory" to place oneself in one of these groups (1960: 40). This did not come without struggle and bigotry – infamously, before John F. Kennedy's election in 1960 it was unconceivable for a Catholic to become president. But the trend toward it was built into American "denominational pluralism" (p. 86) from the start, a pluralism that forced religionists to relax their respective religious truth claims. Herberg called the ensuing disposition "latitudinarianism," which he describes, with immigrant historian Oscar Handlin, as Americans' belief that "ethical behavior and a good life, rather than adherence to a specific creed, [will] earn a share in the heavenly kingdom" (Handlin quoted on p. 83).

This "religiousness without religion" (Herberg 1960: 260), which Herberg also called, notably before Bellah (1967), a "civic religion" or "American culture-religion" (Herberg 1960: 262), has the paradoxical effect of being exacted on everyone but at the same time leaving everyday life resolutely secular. With respect to its universal reach, in America "overt anti-religion is all but inconceivable" (p. 260). Note that, in the early nineteenth century, barely 10 to 15 percent of Americans were members of a church, whereas today the percentage of "nones," that is, Americans without religious affiliation, is in the same smallish range (though increasing recently) and the vast remainder are church members.[7] At the same time, Herberg observed that "mounting religiosity" was complemented by "pervasive secularism" (1960: 22) and an "irrelevance of religion to business and politics" (p. 73). Tocqueville had observed a worldly disposition even on the part of American priests, who "take an interest in the progress of industry and praise its achievements," and who "seek to discover the point of connection and alliance" between the two worlds (1969 [1835–40]: 449). In America, the two worlds, the religious and the secular, are in a way one, a condition that Herberg aptly called "secularism within a religious framework, the secularism of a religious people" (1960: 271).

Legal Secularism

Since 1789, the unchanging core of the American religion–state regime has been the First Amendment's religion clauses. They state, as briefly as it could be, that "Congress shall make no law respecting an establishment of religion, or prohibiting the free exercise thereof." The first half of this phrase has become known as the "Establishment Clause" (illogically, as it should really be the "No-Establishment Clause"), and the second as the "Free Exercise Clause." Almost every word in the innocent-sounding half-sentence containing the religion clauses is significant, and combined they make for one of the most contested and legally belabored sites in American legal history.

First, the religion clauses notionally constrain only "Congress," that is, the federal government, but not state governments. Only in 1940 was the Free Exercise Clause applied to the states, through the Due Process Clause of the Fourteenth Amendment, and in 1947 the Establishment Clause followed suit.[8] Up to then, established churches, arguably the target of the First Amendment's ire, were technically possible, even though the last establishment, the "soft" multiple establishment of Massachusetts,[9] fell in 1833. But as long as the First Amendment did not apply to states, that is, well into the middle of the twentieth century, the American reality was prayer and Bible readings in public schools[10] and religiously motivated laws prohibiting the teaching of Darwinian biology, a legacy of 1920s Protestant Fundamentalism. Even today some conservative legal scholars and justices, like Supreme Court Justice Clarence Thomas, deny the applicability of the First Amendment's Establishment Clause to states, arguing that its content was merely a compromise to protect state-level establishments from federal interference.[11] This would formally clear the way for state governments under the sway of the Christian Right, say, Texas, to reintroduce establishments or declare themselves as "Christian states" (see Nussbaum 2008: 7).

Secondly, it is significant that the First Amendment deals with "religion" explicitly and separately, apart from other half-sentences in the same amendment that protect the freedom of speech and assembly in general (and that could, in principle, cover the fact of religion). The Framers thus seemed to view religion as "special," especially worthy of protection but also especially dangerous, if exercised by majorities against dissenters. The religion clauses express a "constitutional dualism" (Cohen 2013b: 514), containing special protection of religious conscience and free exercise that other forms of human expression do not enjoy *and* special restrictions and liabilities for religious organizations that other types of social organization do not face, to preclude establishment. As to "special protection," it is noteworthy that an alternative formulation, considered at the time, to protect the "rights of conscience" more generally,[12] which would adequately denote the Lockean sources of institutionalizing religion in America (see Feldman 2002a), was explicitly discarded in favor of the more specific yet also more encompassing formulation "free exercise of religion" (see Nussbaum 2008: 102).[13]

With respect to "special restrictions," it must be noted that the Establishment Clause does not just preclude the establishment of churches or of "a" religion, but any law "respecting [of] an establishment of religion," in this generality. This is a much more far-reaching prohibition of contact between state and "religion" at large. It allowed the possibility of a "wall of separation" between religion and state, which would make America, together with France, the only "truly secular" among Western states (Zoller 2006: 563). The American separation regime even erased any distinction between preferred majority religions and minority religions trying to rise to the level of the former, which had always been the reverse side of French *laïcité*. In doing so, the American variant of strict separation would operate "in an infinitely harder and more rigid manner" than the French (p. 592). Conversely, the complete removal of majority privileges in American laicity allowed the possibility of aggrieved majority religions adopting the posture of a persecuted minority of the "religious." In the context of the American race paradigm, that is, of strong civil rights and antidiscrimination provisions, this is a highly lucrative stance that, as we shall see, the Christian Right would take on with gusto and to great effect.

It must be conceded, however, that the possibility of religious majorities masquerading as minorities grows out of a real tension between the Establishment and Free Exercise Clauses, in that disadvantages arising under the Establishment Clause could be easily construed as unconstitutional impairments of free exercise rights. Conversely formulated, strong free exercise rights require the minimizing of establishment constraints. To point to this tension inherent in the religion clauses has likewise been a preferred strategy of conservative jurists allied with the Christian Right. Their undisputed legal mastermind, the respected constitutional lawyer Michael McConnell, thus argued that "religious liberty" is the key value of the First Amendment's religion clauses, while the notion of "separation" of church and state does not even appear in the Constitution (McConnell 1985: 1). The attempts to demolish the Establishment Clause have been multiple and perennial. The Christian Right's advocates in the Supreme Court, for instance, who have been gaining strength since the days of Ronald Reagan, hold to a minimalist view of the Establishment Clause. This holds that the only thing the government is not allowed to do is to "coerce anyone to support or participate in any religion."[14] So the only function of the Establishment Clause is to prevent America from becoming like the Islamic Republic of Iran. A complementary strategy was to argue that not *any* contact between government and religion, but only a *prioritizing* of one religion over other religions was barred under the Establishment Clause. As Steven Bruce pointed out, such a "conservative" view makes no sense because already by 1789 only five states still had legal establishments, and all were "multiple" (1988: 37). According to Bruce, this fact rather supports a "liberal" reading of the Establishment Clause as being "opposed...[to] government support for religion per se" (p. 37). However implausible it may be, an anodyne reading of the Establishment Clause allowed it to be turned on its head. The latter now could – some even argue: should – entail the state's privileging of religion over non-religion. While the attempts to minimize if not demolish the Establishment Clause have varied over the last few decades, its status as main legal enemy of the Christian Right has persisted.

Between the late 1940s and the mid-1980s, "legal secularism" (Feldman 2005: ch. 5) was the dominant approach in American religion–state relations. It was, indeed, a "legal" secularism as it centered on the Supreme-Court-ordered "incorporation" of the First Amendment's religion clauses into the Fourteenth Amendment's Due Process Clause and thus into state law. However, this was never a militantly anti-religious secularism, as in France. Instead, it was, to quote Will Herberg again, the "secularism of a religious people" (1960: 271). It had little in common with the reign of "secular humanism" as "*ersatz* religion" (Neuhaus 1984: 82), as which this period tends to be demonized by the Christian Right. While the Supreme Court rolled back the biggest violations of the "no-establishment" principle in the early 1960s, the rise of legal secularism, after all, strangely coincided with the adding of "under God" to the Pledge of Allegiance (in 1954) and Congress's declaration of "In God we trust" as national motto (in 1956), which were motivated by the anti-Communism of the period. Note, moreover, that the High Noon of American secularism coincided with Robert Bellah's (1967) codification of the "civil religion," incidentally at the height of the anti-Vietnam turmoil. But not just other actors (like Congress and certain intellectuals) would carry the religion torch but the *same* Supreme Court that had instantiated legal secularism *simultaneously* acknowledged and accommodated the high religious temperature of American society.

In retrospect, "separation" and "accommodation" tend to be set up as rival approaches to religion–state relations (especially by McConnell 1985). In reality, however, they are better understood as a package, at least in America. Symptomatic of the complementarity, rather than antagonism, of separation and accommodation are two early benchmark Supreme Court rules, *Everson v. Board of Education* (1947) and *Zorach v. Clauson* (1952). The first of these judgments became famous not just for "incorporating" the Establishment Clause into state law but also for providing the leitmotif for the entire period of legal secularism: that the Establishment Clause "was intended to erect 'a wall of separation between church and State.'"[15] Moreover, the court influentially took the Establishment Clause as a comprehensive "no aid" maxim, which

> means at least this: neither a State nor the Federal Government can set up a church. Neither can pass laws which aid one religion, aid all religions, or prefer one religion over another. Neither can force nor influence a person to go to or to remain away from church against his will or force him to profess a belief or disbelief in any religion.[16]

At the same time, however, that the "wall" between church and state had to "be kept high and impregnable," *Everson v. Board of Education* stressed that the state had to be "neutral" toward religious believers (and unbelievers) but not "their adversary."[17] After recapitulating, through the lens of the Jewish Holocaust, the dark story of the persecution of religious minorities in Europe and thereafter even in colonial America, the *Everson v. Board of Education* court took the point of the First Amendment to be "protection against governmental intrusion on religious liberty,"[18] which could be from the notebook of "accommodation" (McConnell 1985: 1). Last but not least, the outcome of *Everson v. Board of Education* should not be forgotten: it *validated* a New Jersey law that subsidized the bus bills for Catholic schools (along with those for public schools), which had been attacked as a violation of the Establishment Clause. As the court defended its surprising decision, the law in question was but a "general program to help parents...," regardless of their religion," so that the "wall" that did not permit "slightest breach" had "not," in fact, "[been] breached...here."[19]

Everson v. Board of Education, as a classically separationist rule, is often contrasted with *Zorach v. Clauson* (1952) as a paragon of "accommodation." This word was explicitly produced in *Zorach v. Clauson,* its "purpose" described as "facilitating the free exercise of religion" (McConnell 1985: 3–4). This most-favored Supreme Court decision of the Christian Right, quoted wherever separationism and secularism stand to be repudiated, indeed contains the very peculiar line that "We are a religious people whose institutions presuppose a Supreme Being."[20] *Zorach v. Clauson* validated the "released time" program in New York City's public schools, according to which, on written request by parents, students were granted one hour off per week for off-site religious instruction. A clear six to three majority of the Supreme Court considered this a measure of "respect" for the "religious nature of our people," which "accommodates the public service to their spiritual needs."[21] To show "callous indifference to religious groups" or "to be hostile to religion," concluded Justice Douglas in by now famous lines for the court majority in *Zorach v. Clauson*, is "no constitutional requirement."[22] But this was no goodbye to the "wall of separation" that had been enunciated by *Everson v. Board of Education* five years earlier. Instead, *Zorach v. Clauson* stayed *within* a separationist framework: "There cannot be the slightest doubt that the 1st Amendment reflects the philosophy that church and state should be separated....The separation must be complete and unequivocal....The prohibition is absolute."[23]

Legal secularism first showed its teeth in the so-called "prayer cases" of the early 1960s. They put an end to a subtle sectarianism of the public school system, which lingered under the guise of a non-denominational deism that was meant to bolster citizenship and social cohesion. Since the introduction of the public school system in the early nineteenth century, its spirit had been to instill "individual autonomy" and "self-discipline" (see Lacorne 2011: 75). Rather than an economic project of providing skilled workers for corporate America, the new public schools were a political project, to provide unskilled immigrants with a civic education. A staple of the enterprise of bolstering a common morale was non-sectarian Bible reading, without any comment by teachers. As Noah Feldman put it, this notional non-sectarianism functioned as "ideology of inclusiveness that was fully prepared to exclude" (2005: 85). The Catholic Church understood this. From the start, it wanted the Bible out of the school, because the readings were based on the Anglican King James version. In contrast to the Catholic version of the Bible, the King James Bible contained the Old Testament's Second Commandment: "Thou shalt not make unto thee any graven image, or any likeness of any thing that is in heaven above, or that is in the earth beneath, or that is in the water under the earth. Thou shalt not bow down thyself to them, nor serve them." This *Bilderverbot* (pictorial prohibition) conflicted with the cult of saints, the paintings and frescoes that adorn Catholic Churches, the ornate life stories of Jesus and Mary, and so on, that have marked the

Catholic tradition since St. Augustine, who had taken the Second Commandment out of the Catholic catechism (Lacorne 2011: 70). In the 1850s, there was a veritable Bible War in America, with heroic acts of civil disobedience on the part of some Catholic pupils who refused to read from the Protestant Bible, and ever since Catholics have tended to opt out of public schools and push for parochial schools instead. Apart from the Second Commandment disagreement, the (Irish-dominated) Catholic hierarchy would not give up its "authority" as guide to the Bible, which was undermined by its "secular" reading in the public schools. Much like feminists or multiculturalists today, the Catholic hierarchy attacked the latent sectarianism behind a façade of neutrality: "The sects say, read the Bible, judge for yourselves.... The Protestant principle is therefore acted upon, slyly inculcated, and the schools are sectarian" (Lacorne 2011: 76).

The first prayer case, *Engel v. Vitale* (1962), concerned an obligation imposed by the New York City Board of Education to begin each school day with a non-denominational prayer: "Almighty God, we acknowledge our dependence upon Thee, and we beg Thy blessings upon us, our parents, our teachers and our Country."[24] For its defenders, the prayer was religious, certainly, but "based on our spiritual heritage" and, moreover, it was cross-faith and voluntary.[25] However, "as a matter of history," countered Justice Black for the majority of the court, state-ordered prayer had "caused many of our early colonists to leave England and seek religious freedom in America."[26] In barely five pages, unusually short for a decision that would change a century-long tradition, known and cherished since the inception of American public schools, Justice Black hammered home the point that the government's "official stamp of approval" amounted to "one of the greatest dangers to the freedom of the individual to worship in his own way,"[27] thus confirming the centrality of liberty for the Constitution's religion clauses. More technically, *Engel v. Vitale* established as the baseline of a separationist reading of the Establishment Clause that the latter did not only prohibit "direct governmental compulsion," as the Supreme Court under the sway of the Christian Right would argue a few decades later,[28] but also "indirect coercive pressure upon religious minorities." The beast to beat was a "union of government and religion" that "tends to destroy government and to degrade religion."[29] Here is the typically separationist view that religion was not only bliss but also potential danger at the hand of the majority. A lone dissenter on the court, Justice Stewart, who, however, happened to represent the opinion of the vast majority of the American public on this issue, held against the court majority that the contested prayer did not amount to "establishment of a state church" – this was a typically conservative, narrow reading of the Establishment Clause. Moreover, Justice Stewart argued, the suppression

of the prayer denied "the opportunity of sharing in the spiritual heritage of our nation."[30]

One year later, the second prayer case, *School District of Abington
Township v. Schempp* (1963), was about Bible readings in Pennsylvania
public schools, "without comment" and excusable upon written request,
though on the basis of the King James version, and followed by
recitation of the Lord's Prayer. In outlawing this practice, *School District of Abington Township v. Schempp* fixed more clearly than previous Supreme Court rules two doctrinal essentials of legal secularism.
First, the Establishment Clause did not just forbid the "governmental
preference of one religion over another"[31] and thus amount to a norm
to "treat them equally."[32] Instead, it was a norm to "abstain from
fusing functions of Government and of religious sect."[33] Secondly, the
Establishment Clause was not just about the "separation of Church
and State" but it "forbade all laws respecting an establishment of
religion,"[34] which amounted to a much stricter mandate of "whole-
some neutrality."[35]

Hitting America at the summit of its "end of ideology" slumber, well
ahead of the 1960s turmoil of student protest, racial unrest, and sexual
revolution, the Supreme Court's ordering of legal secularism was hugely
unpopular. A Gallup poll found 79 percent of the American public in
support of school prayer after its prohibition under *Engel v. Vitale*
(Daniel Williams 2010: 62). What could possibly be wrong with the
"inclusive" and "innocuous" prayer expelled from the public school by
Engel v. Vitale, as Kent Greenawalt paraphrases the popular reaction
(2009: 106)? Greenawalt sees the impact of the prayer cases thus:
"Widely disobeyed, they also sparked a sharp increase in political
involvement by evangelical conservative Christian groups dismayed over
the country's drift toward secularism and amorality" (pp. 103–4).
However, the religious reaction subtly differed in both cases. *Engel v.
Vitale*'s interdiction of prayer proper was mostly attacked by Catholic
clerics, who found this to be "the establishment of a new religion of
secularism" (quoted in Daniel Williams 2010: 63). Protestant Evangelicals, by contrast, had always denounced the non-denominational prayer
without "Jesus Christ" as "pagan prayer." They also welcomed the
decision to counter the mounting influence of Catholics, who just at
this moment were stepping up their campaign for parochial schools.
Only *School District of Abington Township v. Schempp* met the wholesale disapproval of Evangelicals, as it hit "a hallmark of the nation's
Protestant-designed public school curriculum since the early nineteenth
century" (p. 64). But among Evangelicals there was differentiation too.
The Southern Baptist Convention, which two decades later would grow
into the bastion of the Christian Right, did not join in the opposition

to *School District of Abington Township v. Schempp*, as it was still more beholden to the dissenters' tradition of religious freedom than to the public display and politicization of faith that it would embrace later (p. 66). The Southern Baptists even actively opposed the school prayer amendment that was proposed by the Congressional opposition to *School District of Abington Township v. Schempp*. While the amendment never came, this did not matter much because as late as 1972, about a quarter of public schools in the United States were not complying with *Engel v. Vitale* and *School District of Abington Township v. Schempp*, and in the Southern states noncompliance was even more widespread (p. 67).

Always in the terrain of public schools, where up to the present day its roots are strongest, legal secularism would also impose itself on the last remnants of 1920s fundamentalism. In *Epperson v. Arkansas* (1968), the Supreme Court affirmed a school teacher's challenge to an Arkansas anti-evolution statute that prohibited textbooks that teach "that mankind ascended or descended from a lower order of animals."[36] The Arkansas statute was an adaptation of the infamous Tennessee "Monkey Law" of 1925, in force since 1928, and by 1968 one of two such state laws still existing in the United States (the other being a "monkey law" in Mississippi). It made the teaching of evolutionary theory a criminal offense for the teacher, on pain of his or her immediate dismissal. "It is possible," remarked a rather subdued majority court, "that the statute is presently more of a curiosity than a vital fact of life in these states."[37] From a doctrinal point of view, however, *Epperson v. Arkansas* confirmed a comprehensive understanding of the Establishment Clause as mandating not only "governmental neutrality" between "religion and religion," as minimalist conservatives prefer to argue, but also neutrality "between religion and nonreligion." Otherwise there simply would be no possibility for the federal government to go against a law that does not violate the rights of another religion but that opposes secularism in the name of religion.

However, the undisputed peak of legal secularism was the Supreme Court's *Lemon v. Kurtzman* (1971) decision. It concerned state aid to church-led elementary and secondary schools. This was, next to the display of religious symbols in the public square, one of two permanently controversial issues surrounding the Establishment Clause over the next four decades. Never before had a flimsier, at best indirect and only potential (not actually demonstrated) "entanglement" between state and religion been deemed an unconstitutional "establishment of religion." Concretely, *Lemon v. Kurtzman* incriminated statutes in Pennsylvania and Rhode Island that partially reimbursed parochial school teachers' salaries, textbooks, and instructional materials, even if to be used only in specified secular subjects and for secular purposes, because of their vague "potential" to draw state and religion too close together. Teachers are not "neutrals," argued Justice Burger for the court majority, and a "comprehensive, discriminating, and continuing state surveillance will inevitably be required to ensure that these restrictions are obeyed."[38] In addition to this hypothesized "entanglement," in the court's view there was also the prospect of "divisive political potential of these state programs,"[39] and the threat of "development by momentum."[40] To add insult to the injury of religionists, the court declared that "religion must be a private matter...and that...lines must be drawn."[41]

That religion is private was the leitmotif of legal secularism all along, but rarely had it been stated so directly. For the next two decades, the court would follow the so-called "Lemon Test," which was formulated here not *ex nihilo* but in compilation of the principles underlying the court's previous case law. According to this test, a statute was unconstitutional if one of the following three conditions were not fulfilled: the law needed a "secular purpose"; it had a "primary effect" that "neither advances nor inhibits religion"; and it did not foster "an excessive government entanglement with religion"[42] – which was deemed to be the risk of the statutes in question in *Lemon v. Kurtzman*. No wonder that this maximally secularist rule would become the central negative reference point as the Supreme Court, from the Reagan presidency on, moved toward the Christian Right. However, even in *Lemon v. Kurtzman* the *Zorach v. Clauson* line that "some relationship" between state and religion "is inevitable" was not discarded.[43] As if sensing that from now on the reverse gear was more likely to be taken, the court conceded that "the line of separation, far from being a 'wall,' is a blurred, indistinct, and variable barrier depending on all the circumstances of a particular relationship."[44]

The best proof that legal secularism's insistence on line-drawing and privatizing religion was never far away from accommodation is the famous *Sherbert v. Verner* (1963) rule. Following on the heels of the early 1960s separationist "prayer cases," *Sherbert v. Verner* was one of the most accommodationist Supreme Court decisions ever, though grounded in the Free Exercise Clause. The link between separation on the Establishment Clause and accommodation on the Free Exercise Clause is obvious: the threat *of* religion was mostly originating under its majority guise, which stood to be restricted under the Establishment Clause; by contrast, threats *to* religion mostly concerned minority religions that needed special protections under the Free Exercise Clause. As we shall see, this constellation would be exactly reversed once the Christian Right came to exert its influence, when religious minority rights were diminished under a diluted Free Exercise Clause and religious majorities imposed themselves under an "accommodationist" Establishment Clause.

Sherbert v. Verner concerned a member of the sectarian Seventh-Day Adventist Church who had been discharged for not working on Saturday, the sect's holy day, and subsequently she was denied unemployment benefits because of her lawful dismissal. This was an "unconstitutional burden on the free exercise of her religion," argued the court, and there existed "no compelling state interest" to overrule her religious liberty right.[45] The unacceptable choice of having to "abandon" her precepts of religion for the sake of "accept[ing] work" was "compounded" by "religious discrimination," because under South Carolina law "Sunday worshippers" (the word for mainstream Christians) were expressly exempted "from having to make [that] kind of choice."[46] That "neutrality," the lodestar of legal secularism, also worked in favor of religion is expressed in the fact that the court-ordered "extension" of unemployment benefits to Sabbatarians, to bring them into line with the benefits already granted to ordinary Christians, was deemed to reflect "nothing more than the governmental obligation of neutrality in the face of religious differences."[47]

The Rise of the Christian Right

The Tocquevillian marriage of Christianity and democracy in America rested, we saw, on the political self-limitation of religion. The marriage is put to the test today by a politically assertive Christian Right, which has made huge inroads into the Republican Party – one influential commentator called the Republicans under President George W. Bush the "first religious party in US history" (Phillips 2006: x–xi). However, it would be wrong to assume that the Christian Right is the crest of a broader resurgence of religion. "If there is a trend," argues a perceptive survey of contemporary trends in American religion, "it is toward less religion" (Chaves 2011: 110). Instead, a true novelty on the American scene is the "tight connection" between religiosity and political and social conservatism (p. 111). It puts at risk the kind of "agreement" between religion and politics that Tocqueville observed in the 1830s, and which he, paradoxically, identified with their separation (1969 [1835–40]: 288). If initially Christianity and democracy reinforced one another, like a "double-stranded helix spiraling through time" (Heclo 2007: 35), they now threaten to part ways. The religionists attack a godless "secular humanism" that they see dominant among elites and in public institutions, and democrats distance themselves from bigoted

"Christian theocrats" (p. 205). This confrontation has become known as "culture war" (see Hunter and Wolfe 2006). However, the metaphor is mistaken because the polarization is more between a small number of "cultural warriors" and a large majority of "disgusted bystanders" (Heclo 2007: 120), many of the latter religious themselves. Perhaps a touch too dramatic, Hugh Heclo found this condition reminiscent of the post-revolutionary France that Tocqueville had left to find wisdom in America: "[A] condition of devout, serious Christians alienated from the quest for democracy, and of devout, serious democrats hostile to Christianity" (pp. 143–4).

The Christian Right's shrillest moment was after the terrorist attacks of September 11, 2001, when two of their leaders were in perfect agreement about who "helped this happen": "The pagans, and the abortionists, and the feminists, and the gays and the lesbians who are actively trying to make that an alternative lifestyle, the ACLU, People for the American Way, all of them who have tried to secularize America, I point the finger in their face and say, 'You helped this happen.'" This was Jerry Falwell (quoted in Daniel Williams 2010: 254). "I totally concur," replied Pat Robertson, on whose *700 Club* TV show this strange exchange took place, just two days after the murderous event (quoted in Goldberg 2007: 8).

As shrill as the statement is, its cascading, obsessive reference to "abortionists," "feminists," "gays and lesbians," and "alternative lifestyles" confirms that "personal sexual morality" is a key concern of the Christian Right (Putnam and Campbell 2010: 82) – interestingly, very similar to pious Muslims in Europe and the West (see Chapter 4). In the most important survey on American religion to appear in decades, Robert Putnam and David Campbell depicted the development of American religiosity since the 1950s as "one major shock and two aftershocks" (p. 81). The "major shock" was the 1960s "earthquake" of the "counterculture." Already Hugh Heclo's (2007) diagnosis of the parting of religion and democracy had centered on the counterculture, calling the latter "America's first secular Awakening," with "authenticity" as a "self-referential" key value (p. 99). Heclo thus suggests that an opposition to it was likely to be religious, in terms of anti-secularism. It happened in the first "aftershock" of the 1980s, when "conservative politics" became "the most visible aspect of religion in America" (Putnam and Campbell 2010: 81). Finally, the second "aftershock" was the reactive trend, beginning in the 1990s, of young Americans, aghast at the conservative religionists, turning "decidedly nonreligious" (p. 82).

The key dynamic for Putnam and Campbell is that of "libertines" and "prudes" locked in a reactive chain: "Liberal sexual morality provoked...[the] assert[ion of] conservative religious beliefs...and then conservative sexual morality provoked...secular beliefs" (2010: 82). Consider that 80 percent of the "boomers," who drove the 1960s youth counterculture, endorsed premarital sex, while precisely 80 percent of the older generation rejected this – this was "literally a revolution in traditional moral views" (p. 94). According to Putnam and Campbell, the rise of religious conservatism in the "first aftershock" of the 1960s counterculture earthquake is a complex concatenation of demography (Evangelicals having more children),[48] "greater organizational energy and inventiveness" (like the use of rock music, marketing, and contemporary liturgy), but above all an urgent sense to "stand up for your values," a sense that the "world is sinful" with "God as a harsh judge" (pp. 113–14). Two-thirds of Evangelical Protestants surveyed by Putnam in 2006 found their values "seriously" or at least "moderately threatened" (p. 114), the key source of that threat being a "collapsing sexual morality." Putnam even ranks the latter ahead of a dislike for the court-ordered "legal secularism" that started with the early 1960s prayer cases (p. 117).

In fact, more than the prayer cases, which have long faded in memory and are known today at best to historians and constitutional lawyers, it is another Supreme Court decision, Roe v. Wade (1973), which legalized abortion as a matter of a "right to privacy," which became a perennial fixation for the Christian Right. It galvanized a "right to life" movement that accomplished something unseen so far, a coalition between conservative Catholics (the traditional opponents to abortion) and conservative Protestants, who were drawn into the fold only recently. The very notion of a "right to life" suggests the centrality of values, rather than creed, in this religious mobilization. When Jerry Falwell entered the political scene in the late 1970s, significantly, he would call his movement the "Moral Majority" not the "Religious Majority." This signals the "transmutation of religion into values" (Feldman 2005: 193). Noah Feldman (ch. 6) consequently called the Christian Right "values evangelicals," who in his scenario have come to challenge the "legal secularism" of the 1960s. Their characteristic is a paradoxical sense of "moral majority" lingering as besieged "minority" in an America ruled by secular and amoral elites.[49] Strangely, when he withdrew from politics after a fulminant decade that had seen Ronald Reagan being elected president twice with the help of his movement, Jerry Falwell would still incant, "We are the last minority" (quoted in Daniel Williams 2010: 223).

But who exactly is the Christian Right, what does it want, what has it achieved? In tackling its origins, several layers of ferment have to be distinguished. The most general layer is an extraordinarily high degree of religiosity in America. Between 1988 and 2008, on average 93 percent of Americans said they "believe in God or a higher power" (Chaves 2011: 11). More prosaically, in 2008 86 percent of Americans believed in "heaven," while 73 percent believed in "hell" (p. 33). At the same time, 40 percent reported attending religious service "nearly every week or more," which would make America the West's most heavily church-going nation – topped only by Poland (with nearly 60 percent), but over four times more than church attendance in utterly secularized Germany, France, and Sweden (Putnam and Campbell 2010: 7).[50] More strikingly still, a December 2004 *Newsweek* poll (reported in Phillips 2006: 100) found 55 percent of a national sample responding with "yes" to the question whether the Bible is "literally accurate" (predict-ably, an even higher proportion of Evangelical Protestants, 83 percent, responded this way). Even if these data are only nearly correct, it would qualify about half of Americans as "fundamentalist" in the original sense of the word (see Marty 2000: 13120). No surprise, then, that 60 percent of respondents in a February 2004 ABC Prime Time poll believed that Noah's Ark really existed, and that 61 percent believed that God created the earth in six days (Phillips 2006: 102) – also a view that had energized the 1920s Fundamentalist movement in the United States, and which has received a second lease of life in today's so-called "creation science" (or "intelligent design," see Goldberg 2007: ch. 3). It may be exaggerated to conclude that America is "the world's leading Bible-reading Crusader State," as does Kevin Phillips (2006: 103), but attitudes like these are obviously fertile ground for conserva-tive Christian mobilization.

A second layer of ferment refers to changes in the denominational distribution of American religions. The most significant development here is the spectacular decline of "white liberal Protestants," the previous religious mainstream in America, who shrank from above 25 percent of the American populace in the early 1970s to under 15 percent by 2008 (Chaves 2011: 83).[51] Conversely, "white conservative Protestants" could stabilize their share among America's socio-religious groups, from under 25 percent in the early 1970s to above 25 percent in 2008 (p. 86). In an increasingly fractured – though still overwhelmingly Christian – Ameri-can religious landscape, conservative Protestants now form the dominant religious bloc, ahead of Catholics, who have likewise diminished in recent years. Conservative Protestants' increasing concentration in the churchgoing population has even led to the popular association of "Christian" with "evangelical Protestant" (p. 104). To this must be added yet another close association, that of "evangelical Protestant" with "Republican Party."[52] Putnam and Campbell called it the "God gap," meaning that "religiosity has partisan overtones now that it did not have in the past" (2010: 360). Concretely, the political right is identified with

"evangelicals," the left with "nones" (shorthand for "no religious affiliation"), while the "moderate religious middle [is] seriously weakened"
(p. 132). Between a quarter and a third of the American electorate is
estimated to be Evangelical,[53] and around 80 percent of them have solidly
voted for Republican presidents between 1984 and 2004 (Lacorne 2011:
136).

If Evangelicals today form the heart of the Christian Right and are
closely allied with the Republican Party, this is a spectacular transformation of their dissident origins during the days of Jefferson and Madison.
As late as the Progressive Era preceding World War I, Evangelicals were
on the left side of the political spectrum, supporting women's suffrage,
the regulation of corporate capitalism, the arbitration of international
conflict, direct democracy, and, of course, they had opposed slavery all
along, even provided a churchly home for freed slaves (see Wald and
Calhoun-Brown 2011: 202).[54] This transformation is symbolized by the
Southern Baptist Convention (SBC), today the largest Protestant denomination and "de facto Church of the South" (Phillips 2006: 156). Not
only was the SBC, as mentioned earlier, unbothered by the secularization
of public schools in the early 1960s, initially Southern Baptists also had
no qualms with the court-ordered legalization of abortion in 1973. In
fact, in 1971 the SBC had urged states to liberalize their abortion laws
(Daniel Williams 2010: 115), and as late as 1976, when the religious
opposition to *Roe v. Wade* was in high gear, it rejected anti-abortion
resolutions (p. 156). However, when Jerry Falwell launched his Moral
Majority in the late 1970s, its constituency was almost entirely Baptist,
and from 1982 on the SBC would exclusively support Republican can-
didates for the presidency. Note in this context that in 1980 only 29
percent of Southern Baptist pastors were registered Republican, while in
1984 an impressive 66 percent were (pp. 206–7).

If one looks closely, however, one notices a disjunction between the
militant elite politics of Evangelicals and the more moderate and centrist
views and leanings of the rank and file (see Smith 1998 and 2002; also
Greeley and Hout 2006). In Christian Smith's detailed account of the
views of ordinary Evangelicals, two themes emerge very clearly: first, a
widespread feeling of being "excluded, marginalized, or discriminated
against by secular institutions and elites" (Smith 2002: 4), which does
constitute a communality with Evangelical elite discourse; secondly,
however, a profoundly apolitical orientation, with an investment more
in "the power of individual good examples" than in "gain[ing] control
of the reins of politics" (p. 45). In this second respect there *is* an obvious
disjunction between elite and rank-and-file views. Of the Evangelical
Christians interviewed by Smith, 50 percent even expressed "outright
opposition" to the Christian Right (p. 122). As one memorably remarked,

"I kind of get sick of hearing about the Moral Majority and Christian Coalition. I just tune it out when I hear it on television....I suppose it's okay for them to do that.... This is America. I wouldn't really be a part of it" (p. 122).

Three elements conventionally define an Evangelical Christian: a literalist reading of the Bible; a "born-again" experience, which makes voluntarism, but also the zeal of the converted, the heart of this branch of Christianity, and which provides an unbreakable link to its dissident origins; and, thirdly, the mission of evangelizing others with the Christian gospel, which for an Evangelical revolves around a "personal relationship" with Jesus. It is elements two and three that militate against the politicization of religion, for which, however, the Christian Right has become known in America. Astonishingly, 40 percent of the Evangelicals interviewed by Smith even denied or "somewhat doubted" that America had once been a "Christian nation" (2002: 24), the recovery of which is the undisputed center goal of the Christian Right. Instead, when asked what "Christian America" above all meant to them, the most frequent answer, reminiscent of Evangelicalism's dissident past, was: "religious freedom." And Smith reports that the "almost unanimous" attitude toward their perceived enemies was "civility, tolerance, and voluntary persuasion" (p. 37). This is the exact opposite of the "massive spiritual aggression" prescribed by Jerry Falwell (Lambert 2008: 184). In fact, the dominant mindset that Smith (2002: 45) identified among ordinary Evangelicals was that of "strategic relationalism," which builds on the power of individual example and on a "personal relationship with God." It also resonates with "the Christian tradition itself," which, as Smith reminds us (pp. 57–8), resists politicization. In conclusion, "a unified,...Christian campaign to 'reclaim' the nation for Christ...is simply not in evangelicalism's organizational 'cards' or its cultural 'DNA'" (p. 57).

At the same time, however, the perception of being an embattled minority is in tension with the Pauline gospel of good example and of not separating oneself from non-believers. Here is the main linkage between elite and rank-and-file views. When Harold Ockenga assembled the self-declared "Evangelicals" as a moderate breakaway from Protestant "Fundamentalists" in St. Louis' Corona Hotel on April 7, 1942, he saw "clouds of battle which spell annihilation unless we are willing to run in a pack" (Smith 1998: 121). Indeed, Evangelicalism "flourishes on difference, engagement, tension, conflict, and threat," argues Smith (p. 121). A "sense of strong boundaries" even sets the Evangelicals apart from other Christians, the positive distinction being the "personal relationship" they claim to entertain with Jesus Christ and the authority of the Bible (pp. 124–5). Negatively, though, Evangelicals inherited from fundamentalists the self-perception of being a "persecuted group" (p. 131) and of facing "menacing external threats," particularly by "homosexuals" and "liberals." Smith proposes the evocative metaphor of "spurned lover" to catch Evangelicals' simultaneous engagement with and disengagement from their environment, as they "passionately pursu[e] a culture which...disregards and mistreats them" (p. 145). This ambivalence is even seen as their secret of success, because Evangelicals thus equally avoid the "sectarian" withdrawal of the fundamentalists and the "churchly" merging with mainstream society that has made liberal Protestants almost invisible (p. 150).

Considering the rank and file's apolitical leanings, the noisy and often unappetizing elite politics of the Christian Right has to be taken as a wholly separate phenomenon, driven more by mundane interests than by anything identifiably religious. The history of the "Moral Majority" started, appositely, not from the grassroots but top-down, as the project of three well-known New Right strategists – Paul Weyrich, Richard Viguerie, and Howard Phillips[55] – to tap new voters for the Republican Party, particularly in the Southern states, in continuation of the Republicans' "Southern Strategy," known since the days of Nixon. Not incidentally, Jerry Falwell was approached by the three strategists in the very year that the first openly religious president in US history, the Southern Baptist Jimmy Carter, had ingratiated himself among conservative religionists with a clumsy attempt to appear "both humble and complex" (Harding 2000: 128), confessing to journalists of *Playboy* magazine to have "looked on a lot of women with lust." Falwell reportedly at first "declined" the strategists' offer, "but the idea apparently took root" (p. 128).

However, to cut a long and eventful story short, the Christian Right's spectacular electoral successes, culminating in the two presidential election victories of "born-again" George W. Bush in 2000 and 2004, have not been followed by much success in changing the direction of law and public policy. As to the Christian Right's electoral successes, particularly noteworthy is the so-called "Christian Coalition," TV Evangelical Pat Robertson's follow-up to Falwell's Moral Majority, which had exhausted itself in less than a decade. Between 1989 and 1997, the Christian Coalition was managed by a young political talent, Ralph Reed, described by historian Daniel Williams as a "hard-driving, chain-smoking, wheeling-dealing, dirty politician" until he found Jesus (2010: 227). Reed tapped on, and reinforced, Evangelicals' deeply engrained perception of being a shunned minority, and cleverly prescribed the language of "rights, equality, and opportunity" as a cure; he even claimed to be in favor of church–state separation and for a "nation that is not officially Christian, Jewish, or Muslim" (Wald and Calhoun-Brown 2011: 215). However, these were stealth tactics. The real intention was to take "back [this nation] one precinct at a time, one neighborhood at a time, and one state at a time" (quoted in Daniel Williams 2010: 229). Reed described himself as in "guerilla warfare": "I paint my face and travel at night" (p. 230). To give a taste of the impressive resourcefulness of the Christian Coalition, for the 1994 Congressional election it distributed 35 million voter guides and 17 million Congressional scorecards, while conducting 3 million phone calls to voters (p. 230). No wonder that, by 1994, it "controlled" 18 state Republican parties and exercised a "strong influence" in 13 others (p. 232). Having amassed electoral clout, the next step was to control the political agenda. In 2004, all seven of the top Republican leaders in the US Senate had 100 percent approval ratings from the Christian Coalition (Phillips 2006: 216). The Republican House majority leader professed that "God is using me all the time, everywhere, to stand up for a biblical world view in everything that I do and everywhere that I am" (Tom de Lay, quoted on p. 216). Not to mention that the White House was held by someone whose "favorite philosopher" was "Christ" (George W. Bush, quoted in Lacorne 2011: 129), and who would assemble his staff for (not so voluntary) weekly Bible studies and prayer meetings (Daniel Williams 2010: 252). Under the most religious of all US presidencies, the General Attorney referred to church–state separation as "a wall of religious oppression" (John Ashcroft, quoted in Phillips 2006: 233), and a senior official dismissed the intellectual elites, bizarrely, as "a what we call the reality-based community...[people] who believe that solutions emerge from your judicious study of discernible reality" (quoted on p. 235). Evidently, Oval Office wisdom at the time had other sources.

With respect to law-making and public policy, however, the successes of the Christian Right are negligible, and a sense of failure and disappointment has followed the movement from the beginning. Constitutional amendments to bring back prayer to schools (to mention one of the earliest campaign issues), to stop abortion (repeatedly tried since 1973), and to prevent homosexual marriage (the latest high-octane issue) have all failed, by large margins. Until Bush Jr. arrived in the White House, the tenor was "how little [the Christian Right] had changed public policy" (Wald and Calhoun-Brown 2011: 221). But even under Bush this did not change much. Daniel Williams noted the "failure of the Bush administration to pass even one socially conservative bill during the president's second term" (2010: 263). Most successes were by way not of law- but of decree making, that is, at the administrative level only, such as vetoing federal funds for stem-cell research or the so-called "Faith-Based Initiative," the centerpiece of Bush's "compassionate conservatism." This is not to say that these policies were without effect, with the former impairing medical progress for a while and the latter continuing the dismantling of the American welfare state by other means.

The Faith-Based Initiative, in particular, which typically, after failing in Congress, could be realized only by executive order, amounted to a "spoils system for evangelical ministries" (Goldberg 2007: 107), without the slightest federal monitoring of policy effectiveness. Controversially, faith-based groups were exempted by executive decree from a 1965 executive order that bars religious discrimination in federally funded hiring. Subsequently, religious membership blatantly trumped professional credentials in hiring decisions. The Salvation Army, for instance, would use this as license to "Christianize" the agency, ridding itself of undesired gay and non-Evangelical employees (pp. 129–31). These open discriminations were justified in the name of "religious freedom." And one should not belittle the enormity of $2 billion of federal funding in 2004 alone for the "faith-based gravy train," which was money by definition *not* available to the secular welfare sector, thus indirectly squeezing out the latter (p. 108). Finally, doubts must be raised about an approach to welfare in which "the poor and addicted are sinners who need to be redeemed by Jesus Christ," as Michelle Goldberg paraphrases the teachings of Marvin Olasky, the intellectual father of "compassionate conservatism" (p. 109).

Approved by a conservative Supreme Court majority,[56] the Faith-Based Initiative strangely continues under a Democratic president – in fact, one might well argue that it had enjoyed subterraneous bipartisan support from the start.[57] However, this most visible success in three decades of Christian Right mobilization is too little to offset a general sense of failure. A leader of the Christian Coalition tellingly felt "left to conclude that our greatest problem is not in the Oval Office....It is with the people of this land" (James Dobson, quoted in Daniel Williams 2010: 244). Indeed, perhaps the most significant religious development since the 1990s in the United States has been the dramatic increase in the share of Americans expressing "no religious preference," rising from just 8 percent in 1990 to 20 percent in 2012. Importantly, this increase has not been accompanied by rising levels of atheism – in 2012, only 3 percent of Americans did not believe in God, not much more than in previous years (Hout et al. 2013). Accordingly, Michael Hout et al. conclude that unchurched Americans' "quarrel appears to be with organized religion" (p. 6). This confirms Putnam and Campbell's thesis of the "second aftershock," according to which young Americans have reacted negatively to the political excesses of the Christian Right (Putnam and Campbell 2010: 120–32).[58] As America's exceptional religiosity shows no sign of weakening, there seems to be a self-correctional mechanism built into it that works against the Christian Right's overt politicization of religion.

Toward Legal Theocracy?

While the Christian Right, despite its electoral clout, may not have scored any major legislative victory on its core concerns, from school prayer to restricting abortion and gay rights, it did have one major effect: it helped turn the Supreme Court to the right. The causality is obvious. Under Republican presidents, from Ronald Reagan on, the court was staffed by appointees near or dear to the agenda of the Christian Right, which exerted an ever-growing influence within the Republican Party. Reagan brought William Rehnquist (1986), Antonin Scalia (1986), and Anthony Kennedy (1988) onto the court; George Bush Sr. brought in Clarence Thomas (1991); and Bush Jr. appointed John G. Roberts (2005) and Samuel Alito (2006). Interestingly, none of these new appointments is Evangelical – in fact, all are Roman Catholic. But all were decidedly critical of the legal secularism epitomized by *Lemon v. Kurtzman*, and all repudiated the "wall of separation" between church and state in favor of something more akin to legal theocracy, which is the inevitably American variant of a closer connection between religion and state (see Cohen 2013a: 460).

To put things into perspective, until the more recent appointments of Justices Roberts and Alito, there was no clear conservative majority on religion–state relations in the Supreme Court; instead, the court was deeply divided between liberal "separationists" and conservative "integrationists" (Gey 2007), and its decisions would go in either direction, often unpredictably. John Witte and Joel Nichols thus speak of a "massive jumble of divided and discordant opinions" (2011: xxi), and Noah Feldman (2005) argues that "no single, unified theory or logical reason can explain the arrangements that we now have...disorder reigns" (2005: 216). However, as even the classically separationist decisions of the Supreme Court, as we saw, were shot through with ambiguity and always included a modicum of accommodation, and as case particularism had explicitly been preferred over a clear line,[59] "disorder" is exactly what one should expect in this domain.

The pressure of the Christian Right was always more on the Establishment than the Free Exercise prong of the First Amendment religion clauses (even though, as we shall see, the latter did not go unaffected). This is because the project was to move religion, particularly (but not exclusively) majority religion, closer to the state, desiring recognition and support by the state that is explicitly denied in the Establishment Clause.

While the Free Exercise Clause is at heart a minority protector, the Establishment Clause is a majority stopper.[60] This is why the latter came to be subject to "particularly controversial" judgments (see Greenawalt 2009: 2), which – for good or ill – had to reckon with the strong religious sentiments of the large majority of Americans.

In the Christian Right's attack on the Establishment Clause, one must distinguish between three directions. The first is to reinject religion into the core of the public school experience, from which it had been shut out by the 1960s prayer cases and the invalidation of anti-evolution statutes. The second is to grant religious groups "equal access" to government funding and public facilities (such as public school buildings for religious meetings). And the third is to secure religion a symbolic presence in the public forum, to counteract the secularist vice of a "naked public sphere" (Neuhaus 1984). As I shall discuss in the remainder of this chapter, only with respect to the public school classroom did the Supreme Court hold its secularist line, although with a good measure of ambiguity that reflects the advances of anti-separationist revisionism. With respect to funding, the "wall of separation" has been "breached"; with respect to symbols, it has been "battered." But, beforehand, it must be stated that the more provocative (to put it mildly) propositions placed on the Supreme Court agenda by the Christian Right were always rejected, if by increasingly narrow margins.

Repudiating Christian extremism

In *Edwards v. Aguillard* (1987), a sound 7:2 majority rejected Louisiana's "Creationism Act," which forbad the teaching of the theory of evolution in public schools unless it was accompanied by instruction in "creation science." Hostility to Darwin's evolutionism, which discredited the Bible's creation story, provided a link between 1920s fundamentalism and latter-day Evangelicalism, and it was shared by President Reagan at the time. To fulfill the "secular purpose" prong of the Lemon Test, Louisiana Senator Bill Keith had slyly justified the Creationism Act as in favor of "academic freedom." This was hardly credible, however, because Keith had also stated before the Louisiana state legislature that his "preference" would be "that neither [creationism nor evolution] be taught."[61] To the court majority, the fact that creationism was only to be taught when evolution was taught proved the "purpose of discrediting 'evolution' by counterbalancing its teaching at every turn with the teaching of creationism."[62] Accordingly, the act's purpose was "to advance a particular religious belief" and thus it ran afoul of the Establishment Clause.[63] Of course, for a politicized Southern Baptist like Senator Keith, the constellation was not secularism versus religion but religion versus religion, because the theory of evolution simply constituted another set of "religious beliefs," one that is consonant with the "cardinal principle[s] of religious humanism, secular humanism, theological liberalism, aetheistism [sic]."[64] It is difficult to imagine that the patently religious view that the world was "created ex nihilo and fixed by God"[65] could ever pass constitutional muster. In a fiery dissent, however, Justice Scalia (joined by Chief Justice Rehnquist) still thought so. Using a clever interpretation of case law, he argued that it was sufficient, under the Lemon Test, to identify "a" secular purpose behind a law, among other (religious) purposes. And that secular purpose, in this case, was not teachers' but students' "academic freedom," in terms of "students' freedom from indoctrination."[66] In depriving students of learning about "one of the two scientific explanations for the origin of life," fired Scalia, this was an "illiberal judgment," a "Scopes-in-reverse."[67]

Almost two decades later, and now with the smallest possible majority, the Supreme Court still repudiated a second provocation by the Christian Right, in McCreary County v. ACLU of Kentucky (2005). The case concerned the posting of large copies of the Ten Commandments in Kentucky courthouses, declaring them the "precedent legal code" of the state of Kentucky and "in remembrance and honor of Jesus Christ, the Prince of Ethics."[68] The posting of the commandments was in explicit defense of controversial Alabama judge Roy Moore, who had placed a 2.6-ton Ten Commandments monument in his courthouse, in a self-avowed act of "Christian nationalism," and who had been dismissed for his refusal to remove what became known as "Roy's Rock" (see Goldberg 2007: 25–7). Overall, argued the responsible Kentucky county officials, the "Founding Father[s] [had an] explicit understanding of the duty of elected officials to publicly acknowledge God as the source of America's strength and direction."[69] Immediately sued by the American Civil Liberties Union, the county officials meant to redress Establishment Clause objections by placing the singular exhibit within a larger display on "The Foundations of American Law and Government" – which, a provocation again, included a copy of the 1215 Magna Carta (including its odd anachronism that "fish-weirs shall be removed from the Thames") but not the Fourteenth Amendment or the Constitution of 1787.[70] For the narrow court majority, this was an obvious occasion to reassert the secularist principle, as enunciated in the classic Everson v. Board of Education case (1947). According to it, "state neutrality" did not only forbid the establishment of a "single national religion" and insist that the state had to be neutral (or non-preferential) within the umbrella of religion, which the budding integrationists on the court were close to establishing as orthodoxy. No, the state was also to be neutral with respect to "religion vs. non-religion," and accordingly the prohibition of state support extended to " 'religion' in general,"[71] to "guard against the civic divisiveness that follows when the Government weighs in on one side of religious debate."[72]

But contrary to the *Edwards v. Aguillard* decision, *McCreary County v. ACLU of Kentucky* was a rather close and contested decision that shows how much the court had moved to the right in the meantime. Particularly noteworthy in Justice Scalia's, even by his standards, firebrand dissent (joined in full by William Rehnquist and Clarence Thomas, and in part by Anthony Kennedy) is his claim that government can "favor religious practice," thus flatly questioning the cornerstone of legal secularism. "[E]ncouragement of religion," argued Scalia, is "the best way to foster morality."[73] He cited in support Founding Father John Adams: "Our Constitution was made only for a moral and religious people. It is wholly inadequate to the government of any other."[74] And consider the legions of exceptions to the "brain-spun" Lemon Test with its "supposed principle of neutrality between religion and irreligion":[75] if churches are released from property taxes (but not tennis clubs), students enjoy "release time" for the catechism (but not for cinema), and the Pledge of Allegiance declares America to be "one nation under God," among too many other exemptions to count, this is all a preference of religion over irreligion. But even more noteworthy was Scalia's response to the charge, made by the liberal court majority, that the Ten Commandments display also favored one religion over other religions, thus violating the other prong of the "no establishment" principle as seen through the classic legal secularism lens.[76] This had to be a provocation even for religionists, to the degree that they are ecumenically minded. But it was no problem for Scalia. In the "public forum" (though *not* with respect to "public aid" and "free exercise," conceded Scalia), a preference for monotheism is unavoidable as an "entirely nondenominational" religion does not exist.[77] Conversely, the "Establishment Clause permits this disregard of polytheists and believers in unconcerned deities, just as it permits the disregard of devout atheists."[78] Not only was this an astonishingly theological discourse for a secular court judge, but it was also ruthlessly majoritarian and intentionally discriminatory. As, by Scalia's count, "97.7% of all believers...are monotheistic," their interest "in being able to give God thanks and supplication as a people" counted more than the tiny minority's counter-interest "in not being 'excluded' " – this balancing of the involved interests was dictated by "[o]ur national tradition."[79] Strangely, Scalia held the desired governmental "acknowledgment of a single Creator" *not* to be the "establishment of a religion."[80] This must count as one of the most breathtakingly theocratic broadsides[81] ever fired by a high court judge against the essentials of a secular state.

The ambivalent defense of secularism in the public classroom

With respect to keeping religion out of the public classroom, and thus to ward off a perennial key concern of the Christian Right since the early 1960s, the Supreme Court has stayed "remarkably firm and constant" (Eisgruber and Sager 2007: 160). This line was affirmed in *Lee et al. v. Weisman* (1992), which interdicted state-directed prayers at public high school graduation ceremonies, based on a case in Providence, Rhode Island. However, behind the façade of continuity there has been a significant shift of doctrine that bears the imprint of the conservative attack on legal secularism. Significantly, the majority opinion by Justice Anthony Kennedy, who notably belonged to the side of critics of legal secularism on the Supreme Court, shoved aside the secularist Lemon Test in favor of his long-held "coercion" theory. According to it, the only thing that government was not allowed to do under the Establishment Clause was to "coerce anyone to support or participate in any religion."[82] Apart from the limiting case of coercion, the correct stance of the state was "accommodation, acknowledgment, and support of religion" as "an accepted part of our political and cultural heritage."[83] The coercion theory is an explicit repudiation of the "no aid" principle enunciated in legal secularism's foundational *Everson v. Board of Education* case. In Kennedy's view, the "no aid" principle "would require a relentless extirpation of all contact between government and religion" that had become anachronistic in the "modern administrative state," which reached deeply into people's lives. The coercion theory amounted to a significant weakening of the Establishment Clause, and on its basis Kennedy would consistently side with those who attacked the "wall of separation" with respect to state funding and the public recognition of religious symbols. Constitutional scholar Steven Shiffrin aptly characterized it as "a communitarian perspective favoring majority religions over minority religions because the majority is deemed entitled to express their religious views through the state" (2009: 29).

The irony is that the coercion theory, which was meant to be a religion-friendly instrument of accommodation, had rather harsh and notably anti-majoritarian implications in *Lee et al. v. Weisman*. Participation in the graduation ceremony, one must know, was voluntary, and the prayer in question – entrusted by the school principal to a liberal Jewish rabbi – was non-sectarian, spiked with secular references to "America where diversity is celebrated and the rights of minorities are protected,"[84] and it was barely two minutes long. Still, through its formatting by school officials, the prayer "bore the imprint of the State," which in this way helped "enforce a religious orthodoxy."[85] Most importantly, "pressure," however "subtle and indirect," was exerted on students to "stand as a group or, at least, maintain respectful silence."[86] The "public" and "peer pressure" at play here was obviously at best psychological, but – as Kennedy argued for the court majority – this "can be as real as any overt compulsion."[87]

Lee et al. v. Weisman was a Janus-like decision: in content it affirmed legal secularism, but in form it moved away from it. Thus it had to enrage both the staunch religionists but also the (dwindling) defenders of legal secularism on the court. As for the latter, Justice Souter, while naturally agreeing with the outcome, took the occasion to incant what in retrospect must appear as legal secularism's swan song. By now the voices on the court were growing strong (and would soon prevail) that argued that the Establishment Clause permitted the "nonpreferential" state promotion of religion.[88] "Neutrality," in this view, thinned down from the obligation of the state to stay away from religion to the much weaker mandate to be evenhanded and fair when dealing with religion and irreligion; in some respects neutrality might even be bracketed by a preference of religion over irreligion. In Souter's rather hopeful view, this conservative revisionism was rebutted here. Conversely, as not aid to a particular religion but aid to religion in general was rejected in *Lee et al. v. Weisman*, the latter "affirm[ed]" the "no aid" principle that is central to legal secularism.[89] However, this "affirmation" was unintended and ephemeral, and it remained limited to the narrow context of the public school classroom.

More indicative of the direction in which the Supreme Court would move in the future was Justice Scalia's predictably acidic dissent. "Psychological coercion" could not be equated with "legal coercion," and non-denominational prayer at public ceremonies, such as the one at issue here, is "so characteristically American [it] could have come from the pen of George Washington or Abraham Lincoln himself."[90] As he would also do later in *McCreary County v. ACLU of Kentucky* (2005), Scalia contrasted the "desire of a religious majority" with the interests of a minority of "nonbelievers," and he held that a preference for the former was "mandat[ed]" by the "US constitution" itself.[91] In his indictment of the court "bulldozer of…social engineering," Scalia mixed Puritan-theocratic with Republican-instrumental motives of the American tradition (as identified by Witte and Nicols 2011: 34–6). According to Scalia, the Founding Fathers "knew that nothing, absolutely nothing, is so inclined to foster among religious believers of various faiths a toleration – no, an affection – for one another than voluntarily joining in prayer together, to the God whom they all worship and seek." The court's pro-hibition of the prayer deprived "our society" of "that important unifying mechanism."[92]

There is, of course, one nagging exception to the legally ordained exclusion of religion from the American public classroom: the Pledge of Allegiance. Or is its best-known line, that America is "one Nation under God," which American school children are asked to recite at the begin-ning of each school day, not "religion" but mere "patriotism"? This was the issue in *Elk Grove Unified School District v. Newdow et al.* (2004). It seems inconceivable that this badge of American everyday nationalism would ever be found unconstitutional, but its invocation of "God" still raises prickly issues under the Establishment Clause.[93] The court in *Elk Grove Unified School District v. Newdow et al.* predictably retained the Pledge in its disputed form, if only on procedural grounds that avoided the substantive religion question.[94] However, three judges argued "on the merits" that the "under God" phrase of the Pledge was constitutional, if in instructively different ways. For Clarence Thomas, together with Antonin Scalia the staunchest religionist on the current Supreme Court, it was obvious that the meaning of "under God" was religious, had it been inserted only in the 1950s into a previously purely secular version of the Pledge. The added value could logically only be religious. Indeed, the 1954 House Report introducing the change confirms that it "reflected the traditional concept that our Nation was founded on a fundamental belief in God."[95] Further consider that, when the Supreme Court had ruled, back in 1943, and on the basis of the secular first version of the Pledge, that states were not allowed to compel students to take the Pledge, the court called the unconstitutional element "compulsion to declare a belief." Now that "under God" was added, argued Thomas, plausibly, "[i]t is difficult to see how this does not entail an affirmation that God exists."[96] However, he upped the ante in considering the fact moot, because the Establishment Clause, in his view, did not apply to states at all. Accordingly, states were free to deal with the fact of religion as they saw fit, for instance, officially declaring themselves to be "Christian."

By contrast, Justice O'Connor and Chief Justice Rehnquist, in two separate opinions, sought to salvage the "under God" in the Pledge by declaring the phrase to have a cultural ("patriotic") rather than religious meaning. This happened to be the main line whereby Supreme Court jurisdiction has recently permitted the American federal state to associate itself symbolically with religion (close parallels for which can be found in Europe; see the Conclusion). Citing a long list of presidential invo-cations of "Almighty God," from George Washington to Lincoln, Roosevelt, and Eisenhower, among others, Chief Justice Rehnquist held them all to be "patriotic" but not religious. Still, the main legal task for the Pledge defenders was showing how "under God" was different from the "religious exercise" that had been declared unconstitutional in *Lee et al. v. Weisman*. For Rehnquist, the recitation of "under God" was "in no sense a prayer, nor an endorsement of any religion, but a simple recognition of the fact noted in H.R. Rep. No. 1693, at 2: 'From the time of our earliest history our peoples and our institutions have reflected the traditional concept that our Nation was founded on a fundamental belief in God.'"[97] But this way of rendering "under God" descriptive, and thus to evacuate from it a religious commitment, is unconvincing. As Kent Greenawalt noted, "The language of the pledge is not historical. It sounds as if the Nation *is* 'under God', not that historically many citizens have believed that the nation is under God" (2009: 98).

In her parallel opinion, Justice O'Connor similarly characterized the pledge as "merely descriptive": "[I]t purports only to identify the United States as a Nation subject to divine authority. That cannot be seen as a serious invocation of God or as an expression of individual submission to divine authority."[98] But if the "Nation" is declared "subject to divine authority" (which, strictly speaking, declares the United States to be a theocracy), one must ask, how can this *not* entail "individual submission," and thus *not* be religious in meaning? The dissociation of the Pledge from "individual submission" to God, and the claim that it is not a "serious invocation of God," is also unconvincing because this dodges the nature of a pledge, which is by nature a commitment that resists trivialization. In particular, O'Connor tried to trivialize the ineradicably religious meaning of the pledge by equating it with "ceremonial deism," if not blind and non-committal "rote repetition." Kent Greenawalt correctly objected to this that "in a pledge, we are undertaking to affirm the content of the pledge. That is what a pledge is" (2009: 100). But then the individual "pledge[s] allegiance to...one Nation under God," however one tries to twist and tweak the meaning of this phrase. O'Connor is probably right that "some references to religion in public life and government are the inevitable consequence of our Nation's origins."[99] But if, indeed, as she claims, there are "no de minimis violations of the Constitution,"[100] here obviously is one, because all attempts to take religion out of "under God" are doomed to fail. The religious moment of the Pledge, strenuously attempted to be muted in favor of "patriotic,"[101] even slips back in explicitly when the charge is rebutted that a "particular religion" is favored. Surely, "Buddhism" is not accommodated by the invocation of "God," but some such exclusion is unavoidable: "The phrase 'under God,' conceived and added at a time when our national religious diversity was neither as robust nor as well recognized as it is now, represents a tolerable attempt to acknowledge religion...without favoring any individual religious sect or belief system."[102] But then the Pledge "acknowledged" religion after all!

Breaching the wall: access and funding

Aside from its grand Christian restoration agenda, mundane pocketbook issues of access to state funds and facilities have from the start featured centrally on the Christian Right's agenda. Even more than abortion, the "principal motivating issue" in the rise of the Moral Majority in the late 1970s was the withdrawal by the Internal Revenue Service of tax-exempt status from Christian schools and universities that practiced racial discrimination or segregation (and sometimes had precisely been created to do that under religious cover) (Greenhouse and Siegel 2011: 2066, fn. 141). One must concede that the teeth of legal secularism were in no domain more painfully felt than with respect to material resources denied by the state to Christian or other religious constituencies, but which were accessible to secular groups. Particularly galling was the Supreme Court's *Aguilar v. Felton* decision of 1985, which deprived an annual number of 20,0000 underprivileged students in New York City's parochial schools of so-called "Title 1" benefits under the federal Elementary and Secondary Education Act of 1965. Under this program, public school teachers were sent into parochial schools for remedial teaching. After having quietly operated for 19 years, the program came to be outlawed under the Lemon Test's rather capricious "excessive entanglement" prong. As Chief Justice Rehnquist wrote in a bitter dissent, this prong of the test created a "Catch-22" situation in that the "supervision" exacted by the state to keep the program secular was itself held to be an instance of illicit "entanglement" between religion and state (see Witte and Nicols 2011: 213). *Aguilar v. Felton* may have helped the cause of church–state separation, criticizes legal scholar Michael McConnell, but "the most obvious consequence...was to penalize poor families who decide to educate their children in religious schools" (1985: 2).

Aguilar v. Felton was overruled in 1997, and similar inequities in access to public funds and facilities have almost completely disappeared. The breaching of the wall of separation with respect to access to public money and facilities must be considered the Christian Right's single biggest success. It was interestingly achieved by playing the minority card, and by mobilizing the free speech clause of the First Amendment. The lead case in this respect is *Rosenberger v. University of Virginia* (1995), which was pleaded before the Supreme Court by Michael McConnell (see the discussion in Fish 1997: 2315–19). Here the Supreme Court decided that the denial of university funding for an Evangelical student newspaper, while such funding (drawn from a general student tax) was available to a non-religious student newspaper, constituted unlawful "viewpoint discrimination" under the Free Speech Clause of the First Amendment. This meant that, for the first time, state aid was available for a religious cause. This is because *Wide Awake*, the Evangelical newspaper in question, did not so much spread information as "encourage students to consider what a personal relationship with Jesus Christ means."[103] Under previous court jurisdiction, only "equal access" to public facilities (like public school rooms for religious meetings) had to be made available to religious groups; the novelty of *Rosenberger v. University of Virginia* was to extend this logic to "funds." This was a small logical step. But it made all the difference. As Justice Souter pointed out in dissent, "Using public funds for the direct subsidization of preaching the word is categorically forbidden under the Establishment Clause."[104] He drew support from James Madison's famous "Memorial and Remonstrance" (1775), which had thundered against "three pence only" as sufficient for a "no establishment" violation.[105]

Underlying this breach of the wall of separation is a new concept of neutrality. Neutrality no longer connotes secularity (as in *Lemon v. Kurtzman*) and the prohibition on aiding (or hindering) religion (as in *Everson v. Board of Education*); instead, it connotes evenhandedness (or non-preferentialism) in the treatment of religion and non-religion. This was possible once the focus had shifted from the Establishment Clause logic to forgo state contact with religion to the Free Speech logic that the religious viewpoint had to be treated equally to other viewpoints. Constitutional scholar Stanley Fish put it crisply: "So the rule is changed from 'no aid to religion' to 'no aid that is not also given to secular entities'; evenhanded equality in aid replaces the older policy of prohibiting aid."[106] Under this logic, there is no stopping point to support religion other than that such support is also available to non-religious causes. More like a token shadow of the past, the "primacy of the no-direct-funding rule over the evenhandedness principle"[107] still lingered, in that "private choice" had to mediate between state and the religion to be benefited – which in *Rosenberger v. University of Virginia* was the rather forced construction that the University of Virginia did not fund the Evangelicals directly, but only the printers who produced their newspaper. So the next step was to shed this limitation, and to make neutrality as evenhandedness the sole and freestanding principle. This happened in *Mitchell et al. v. Helms et al.* (2000), when any further scrutiny of giving "otherwise permissible" state aid to "pervasively sectarian" schools was declared a "doctrine, born of bigotry, [that] should be buried now."[108]

However, there was a price to pay for breaching the wall of separation with respect to state aid: religion was no longer special, but just one of several "viewpoints" that had to be treated equally. Neutrality as even-handedness had to be disastrous when applied to the Free Exercise Clause, which previously had protected minority religions from the crutches of general (and thus neutral) laws under the premise that religion was "special" – in this respect, especially in need of protection. Accordingly, it is no coincidence that the advance of majority religions on the Establishment Clause front (*nota bene*, in the minority-protection guise of preventing "viewpoint discrimination") was complemented by a serious setback for minority religions on the Free Exercise front. Representative here is perhaps the most ill-famed of all Supreme Court decisions on religion: *Employment Division v. Smith* (1990). It affirmed the denial of unemployment compensation to two social workers (delicately specializing in drug rehabilitation) who had smoked peyote, yet within a religious ceremony of the Native American Church of which they were members. Importantly, the "seriously held belief" of the plaintiffs was not in question.[109] However, as Justice Scalia argued for the court majority, "We have never held that an individual's religious beliefs excuse him from compliance with an otherwise valid law prohibiting conduct that the State is free to regulate."[110] Oregon's anti-drug law, under which the plaintiffs had lost their jobs, was a "neutral law of general applicability," and to break it for the sake of religious belief would make the latter "superior to the law of the land, and in effect...permit every citizen to become a law unto itself." Accommodation was still possible, argued Scalia, but only through the "political process." If this put minorities at a "relative disadvantage," this was an "unavoidable consequence of democratic government."[111]

Masterminded by Justice Scalia, *Employment Division v. Smith* shows the same crude defense of the majority principle that Scalia brought to bear in Establishment Clause cases, where he conversely attacked the blocking of religious majority preferences by separationist rules. Pairing the two types of cases, one notices a fundamental reversal of constellations. Under legal secularism, religious majorities had been blocked under the Establishment Clause while minorities had been strongly protected under the Free Exercise Clause. Now the situation was the reverse: minorities became vulnerable under a diminished Free Exercise Clause, while majorities had their free go under an obliterated Establishment Clause.

Battering the wall: symbols

Noah Feldman argued that his "values evangelicals" won the "war over institutions and economics," as documented in the previous section, but that they lost the "culture war" over symbols in the public sphere, which, however, they happened to "care most about" (2005: 216, 218). His second claim is not quite correct. With respect to symbols, the successes of the Christian Right have been more significant than depicted by Feldman (writing around 2004, of course, when jurisdiction was still evolving). If there has been no "breaching" of the wall of separation, as with respect to access and funding, a "battering" of the wall is still undeniable.

First, the centrality of symbols for the Christian Right stands to be underlined. One of their most serious theorists, Richard John Neuhaus, actually argued that the "naked public square" he so much worried about is "impossible" – either it is filled by the state hyping itself up "as church," pushing "secular humanism" as idolatrous "*ersatz* religion" (1984: 82); or it is filled by its rightful owner, the "very new-old language of Christian America" (p. 93). *Tertium non datur*. In a different key yet to the same effect, Michael McConnell argued that liberalism was "foremost a regime of fair procedures" (1985: 16), not of ultimate values, and thus insufficient to motivate and bind people. "[A]ny democratic form of society must inevitably reflect the values of its people" (p. 16), which in America happen to be religious values. From this followed that a "preferential treatment for religion in some matters is desirable" (p. 22). Whether depicted as in competition with or as complementary to the liberal state, religion's presence in the public sphere mattered centrally to the Christian Right.

The best-known and most reviled of the religious symbol cases is *Lynch v. Donnelly* (1984), whose forced hermeneutics of "crèches" and "plastic reindeers" has become proverbial. The decision validated a state-financed Christmas display in a small Rhode Island town, on the argument that even the most incriminated element, a Christian crèche or nativity scene, in this particular context, served a "secular purpose," namely, to "celebrate the Holiday"[112] and "engender a friendly community spirit of goodwill in keeping with the season."[113] Legally the case is important for the "endorsement" interpretation of the Establishment Clause, which Justice O'Connor presented in a concurring opinion, and which marks an important step in the move away from legal secularism, if not the demolition of the Establishment Clause itself. Crucially, it does away with the need under the Lemon Test to identify the "secular purpose" of a law or policy to let it pass constitutional muster. Instead, the question becomes whether the measure constitutes an "endorsement" or "disapproval" of religion on the part of the state that thereby excludes people: "Endorsement sends a message to nonadherents that they are outsiders, not full members of the political community, and an accompanying message to adherents that they are insiders, favored members of the political community. Disapproval sends the opposite message."[114]

The endorsement test, which the court officially adopted in subsequent Establishment Clause decisions, fundamentally shifts the central value to be furthered by the Establishment Clause from "liberty" to "equality" (see Feldman 2002a, 2002b). With its focus on individual equality, "endorsement" was a timely formula that articulated the dominant constitutional value of the time and was minority-sensitive, resembling the "paradigm of race" with its concern about combating racial inequality (Feldman 2002b: 703). The whole tenor of endorsement is minority protection, and as "disapproval" of religion was also outlawed, it even allowed religious majorities to refashion themselves as aggrieved minorities. But perhaps the most important victory for "values evangelicals" and the Christian Right signaled by the shift to endorsement was that it did away with the detested "secular purpose" requirement of the Lemon Test, which had rested on legal secularism's central idea that, in some respects, the state should "disfavor" religion (Feldman 2005: 205). Under "endorsement," the new direction was that the state "must treat religion and nonreligion equally" (p. 205). This subverted the original purpose of the Establishment Clause, which had been the separation of religion and state. Feldman draws the hilarious scenario of the state, under the endorsement test, getting away with paying all clergy of the land as long as it also paid "ballet teachers and university professors under the rubric of a fund for 'general moral and aesthetic education'" (2002b: 678). In its minority-sensitive garb, endorsement analysis allowed the weird possibility of a forward-looking "egalitarian establishment of religion" (p. 729).

However, the concrete outcome of *Lynch v. Donnelly* was more crudely majoritarian, as was the entire Supreme Court's move away from legal secularism, for which *Lynch v. Donnelly* was an important milestone. Note that the mayor of Pawtucket, Rhode Island, had declared that the point of the crèche was to "keep Christ in Christmas," and that his opponents' attempt to get Christ out would be "a step towards establishing another religion, non-religion that it may be."[115] This was unmistakably the language of the Christian Right, which scored an important victory in *Lynch v. Donnelly*. Indeed, this was the "sort of religious chauvinism that the Establishment Clause was intended forever to prohibit," as Justice Brennan argued in dissent.[116] Brennan severely accused the court majority that its decision harked back to the days when it could be declared that "this is a Christian nation,"[117] and he warned that the city action condoned by *Lynch v. Donnelly* was "a coercive, though perhaps small, step toward establishing the sectarian preferences of the majority at the expense of the minority."[118]

But the string attached to the favoring of majority preferences under the endorsement test was the transformation of religious into cultural symbol. This is why in *County of Allegheny v. ACLU* (1989), which was the first Establishment Clause case decided on the basis of the endorsement test, the Christian crèche in a Pittsburgh courthouse did *not* pass constitutional muster. The objects of contention in this case were two holiday displays, a large crèche in the Allegheny County Courthouse, and an 18-foot Chanukah menorah outside Pittsburgh's City-County Building. If the crèche was rejected while the menorah was accepted, this is because their specific contexts, according to the narrow court majority, left the crèche religious, whereas the menorah was rendered secular. As to the crèche, being exhibited unaccompanied and with the large insignia *Glory to God for the birth of Jesus Christ*, "unlike in Lynch, nothing in the context of the display detracts from the crèche's religious message."[119] By contrast, the menorah, as part of a larger holiday display, was rendered secular by "stand[ing] next to a Christmas tree and a sign saluting liberty";[120] moreover, the Chanukah holiday marked by it "ranks fairly low in religious significance"[121] for Jews and, singled out by American Jews for its proximity to Christmas, was more of a "cultural or secular" event. However, why not the other way around, the Christmas tree rendering the menorah religious? This was the interpretation favored by Justice Brennan, dissenting. He rightly pointed out that the secularization of the menorah rested on the context-free "secularity" of the Christmas tree, which was questionable. Accordingly, Brennan reached the exact opposite conclusion, of the menorah, "unquestionably a religious symbol," reinforcing the "religious significance of the Christmas tree," and he would reject both, the crèche *and* the menorah, as unlawful "double establishment."[122]

The endorsement theory, which became law in *County of Allegheny v. ACLU*, "replaces the bright line of separationism with an uncertain screen, through which many symbols and practices of an obvious religious character will pass" (Lupu 1993: 240). But it did not go far enough for some, who also criticized that in its context dependence it produced a "jurisprudence of minutiae" with a risk of getting lost in the "unguided examination of marginalia."[123] Also in *County of Allegheny v. ACLU*, Justice Kennedy thus proposed his alternative "coercion" theory (discussed above), which was supported by three more justices in this case (including Chief Justice Rehnquist and Justice Scalia) and thus emerged as a serious competitor to the endorsement theory. Importantly, on its basis both menorah *and* crèche came to be affirmed, and particularly the crèche refusal was denounced as "unjustified hostility toward religion."[124] The coercion theory had the advantage of obliterating an inquiry into the meaning of religious symbols, "religious" or "secular," for the simple reason that, qua "symbol," they would *all* be validated because of their inability to "coerce." Accordingly, Kennedy's critique of the endorsement theory was that it would invalidate too many "traditional practices recognizing the part religion plays in our society," from the National Day of Prayer to the Pledge of Allegiance and the national motto "In God we trust." This is not quite correct – the task under the endorsement test would rather be to transform them from "religious" into "cultural." Endorsement was a centrist doctrine, allowing liberals to get onboard, and it precisely reflected Justice O'Connor's mediating position on the court. But it amounted to a brake on the religious conservatives. By contrast, coercion theory was the religious conservatives' battle horse for the state to recognize, even favor, religion *as* religion, without any cultural proviso.

The God frontier and the notion that the state can favor religion over non-religion were pushed mightily in *Van Orden v. Perry* (2005). The object of contention was a 6-foot-high monolith with the Ten Commandments near the Texas State Capitol, which had been donated to the state by a civic organization back in 1961. While surrounded by two dozen other historical markers and monuments, the religious nature of this monument was obvious, at a minimum, from the large and in part capital spelling of the first line engraved in it, "I AM the LORD thy God."[125] Interestingly, the case was decided on the same day as *McCreary County v. ACLU of Kentucky*, which had also been about a Ten Commandments exhibit. But whereas the Kentucky courthouse exhibit had been a "deliberate act of provocation" (Eisgruber and Sager 2007: 133), this could not be said about the Texas monument, which had stood there "unchallenged" for 40 years.[126] If the *McCreary County v. ACLU of Kentucky* variant of the Ten Commandments was defeated by a narrow court majority while an equally narrow majority validated the Texas monolith, the difference was the swing opinion of Justice Breyer. Although declaring the Texas stone a "borderline case," Breyer still found that the "nonreligious aspects of the tablet's message...predominate."[127]

However, more interesting than the modicum of secularism that, ironically, vindicated the constitutionality of the Texas Ten Commandments was the "plurality opinion" by Chief Justice Rehnquist. Rather provocatively, Rehnquist declared that a "preference for religion over irreligion" was not a violation of the Establishment Clause.[128] When the Chief Justice opined that "[o]ur institutions presuppose a Supreme Being," he was notably *not* quoting the very similar, famous line in *Zorach v. Clauson* (1952). His statement thus has to be taken as a free-standing, late twentieth-century affirmation of theocracy. And it was an understatement to find, as Justice Stevens did in his dissent, that the plurality in *Van Orden v. Perry* "wholehearted[ly]" validated "an official state endorsement of the message that there is one, and only one, God"[129] – Rehnquist's statement that America's state institutions "presuppose"

God is a touch stronger. However, there was still an element of secular moderation in Rehnquist's plurality opinion, when he pointed to the "undeniable historical meaning" of the Ten Commandments (beyond their narrowly religious meaning), and notably held the public schoolroom off limits for religious symbols and prayer alike.[130] This apparently annoyed the staunchest religionist on the court, Justice Scalia, who (in a punchy one-paragraph concurring opinion) would have "prefer[red] to reach the same result" by an even more bluntly anti-separationist line: "[T]here is nothing unconstitutional in a State's favoring religion generally, honoring God through public prayer and acknowledgment, or, in a nonproselytizing manner, venerating the Ten Commandments."[131]

Notably, *Van Orden v. Perry*'s latently theocratic "plurality opinion" is just that, the opinion of a "plurality" but not "majority" of the court, and thus no precedent for future decisions of the court. To pass constitutional muster, the Texas Ten Commandments still had to convey, at least to one but decisive judge, "a broader moral and historical message reflective of a cultural heritage."[132] That is, the transformation of a religious into a cultural symbol is still required to deflect an Establishment Clause challenge.[133] As it denied religion qua religion, this is a stronger qualification than the one on the "access and funding" front (where support for religion was conditional on non-religion also being supported by the state). Accordingly, one must conclude that with respect to religious symbols the wall of separation has been battered but not breached.

Conclusion

While the political zenith of the Christian Right has passed, its legal zenith may not have been reached yet. There is irony in this, because the judiciary had previously been the stronghold of the legal secularism that is now being counted out by an increasingly conservative and anti-separationist Supreme Court. Glacier-like, the effect of the court's gradual reconstitution under Republican presidencies beholden to the Christian Right outlasts the latter's electoral fortune. If the staunchest religionists on the court flirt with theocratic positions, this is doubly ironic because the Supreme Court, with its ultimate power of judicial review the true "voice of the popular sovereign" in America (Kahn 2011: 13), itself may be considered a "priesthood" of sorts that guards that "most sacred of texts: the Constitution" (p. 9). From this angle, legal theocracy might actually be vindicated as an act of modesty and self-limitation.

Epitomized by the notion of the wall of separation, the American state had once been the most radical of all secular states in its denial of all contact with religion, even that of the majority. Under the influence of the Christian Right, which has slowly worked its way into America's highest court, the old separationist approach is giving way to a new "integrationist" one (Gey 2007). According to it, the religious society that America empirically is should be formally reflected in its laws and institutions. Steven Gey is still optimistic that the integrationists will not succeed: first, because their vision is "deeply inconsistent with the country's basic history and traditions" (p. 42); but, secondly, because of a changing "religious demography" that, as a direct result of the political excesses of the Christian Right, is boosting "secularists" as the "fastest growing component" of the American populace (p. 45). Indeed, even on its own terms the new integrationism is still embedded within an overall separationist framework. No return to prayer and anti-evolutionism in America's public schools is in the making. And with respect to funding and symbols, state support and recognition, respectively, are "only incidentally religious" (Wald and Calhoun-Brown 2011: 102). This means that, with respect to state funding, the prior existence of non-religious beneficiaries is still required for religious beneficiaries to be "neutrally" treated; and with respect to state recognition, the refashioning of a religious into a cultural symbol is still required for the state to openly associate and identify with religion (which, however, I argued is a stronger proviso than that found on the funding front). Moreover, even in Justice Scalia's populism, the rapprochement between state and religion is non-denominational. This reflects the deep structure of American religiosity that has largely immunized the latter from civic strife and made religion compatible with democracy since the days of Tocqueville. If one brackets the shriller statements of the Christian Right, there is no sign that the Tocquevillian "agreement" between politics and religion in America is giving way to something less desirable. In relaxing its formal distance from religion, the American state – to repeat, in its own non-denominational way – may become a bit more like the "modest establishments" (Laborde 2013) of Europe, within a securely secular framework that is only lightly touched but not rocked by the occasional theocratic rhetoric.

As it moved from the separationist to the accommodationist pole, the biggest change in the American religion–state regime has certainly been with respect to the relative standing of religious majorities and minorities, the former having gained through a diminished (or rather: detoured) Establishment Clause and the latter having lost previous protections under a Free Exercise Clause that is no longer taken to exempt religious minorities from general laws. But the very distinction between "majority" and "minority" is fairly meaningless under the non-denominationalism that is de rigueur in American public life, and it is greatly relativized by the sociological fact of persistent denominational pluralism. More-over, the grossest disadvantages for religious minorities after the Supreme Court's notorious *Employment Division v. Smith* (1990) decision have been rectified through the political process (see Witte and Nichols 2011: 161–3). And "Islam" – to name that most vilified of minority religions in the West – is plainly *within* the "monotheistic" preference zone carved out by Justice Scalia. In his first Inaugural Address, Democratic President Obama depicted America as "a nation of Christians and Muslims, Jews and Hindus, and non-believers" (quoted in Lacorne 2011: 103). This is as much description as vision, to which there is no serious alternative. America is still better equipped than most other countries to fold into one nation believers and non-believers alike.

4

Challenge to the Secular State (II)

Islam in Europe

Islam in Europe is equivalent to the Christian Right in America in being the major challenge to the secular state on the opposite side of the Atlantic. The two challenges, of course, are rather different. The Christian Right grows out of majority society, finding fault with the radical separation between church and state that is America's distinct variant of secularism and that is itself tied up with the history of Latin Christendom. By contrast, with the exception of southeastern Europe, where Islam has indigenous roots, Islam is external to Europe, owing its presence mostly to postcolonial and guest-worker migration after World War II.[1] This fact both lowers and raises the level of challenge to the secular state. Demographically, the Islamic challenge cannot but be smaller because one is dealing here with a minority religion that realistically can aspire to little more than finding a place within Christian-majority society and institutions that, in Europe, are thoroughly secularized and unlikely to be changed much in the process. Conversely, the Christian Right, which grows out of and even explicitly claimed to be the "majority" in America, "wants the whole thing,"[2] even though its modest successes do not live up to its ambitions.

However, from a philosophical and historical angle the challenge of Islam to secular Europe is also more profound than that raised

128

by Christianity's own offshoots in America could ever be. This is because Islam grows out of a different civilizational context and operates on different principles than Christianity, so that its implantation into societies shaped by the latter, including the secularization that followed from it, cannot but cause irritation and friction. Tocqueville, when reflecting on how religion might (and should) support a democratic society, contrasted Islam and Christianity in incisive ways:

> Muhammad brought down from heaven and put into the Koran not religious doctrines only, but political maxims, criminal and civil laws, and scientific theories. The Gospels, on the other hand, deal only with the general relations between man and God and between man and man. Beyond that, they teach nothing and do not oblige people to believe anything. That alone, among a thousand reasons, is enough to show that Islam will not be able to hold its power long in ages of enlightenment and democracy, while Christianity is destined to reign in such ages, as in all others.
>
> (1969 [1835–40]: 445)

Tocqueville got it equally right and wrong. On the right side, the irritation of Islam for a liberal society has never been more crisply articulated. A contemporary author, who has done much to show that Islam is fully compatible with a liberal society, says exactly the same:

> As Islam developed and flourished for the vast majority of its history as the public religion of state power, doctrines of public law and political obligation, no less than matters of worship and ritual, have always been objects of intense practical concern. On this conception of religious morality, a political order is legitimate to the extent that it approximates an ideal legal order as expressed in the idea of *shari'a*. (March 2011: 28)

In short, Islam stipulates a unity of religion and politics, creedal and civic affiliations, which constitutes specific hurdles for integrating it in a secular state. This must not always be felt on the ground, as the process of "legal integration" (Joppke and Torpey 2013) has overall been successful, and as the real integration problem in Europe does not seem to be "Islam" as a religion but "Muslims" as a socioeconomically deprived minority. (For the problem of labeling "Islam" and "Muslims," see Brubaker 2013b.) Having said this, at the level of political thought it is still useful to begin with Islam as "separate from the West and with a logic of its own," as a "paradigmatic alternative to Europe" (Black 2011: 1, 3).

While he grasped the different logics of Islam and Christianity, Toc-queville was less prescient about the two religions' different futures, supposedly blissful for Christianity and distinctly less so for Islam. To begin with, Christianity's political self-limitation did not come automatically but was the result of a struggle that was as long as the history of Europe, lasting at least from the fifth century till well into the 1960s. And this hard-won self-limitation sealed Christianity's demise as a polity-and society-defining force. Representative here is the emergent European Union's refusal to include even a meek symbolic reference to God or Christianity into the preamble of its planned constitution (that never materialized). Conversely, Islam, far from losing its edge in a democratic age, seems to be more ardently embraced than ever, by majorities in Muslim societies no less than by minorities in the West. Ernest Gellner controversially argued that Islam's more comprehensive leanings, combining "both faith and morals," made it "secularization-resistant" (1992: 6; for a critique, see Zubaida 1995). But this "resistance" shows in Islam's persistence as unquestioned legitimizing ideology of Muslim-majority societies (see Ferrari 2012b). And it shows, post-Gellner, in its attractiveness as an oppositional identity option of a marginalized minority in the West (see Roy 2002). Note that Khaled Kelkar, France's most wanted after the lethal bombing of the Paris Metro in 1995, who had discovered Islam as "a great opening of the spirit" in prison, would say, before he was hunted down by the French anti-terror police, that he was "neither Arab nor French, but a Muslim" (Leiken 2012: 12).

When contrasting the religion–politics constellations under Christianity and Islam, it is useful to distinguish between their "original positions," which, however, under the "pressure of historical circumstances," came to be modified "almost to convergence" (Black 2008: 11). Christianity started apolitical, yet in the Papal Revolution it tried no less than to bring secular authority under its control. Islam started political, yet moved in the opposite direction of establishing "some separation between the religious and the political" (p. 21), as in its tenth-century distinction between (religious) Caliph and (political) Sultan, and in a tendency toward "spiritualizing" the *ummah*. But already by the thirteenth century, there was a return to the original positions in both religions. The medieval Muslim scholar Ibn Taymiyya anticipated contemporary political Islamism in his view that "religion without sultan (power), holy war (jihad) and wealth, is as bad as power, wealth and war without religion" (p. 27). And, for Christianity, Thomas Aquinas developed the opposite idea that "in those things that pertain to the civil good, the secular power is to be obeyed rather than the spiritual" (p. 29). Antony Black plausibly concludes: "It seems that the separation of church from state has been nearly always regarded as the norm in Europe and the West, and the integration of politics with religion has nearly always been regarded as the norm in Muslim countries" (p. 32).

In her noted treatise on medieval Islamic political thought, Patricia Crone points out that in the Islamic tradition there is "no word for states," neither qua "Weberian state" nor qua "nation-state" (2004: 3; confirmed by Finer 1997: 678). Medieval Muslims saw themselves ruled by "persons rather than institutions" (Crone 2004: 3), and the "society" over which rule was exercised was either "ummah" or "millet," both connoting a religious community. In contrast to Christian ontology, where government is the result of humanity's fall into sin, for Islam there *always* had been government, with "God rul[ing] in the most literal sense of the word" (p. 6). "Law" is ipso facto religious law, not limited to regulating the relations between God and human beings but extending to all aspects of inter-human relations. This law is revealed by God to human beings through prophets, of which there were many, until the appearance of the last prophet, Muhammad. Surely, the political expanse of his doctrine was also conditioned by the fact that he operated in a "stateless environment," where "every tribesman defended himself and his dependents" (p. 12). While Jesus lived in a society with functioning political authority, so that the idea of "dual membership" (one civic, one religious) could come rather easily to him and his followers, Muhammad's *ummah* had to be "a congregation and a state rolled together" (p. 13). Crone concludes that early Muslim society was marked by "a complete fusion of the religious and the political all the way through: there was no religious community separate from the politically organized society and no ecclesiastical hierarchy separate from the political agency" (p. 15).

Another way to formulate the matter is that in traditional Islamic political theory "the ideal State [is]...a co-operative partnership between governor and governed, both owing a common obedience to the revealed law" (Coulson 1957: 49). As there is "no legislative power as such in Islam" (p. 50), there can in principle be no conflict between ruler and ruled – which also explains the near-absence of "rights of men" in Islam, whereas the "rights of God" pertain to "the whole of the Shari'a" (p. 50). In effect, this constellation entails "broad discretionary powers of the sovereign" (p. 55), "completely subordinat[ing] the principle of the individual liberty to that of the public interest and welfare" (p. 56).

If one factors in the early defeat of natural law and *falsafa* (philosophy) in Islam (briefly discussed in Chapter 2), whereby non-Muslims were categorically excluded from access to morality and truth, this was not a religion easily portable and adjustable across places. It is in fact the most territorial of the three monotheisms, even more territorial than the Jewish, for which, until 1948, the dispersal in the diaspora was constitutive (and in important ways, even after the founding of Israel, it still is). Significantly, the two older monotheisms, Judaism and Christianity, do not know anything akin to the division of the world into the House of Islam and the House of War, along with the obligation for Muslims of something akin to the Prophet's *hijra*, that is, emigration to a Muslim polity where religious overlaps with political law. Moreover, "[t]raditional Islam does not recognize humanity as a significant category" (Black 2008: 148), knowing only the distinction between "Muslims" and "infidels" (*kufir*). The relationship between the two is one of ineradicable inequality, if not lawlessness, because infidels (with the partial exception of *dhimmis*, other People of the Book) were not seen as endowed with morality and as "what we would call truly human" (Crone 2004: 359). In its very first paragraph, the Qur'an sets up a dichotomy between the "righteous" and the "unbelievers," promising "gardens watered by running streams" (2:23) for the first but "grievous punishment" (2:1) for the latter. While this defining text of the last and conclusive monotheism contains something for every taste, the pacifist gospel of Mecca as much as the belligerent commands of Medina, unquestionably there is in it the potential of a group- and opposition-building fighting creed that has energized its followers through the ages. *This* Islam is comparable to the powers of nineteenth-century nationalism (see Gellner 1992) or twentieth-century Communism (see Monnerot 1949). Today, in one prominent reading (Ramadan 2002b), Islam is the main protagonist in the "resistance" to capitalist globalization.

When tackling the question of Islam in Europe, it has become de rigueur to start from the premise of joint roots and Europe's enrichment by Islam. "Islam was never simply the Other, the Orient, but an element of Europeans, not only part of our past but of our present too," writes the British anthropologist Jack Goody (2004: 65). As proof he points to such mundane things as irrigation, hygiene, pasta, coffee, rice, silk, and sugar, all of which owe their presence in Europe to Muslims. Blowing into the same horn of denying a compatibility problem between "Islam" and "Europe," Olivier Roy has forcefully argued that it is wrong in principle to tie up the issue of Muslim integration with "an enquiry into the theological tenets of Islam as a religion" (2013: 6). After all, no one ever asked the Catholic Church, a fierce enemy of liberal democracy until the Second Vatican Council in the early 1960s, to adapt its theology to liberal values. Such theological inquiry, argues Roy, would violate the separation between church and state in a liberal society. Moreover, from the point of view of political liberalism, which this French Islam specialist intriguingly adopts from John Rawls (1993), the assumption of "shared common values" (other than thin procedural values) is a chimera to begin with. Instead, Roy proposes to shift focus from "religion" as dogma to "religiosity" as practice, which would make Islam appear just one of many religions, all alike in being pure "faith" stripped of contingent "culture," a trend that he observes in the youthful versions of all contemporary monotheisms, Jewish, Protestant, Catholic, Islamic (see Roy 2010). As Roy provocatively concludes, "Islam does not bring a new culture or new values, but is the mirror through which Europe is looking at its own identity" (2013: 18), or, rather, discovers that it does not have one except being Islam's Other: "Islam is the negative identity of a Europe that is unable to forge a common – much less positive – identity for itself" (p. 12).

In Roy's tranquilizing view, the entire *problématique* of Islam in Europe and the West shrinks to an "optical illusion" (Roy 2013: 12). One wonders: why all the noise, especially after 2001? Bassam Tibi, the contentious German-Syrian scholar of past and present Islam, takes the opposite view, that "Islamic civilization has problems with modernity" (2009a: 25) and that "Islam has to change" its approach to knowledge, law, human rights, and so on, if the people under its sway want to move ahead. Tibi endorses Jürgen Habermas's view that modernity is marked by the "principle of subjectivity": "In modernity, religious life, state and society, but also science, morality and art transform themselves into instances of the principle of subjectivity" (Habermas 1985: 25). Religion thus becomes "faith" within a human-centered ordering of the world. For Tibi, this means that Islam must transform itself into a thoroughly secularized "Euro-Islam" that respects the separation of religion and politics, secular democracy, human rights, toleration, and pluralism (Tibi 2009b: 44).

If one follows the pronouncements of some of contemporary Islam's best-known voices, a secular Islam will never be. The prominent Egyptian cleric Yusuf al-Qaradawi rules it out categorically: "[A]s Islam is a comprehensive system of worship...and legislation (Shari'ah), the acceptance of secularism means abandonment of Shari'ah, a denial of the divine guidance and a rejection of Allah's injunctions.... [T]he call for secularism among Muslims is atheism and a rejection of Islam" (al-Qaradawi 1987: 38). If al-Qaradawi is correct, political scientist Giovanni Sartori, never mincing his words, is *also* correct to characterize Islam as "an invasive theocratic monolith" that cannot be "integrated" and that, in fact, no non-Muslim society has ever managed to integrate.[3]

Instead of coolly denying any conflict, as does Roy, or heatedly overdrawing it, as do Tibi and Sartori, a more balanced approach is to recognize the mutual accommodations and approximations between Islam-on-the-ground and local host societies, as John Bowen (2010a: ch. 8) has masterfully done for the case of France. However, even by Bowen's own account, any such bridging must first assume that there is something to bridge, namely, "Islamic rules" and "European ones" (p. 165).

Two Civilizations

It is therefore apposite to begin by spelling out these opposite rules, and to explicate the incompatibilities and the ground that is less likely to be shared. Though growing out of the same monotheistic roots as "sister religions" (Lewis 1993: vii), "Islam" and "Christendom" evolved historically as often sharply opposed competitors for a world-changing, universalistic project that addressed, with the intent to convert, all human beings – something that the parent religion of both, an inward-looking, ethnic Judaism, had abandoned early on. (For a comparison of the three "children of Abraham," see Peters 2004.) If, as I shall suggest, one can contrast Islam and Europe (and the "West" that is the offshoot of Europe) as different "civilizations",[4] this is on the premise of a fundamental similarity, in terms of joint historical roots and a shared universalistic ambition, which made both "understand" their differences as no two other religions could: "When Christians and Muslims called each other accursed infidels, each understood exactly what the other meant, because both meant exactly the same thing" (Lewis 1993: 175). In fact, much of the tension between the two arises precisely out of the historical and moral ground they share, in a constellation that Freud aptly called the "narcissism of minor differences."

Historically, "Europe" as a self-reflected entity is an outgrowth of the early medieval confrontation with an expanding Islam. "The very concept of Europe as a cultural rather than geographical expression emerged in the eighth century, during the conflicts between *us* – Latin Christian Europeans – and *them*, namely African and Asian Muslims" (Jenkins 2007: 260). In a classic work on the making of medieval Europe, the Belgian historian Henri Pirenne showed how the seventh-century Islamic conquest of North Africa and Spain had destroyed the unity of the Roman-Mediterranean world around the *Mare Nostrum* (Our Sea) so that "Europe," its center of gravity now pushed to the north, emerged exactly in contradistinction to the Islamic world: "Without Mohammad, Charlemagne would be inconceivable" (Pirenne 1970 [1939]: 175). Pirenne further notes that the earlier Germanic invasions were easily "absorbed" and Christianized, whereas the Arabs were "exalted by a new faith" that rendered them "unassimilable" (p. 109): "The Germanic became Romanized once he entered the Roman lands. The Roman, by contrast, became Arabized once he was conquered by Islam" (p. 111). As a result, "two civilizations, different and hostile," replaced the "Mediterranean unity" of Roman times along the shores of the Mediterranean Sea (p. 111). And between the two civilizations there was not trade but "perpetual war" (p. 128). It would remain that way for one thousand years. Late eighteenth-century English historian Edward Gibbon famously mused that Europe might have turned Islamic had the invading Muslim armies not been decisively repelled twice, in Poitiers (732) and near Vienna (1683): "Perhaps the interpretation of the Koran would now be taught in the schools of Oxford and her pupils might demonstrate to a circumcised people the sanctity and truth of the Revelation of Mahomet" (Gibbon quoted in Pagden 2008: 157).

The aggressive impulse in the confrontation with Islam tends to be attributed to Europe – in the dark optic of Gil Anidjar, the identity of "Europe" rests on its construing of two enemies: Jews as its "internal and theological enemy" and Muslims as "its external and political enemy" (2012: 23). However, prior to Europe's making the world safe for Christianity, which roughly occurred from the late medieval Crusades to the sixteenth-century explorations of the Americas, there had been the experience of colonization and domination by a civilization infinitely more developed and sophisticated. As Bernard Lewis describes it, "Christendom" appeared to conquering Islam as "poor, small, backward, and monochromatic," much as "central Africa looked to Victorian England" (1993: 9, 13). The Crusades, while no doubt more brutish and intolerant than any Muslim domination had ever been, might even be called a "counter-jihad" (Tibi 2009b: 76), a response to a "deep imperialist undercurrent" (Karsh 2007: 235) that had marked Islam no less than the imperialist West. Note that, while not unknown in the Christian tradition, the notion of "Holy War" has rather different connotations in the two religions: "Holy war began in Christianity as metaphor, moved to literal policy, and has on the whole moved back again to metaphor. In Islam it began as practical policy, was used as metaphor by sufis and others, and is now both" (Black 2008: 37). Since the invention of firepower, things "went wrong" for Islam and the "balance of power" came to be reversed in favor of Christian Europe (Lewis 2002: 20). While today's political Islamists are hardly graduates in comparative history (more often, in fact, they are engineers; see Gambetta and Hertog 2009), the stark disjunction between, on the one hand, a creed that was meant to rule and once had ruled and, on the other, the mostly inferior positions of its people today surely colors the present encounter between Islam and Europe and the West.

Despite the fame he garnered for using the notion, the rivalry between Islam and the West as one of "civilizations" is not the invention of Samuel Huntington (1996). While Huntington came to be isolated and shunned in the *juste* academic milieu for his edgy views, many Muslim intellectuals have adopted a civilizational discourse. For the Swiss Muslim scholar Tariq Ramadan, for instance, who has tried more than most to reconcile the two, "Islam" and the "West" still stand sharply apart as separate "civilizations," "so near and so different at the same time" (2001: 213). Strikingly frank and matter of fact, he distinguishes the two in terms of "freedom" versus "submission," the first being the guiding principle of the West, the second that of Islam. In Ramadan's view, Judeo-Christian "doubt" and Islamic "faith" make for "two different universes of reference, two civilizations and two cultures" (p. 219). Not that different from Ernest Gellner's view of Islam as "secularization-resistant" (1992: 5), Ramadan claims that "Muslim thought has never ventured out of the sacred space" (2001: 217).

A "civilization," according to Huntington, is "a culture writ large,"[5] "the broadest cultural entity," "the biggest 'we'" (1996: 41). One may quibble about how many of them there are and whether they really explain the motives and behavior of their people,[6] but this is exactly how the world appears from many a contemporary Islamic point of view. Whether reformist or traditionalist, Islam depicts its adherents as a people apart, thus constituting the quasi-nationalism that Ernest Gellner (1992: 15) had seen in it, at least in the reformed "High Islam" of the scholars. But the language of nationalism, of which there are necessarily several within the ambit of any one "civilization," is still too anodyne to capture the absolute Otherness of Islam. In fact, the language of nationhood, conveying pluralism, is "one of the distinguishing features of European political culture," whereas "in the Islamic world the community of language, faith, shared historical consciousness, and a common awareness of insiders and outsiders...were all projected onto the "umma" (Black 2008: 68). Given the quasi-national nature of the *ummah*, there is no place alongside it for "nationalism" and "nation-state" proper, which appear as "forms of idolatry, worshipping a reified nation as a substitute for God" (Zubaida 2004: 412).

At least two themes can readily be found in self-descriptions of Islam that, from its own point of view, set it apart from the "West." The first is a reluctance to draw distinctions, most notably between the sacred and the secular. If liberalism is an "art of separation," a "world of walls" each "creat[ing] a new liberty," and thus a reflection of the "long-term process of social differentiation," as Michael Walzer (1984: 315, 319) evocatively put it,[7] Islam is the exact opposite, negating separation and favoring a stipulated unity. Joseph Schacht's classic study of Islamic law thus characterizes sharia as "an all-embracing body of religious duties," "regulat[ing] the life of every Muslim in all its aspects," "compris[ing] on an equal footing ordinances regarding worship and ritual, as well as political and...legal rules" (1964: 1). For Schacht, indeed, Islam *is* law (not theology, which is a preoccupation of Christianity, stemming perhaps from its complicated deity), and one that knows no exceptions and is valid everywhere. This conflicts with the logic of secularization, which relegates religion to a "subsystem of society" and is but the "consequence of the high degree of differentiation reached by modern society" (Luhmann 1982: 227–8).

The dislike of differentiation and refusal to accept the sacred–secular distinction (in which Islam and Orthodox Judaism are "remarkably alike"),[8] blends with a second theme: the primacy attributed to the collective over the individual. Middle East historian Carl Brown put it this way: "Islamic political thought emphasizes unity and community with correspondingly less valuation placed on the individual and individualism as in Christian (and Western) political thought" (2000: 79).

The important point is that these themes are not only externally but self-attributed. For Tariq Ramadan, the two themes of unity and community converge in the notion of *tawhid* ("the oneness of God"), which is said to set the "Islamic civilization" apart from the West (Ramadan 2001: 245). Ramadan illustrates the different philosophies of the two civilizations by way of the starkly different renderings of Abraham's sacrificing of his son, Isaac, in the Bible and the Qur'an. What in the Bible appears as a drama of "sin, suffering, anguish and fear," setting Abraham apart from God and from his son, is in the Qur'an no drama at all because "both have submitted," father and son: "Shared Faith, the brotherhood of Faith – which is the foundation of Islam – is opposed to any idea of tragic consciousness" (p. 217). In the holistic world of Islam, "to think is not at all struggling to liberate oneself from God, it is rather coming closer to him" (p. 217). One perhaps cannot understand this unless one believes. Ramadan still insists that "[n]othing in Islam is opposed to modernity," and that an "Islamic modernity" is possible (p. 307). Yet one wonders: can there be modernity without the "principle of subjectivity" (Habermas), with its distinctive *Entzweiung*, the separation of the individual from group and society, which was already bemoaned (and meant to be overcome) by Hegel?

The Iraqi scholar-politician Ali Allawi (2009) also describes Islam as a civilization apart. "The sharp dichotomy between the sacred and the profane…does not hold in Islam" (pp. 10–11), he finds, and according to him Islam rejects the "primacy of individual over collective rights" that is said to mark the "West" (p. 4). Instead, "submission to the decrees of God" constitutes the "basis for public organization," and this "can brook no compromise" (p. 11). Notably *not* flowing from the pen of a radical cleric, this apodictic description by a worldly statesman and intellectual raises doubt about the prospects of current government efforts throughout Europe to domesticate or nationalize Islam. Allawi further notes that the Arabic word for "individual" (*al-fard*) does not connote "purposeful being" but "singularity, aloofness or solitariness" (which incidentally mirrors an idea of freedom as "licentiousness" [Crone 2004: 280]), and that "the entire edifice of individual rights...is alien to the structure of Islamic reasoning" (Allawi 2009: 11). Tariq Ramadan echoes this view, arguing that in Islam "God has rights" while humans have merely "duties" (2001: 24). For Allawi, there is no need for individual rights in Islam's "God-centered community," with its "continuum between the individual and the group, with little possibility of ethical atomization" (2009: 12). These indigenous views of Islam inevitably remind one of Marxism, whose "good" society likewise knew no need for trivial "rights" (see Lukes 1985). As Allawi concludes the conceptual part of his passionate *état des lieux* of the Islamic world, for the sake of retaining its "separate civilizational space" Islam must reject the "ideals of liberalism, democracy and secularism" (2009: 190).

This is strong language that, if accurate, would entail the futility of the entire project of integrating or accommodating Islam and Muslims in Europe and the West. And *Financial Times* editorialist Christopher Caldwell (2009: 129) would be right that the attempt to create a "French" or "German" Islam "answers to a question that Islam does not ask" (2009: 129). Conversely, if "liberalism, democracy and secularism" are not acceptable for Islam, Bassam Tibi (2006) is correct that there are only two alternatives: either the "Islamization of Europe," which he deems to be Tariq Ramadan's project, or to "Europeanize Islam," which would make for a "Euro-Islam" that is "as secular as secular Europe is" (Tibi 2009b: 80) – but that would no longer be the "Islam" of Ramadan, Allawi, or al-Qaradawi, and presumably most other Islamic scholars, clerics, and jurists.

Caldwell argues that in the case of Muslims and Islam in Europe one is "not dealing with an ordinary immigration problem...but with an adversary culture" (2009: 329), which threatens nothing less than the "essence of Europe" (p. 11). In the following, I will argue that there *are* elements of an "adversarial culture," but only at the level of Islamic elite discourse. By contrast, ordinary Muslims hold views that are often not distinguishable from those of average Europeans or, at worst, are similar to those of other religious conservatives.

Islamic Elite Discourse: European Muslims as a "Minority" or as "Citizens"

Traditional Islamic doctrine says much about the conditions of non-Muslims under Muslim rule but little about the opposite conditions of

Muslims living under non-Muslim rule. This reflects the early dominance of Islam as political fact, but also as principled aspiration. Yusuf al-Qaradawi introduces his influential handbook on how to live in a non-Islamic society by arguing that, insofar as the "word of Allah" is "always uppermost," "Islam came to be followed, not to follow; to be dominant, not subordinate" (1960: 2). For traditional Muslim jurists, to live under non-Muslim rule is undesirable, if not forbidden – the only exceptions being short-term visits for trade and conquest by infidels. A long-term residence under non-Muslim rule was not foreseen, and the *hijra* to Muslim-majority lands was either required or recommended, much as the Prophet had originally moved from Mecca to Medina in order not to be ruled by non-Muslims. Note that Year One in the Islamic calendar is the year of Muhammad's flight to Medina, which symbolizes the "Islamic unification...of religious truth and political authority" (March 2009a: 104). The early political success of Islam, which reinforced the creedal rejection of differentiation between the religious and secular spheres, long rendered irrelevant any serious contemplation of Muslims living under non-Muslim rule. "What never seems to have occurred to any of the classical jurists," argues Bernard Lewis, "was that great numbers of Muslims, of their own free will, would go and live under the rule of non-Muslim governments" (1993: 41).

To accommodate the new situation of Muslim immigration to the West, reformist Muslim jurists have created a new "*fiqh* for minorities." This novel jurisprudence differs from the traditional legal schools of Islam in placing a greater emphasis on non-textual reasoning (*ijtihad*) that finds its basis in the "ultimate objectives" (*maqasid*), rather than in the letter, of the Qur'an – without any questioning, however, of the Qur'an as "immutable and incontrovertible" and "offer[ing] solutions and answers to all questions" (al-Alwani 2003: 9, 19). Notwithstanding the presumption of absolute Qur'anic authority, the "*fiqh* for minorities" aims to find a balance between maintaining the faith and the everyday challenges to that aspiration that arise from living in realms in which Muslims and Islamic laws do not predominate.

European Muslims as a "minority"

An important figure in the making of minority *fiqh* is the Qatar-based television cleric Yusuf al-Qaradawi – creator of the popular Islamic website Islam Online, regular presence on the Arabic al-Jazeera TV network, and president of the influential European Council for Fatwa and Research. While "not reputed to be an especially great scholar," he is nonetheless considered "the most important media cleric in the

Arabic-speaking world today" (Feldman 2007: 104), and one who is not given to extremes but who "largely defines the mainstream Muslim position" (Lynch 2010).

In a 2007 *fatwa* (legal opinion), al-Qaradawi summarizes "the duties of Muslims who live in the West" in five points.[9] First and foremost is the "duty to keep one's Muslim identity." From this follows, secondly, the duty to "bring up [one's] children Islamically." Should this not be possible, Muslims have to "go back to their countries of origin, as staying in the west...will cause an irreparable harm to the whole family." Because Muslims in a non-Muslim context cannot but be "a minority," their third duty is "to unite together as one man" and "to reject any form of division that is capable of turning them to an easy prey for others." To the degree that there is a "duty of Muslims towards the society where they reside," this is, fourthly, the obligation "to be sincere callers to their religion," which is an obligation "not only restricted to scholars and Sheikhs." This proviso touches on the basic premise of al-Qaradawi's assent to the presence of Muslims in the West: their proselytizing and active spreading of the Islamic faith. To call proselytizing a "duty" to the host society reveals a minimalist, at best instrumental, engagement of Muslims with their host societies. No wonder that Muslims' fifth and final duty in the West turns back onto themselves, as they are to "champion the rights of the Muslim Ummah," from Palestine to Chechnya: "Nowadays, we see the Jews, from the four corners of the world, championing and backing Israel, and we call on all Muslims in all parts of the world saying that it is high time to champion the rights of their Muslim Ummah." Overall, al-Qaradawi depicts Muslims in the West as a people apart and united. This may be compatible with non-liberal versions of multiculturalism, but it presents a serious challenge to all current Western state policies to "integrate" them.

Al-Qaradawi's 2007 *fatwa* reflects the hardened group identity of Muslims after 2001; little remains in it of the "minority *fiqh*" that he had earlier helped bring about. The minority *fiqh* first provided a framework whereby Muslims could live in the West without giving up their creed. Al-Qaradawi also called it a "*fiqh* of balances," which refers to the "need to balance minor evils against greater or longer-term benefits to Muslims" (quoted in Bowen 2010a: 145). That conception is systematically laid out in al-Qaradawi's classic work, *The Lawful and Prohibited in Islam* (1960). It provides an interpretation of Islam reminiscent of English common law, at least as it touches on the regulation of social life: everything that is not explicitly prohibited (*haram*) by the Qur'an or another "sound" source is permitted (*halal*). Note that the permitted is the default position, because "the things which Allah has created and the benefits derived from them are essentially for man's use, and hence are permissible" (ch. 1, p. 2). The "authority to legislate" the *halal* and the *haram*, of course, is God's alone, which reduces the role of the cleric to that of interpreter (rather than decision-maker). The *halal/haram* distinction is not capricious but made "with people's well-being in view," outlawing only what is "impure" and "harmful" (ch. 1, p. 9). Furthermore, the *halal/haram* distinction is not to be applied differentially according to social situation or status – there are "no privileged classes...in the name of religion," and "true morality...is distinguishable by its universality" (ch. 1, p. 15).

While most of this does not differ much from traditional understandings of Islamic law, the novelty kicks in when considering the role of exceptions: "[N]ecessity removes restrictions" is al-Qaradawi's central line (1960: ch. 1, p. 17). "In permitting the use of [the] haram under necessity," as al-Qaradawi explicates the "11th principle of Islam," "Islam is true to its spirit and general principles. This spirit...is to make life easy and less oppressive for human beings" (ch. 1, p. 17). For instance, while it is forbidden to eat pork or the meat of naturally deceased animals, "if one is compelled by necessity...there is no sin on Him; indeed, Allah is Forgiving, Merciful" (ch. 2, p. 3).

With great simplicity and logical consistency, al-Qaradawi lays out the *halal/haram* dualism, always modifiable by reason of necessity, for all aspects of life, from the merely personal and private to marriage and family life and social relations outside the home. While written before Muslim immigrants had established themselves in large numbers in the West and before the global polarization between Islam and the West, *The Lawful and Prohibited in Islam* is already framed as a riposte to "Christian missionaries" and "Imperialist powers" that have drawn "a very distorted and ugly picture of Islam." Some of its more striking passages depict Muslims as a group that must always seek to stay apart, even visibly. For instance, the growing of beards among Muslim men is said to be based on a *hadith* (recorded word of the Prophet) that prescribes it for the sake of "be[ing] different from the polytheists" (al-Qaradawi 1960: ch. 2, p. 10). Muslims must avoid "resemblance in appearance" to non-believers, as this "produces love, friendship, and affinity in feeling," which would undercut the "distinction from those who do not believe [that] is obligatory for Muslims" (ch. 2, p. 11). Al-Qaradawi cites the Prophet as saying, "Whoever imitates a people is one of them," so that dress and hairstyle fulfill a separationist, group-building function (ch. 2, p. 11). In the closing chapter on social relationships, al-Qaradawi concedes that the Qur'an, while in some passages objecting to Muslims who "take the Jews and Christians as friends" because "they are the friends (only) of each other," *also*, in friendlier sections, "enjoin[s] affection and kindness to the good and peace-loving

peoples of *every* religion" (ch .4, p. 4; emphasis added). But such "affection" and "kindness" does not amount to "loyalty," which is reserved
to fellow Muslims: "Islam does not recognize any loyalty other than to
its belief, any relationship other than that of its brotherhood, or any
differentiation among human beings other than on the basis of belief
and unbelief" (ch. 4, p. 8).

In Andrew March's typology of "theocratic minorities" trying to cope
with a "non-ideal" polity, al-Qaradawi's approach represents a "temporary modus vivendi model" that March finds "dominant" among Islamic
jurists (and that he, interestingly, also attributes to Evangelical Christians
in the United States). Importantly, its self-restraint and its acknowledgment of a "thin social contract" are only tactical concessions to demographic weakness; they are not principles – there is "no permanent,
principled commitment to self-restraint in implementing its own comprehensive theocratic system" (March 2011: 31).

Al-Qaradawi is a hugely contradictory and contested figure. As shown,
the thrust of his minority *fiqh* is to make the ethical life of Muslims in
the West easier, instead of imposing obligations that are difficult or
impossible to meet. On the grounds of necessity or mere expediency for
Muslims, for instance, he has assented to interest-bearing mortgages,
thus lifting the religious prohibition on *riba* (interest) from economic
transactions. He has also agreed to Muslim men's serving in non-Muslim
armies even when attacking Muslim countries, thus breaking one of the
greatest taboos in applied Muslim ethics. A moderate in the eyes of some
(March 2007b), to others he is a dangerous extremist (Berman 2010).
In support of the latter view, Harold Berman adduces al-Qaradawi's
endorsement of female (and unveiled!) suicide bombing in Israel, or his
tirades against "this oppressive Jewish, Zionist band of people," whom
he wishes to see "count[ed]...and kill[ed]...down to the very last one"
(quoted on p. 92).

European Muslims as "citizens"

Even if Tariq Ramadan is widely suspected of "double talk," including
dubious positions on Jews, violence, and women (Berman 2007), he has
never gone to the extremes associated with al-Qaradawi. Ramadan rarely
misses the chance to praise al-Qaradawi, but he has also criticized
Muslims' withdrawal and self-insulation as a minority that follow from
the program of a minority *fiqh* along the lines that al-Qaradawi proposes.[10] If they adopt a "minority consciousness," and thus situate themselves "in the West but outside the West," Muslims become vulnerable
to "suspicions about their allegiance and loyalty" (Ramadan 2004:

107–8). Ramadan thus favors Muslims' positive engagement as citizens in their host societies.

In Andrew March's typology (2011: 31–2), Ramadan moves to a "religious-integralist model" or even "thicker social contract model," which March still considers a "minority position" in contemporary Islamic scholarship. Ramadan's discursive move from a "minority" to a "citizenship" perspective has helped make this Swiss Islamic scholar with his good looks and smooth talk (if often obscure prose) one of *Time Magazine*'s "100 most important innovators" of the twenty-first century, and the "go-to" representative of Muslims for governments from Canada to Britain.

For March, who has argued that contemporary mainstream Muslim reasoning is commensurable with Rawlsian "political liberalism" (2009a), Ramadan's position marks a transition from a purely tactical embrace by Muslims of "resident alienage" to their loyal "citizenship" in host societies. Note that in traditional Muslim jurisprudence, work permits, legal residence, and naturalization figured as "contracts of security" (*aman*) that oblige Muslims to obey the laws of host societies, in return for being granted protection and being allowed to practice their faith freely. Similarly, traditional Muslim law favored residence in non-Muslim societies only for the instrumental reason of *da'wa*, the spreading of the Islamic faith and conversion of non-believers. Does Ramadan allow for Muslims' intrinsic involvement in the public life of host societies, as loyal "citizens" rather than merely aloof and disconnected "residents"?

A normative conception of citizenship as "morally motivated commitment to a political community," which is more than mere "law abidingness" (March 2009a: 136), may be compelling for the political theorist. But it exceeds the legal minimum required by the liberal state, not to mention that doubts are allowed that this is the dominant attitude of ordinary citizens. Worse still, if states require "morally motivated commitment" as a precondition for granting citizenship to immigrants, the reality is more likely to be an illiberal intrusion into a domain that is rightly considered private and outside the ambit of legitimate state intervention (see Joppke 2010: 54–5, 140–2). But even more astounding is the notion that, of all groups, Muslims in the West, or, more precisely, the elites writing and acting for them, should exhibit "morally motivated commitment" to their host societies. Scrutinizing Tariq Ramadan's enigmatic positioning is instructive in this respect.

Ramadan shares with al-Qaradawi a fundamental distinction between "orders of creed and worship" and a "sphere of social affairs" (Ramadan 2009: 264). While the creed is immutable and "subjected to the sole and ultimate authority of the revealed texts," in the social sphere the "whole range of possibilities is open" (p. 264). Accordingly, in the social sphere the al-Qaradawi principle applies that "everything is permitted except what is explicitly forbidden by a text" (Ramadan 2004: 35). This opens up a space for "reason and creativity" (p. 35), and allows the adjusting of Islamic precepts to a changing historical and social context. However, one may quarrel with Ramadan's conclusion, strategically addressed to a Western audience: "So there is indeed a difference in Islam between creed and rationality, the private and the public, the religious and the political" (p. 36). This assertion contradicts his earlier framing of Islam and the West as "two different universes of reference," the first holistic and built on "faith," the second torn and divided by "doubt" (Ramadan 2001: 219). One cannot have it both ways. If a religion–politics distinction is conceded, the critique of secularism and of the disappearance of "spirituality" in Western public spaces (as in Ramadan 2002a: 138) loses its foundation.

While Ramadan shares with al-Qaradawi the basic thrust behind the minority *fiqh* – namely, the aim of making religious obligation more flexible and less burdensome in the everyday life of Muslims in the West – the difference, as said, is to move the emphasis from Muslims as minority to Muslims as citizens. But the great fanfare of this move is itself indicative of a problem. Would anyone doubt that the adherents of other faiths can be "citizens" of their societies? Adherents of certain religious sects may reject and seek to remain apart from their societies (Spinner-Halev 1999 calls them "partial citizens"), but the squaring of faith and citizenship seems to raise particular difficulties for Muslims. Note that Ramadan's programmatic text *To be a European Muslim* (2002a) begins with a vision of "coexistence" (p. 4). This is not the way fellow citizens are expected to relate to one another, who are memorably referred to by German legal scholar Ulrich Preuss as constituting "a kind of community in which aliens can become associates" (1995: 275); and it falls short of the "morally motivated commitment" stipulated by March (2009a: 136). One also finds there an aversion toward "becom[ing] *one of theirs*, an *authentic* European" (Ramadan 2002a: 1).

Of course, Ramadan's opposition to conceiving of Muslims in the West as "reclusive minorities" (Ramadan 2004: 54) is in one sense genuine: a minority stance is rightly seen as conflicting with the universalism of Islam. "The universality of the message of Islam," argues Ramadan (p. 54), "invites us to integrate everything that is positive ... and to act from within, as full members in our society" (p. 55).

Let us pursue the question of whether Muslims' engagement with Western host societies is only instrumental or intrinsic. Islamic reformists have long rejected the traditional dualism between the House of Islam (*dar al-Islam*) and the House of War (*dar al-harb*), stipulating a third abode that is somewhat in between. Al-Qaradawi and others have called it the House of Treaty (*dar al-ahd*), in which the acceptance of secular law is exchanged against security and the guarantee to practice one's belief freely. Another name for it is the House of Proselytizing (*dar ad-da'wa*), which provides a potent Islamic justification for dwelling among non-believers. The problem is that the House of Treaty and the House of Proselytizing entail only a tactical or instrumental relationship to non-Muslims, who figure either not at all or only as objects of conversion.

To chase away the instrumentalism, perhaps even the force, that is often associated with the mandate to convert, Ramadan calls the third abode the House of Testimony (*dar al-shahada*). According to it, Muslims "must remind the people around them of God and Spirituality" (Ramadan 2004: 73), much as the Prophet did in Mecca before the *hijra*. *Shahada* means testimony, and as such it is simply the first of the five pillars of Islam, calling upon every Muslim to pronounce that there is "no God but God and Muhammad is his prophet." The distinction between *da'wa* and *shahada* is cryptic, and Ramadan does not always keep to it strictly – which may not matter because whenever he adopts the notion of *da'wa* he takes it in a non-instrumental way (*"dawa* [is] not a matter of wanting to convert," he says [p. 208]). Ramadan still prefers *shahada* over *da'wa* to rule out an instrumental interpretation of Muslims' relations to their host society. *Shahada* incorporates the Qur'anic notion that there is "No compulsion in matters of religion." If "conversion is something that only God can accomplish" (p. 81), it can never be the result of human action or force. Accordingly, *shahada* accepts non-Muslims as self-authenticating individuals, as subjects and not just objects. However, this does not make the project any less expansive, as from the point of view of giving testimony "the whole world is a mosque" (Ramadan 2002a: 144). It is thus alarmist in tone but logically correct to conclude that Ramadan's project, like that of the traditionalist al-Qaradawi, is the "Islamizing of Europe" (Tibi 2009b: 31) – a ridiculous prospect for a smaller than 5 percent minority in Europe, yet undoubtedly the Islamic elite's intention.

The important difference from al-Qaradawi's minority approach is still Ramadan's repeated insistence that the West "is not in fact a hostile place" (Ramadan 2004: 70), and that Muslims are "at home in Europe" (Ramadan 2002a: 223). One finds in Ramadan an astonishing celebration of the "fundamental rights" that Muslims enjoy in Western societies, especially if one compares their situation with that in Muslim-majority societies. He even avers that "with respect to the parameters of safety and peace...the appellation *dar al-Islam* is applicable to almost all Western nations," while this is not the case "for the great majority of the Islamic countries where the populations are overwhelmingly

Muslim" (Ramadan 2002a: 127). In fact, the problem for Muslims in the West is not at all a problem of deficient "legislation, laws or rules" (p. 138) – these are all fine. Instead, the problem is "how to maintain a spiritual life in a modern...society": "Spirituality is of great significance in Islam and the neutrality of the public space...has often been confused with a total absence of religiosity" (p. 138). This strongly echoes the American Christian Right's lament about the "naked public square" (Neuhaus 1984). But then the problem for Muslims is not one of Western host societies that exclude them, but of Muslims who don't do enough to get their message across. Ramadan concedes this point with admirable frankness: "[R]esponsibility [is thrown] back at the Muslims" (2002a: 138).

Ramadan's advocacy of a citizenship rather than minority stance for Muslims in the West is consistent with, even commanded by, the universalism inherent in the creed. Conversely, it would be self-contradictory to make "universal Islam" only a matter of "eternal foreigners, living in parallel, on the margins or as reclusive minorities" (Ramadan 2004: 54). Thus there seems to be an intrinsically Islamic motivation for a citizenship stance. Ramadan pushes the point even further, claiming that "faith and nationality...are not of the same nature," the first being a question of "being" and the second a question of "geographical attachment" (Ramadan 2002a: 163). Accordingly, an "individual is British, French or Belgian and of Muslim faith, just as others are of Jewish or Christian faith" (p. 163).

However, Ramadan's plea for citizenship is inconsistent with the vision of "coexistence" that had opened up his *To be a European Muslim* (2002a) and that is equally constitutive of his prescriptions. This is a vision of equal but separate, not commensurable with a conception of citizenship that extracts strangers from their primordial groups in order to make them political consociates. There is no question that the allegiance to the *ummah*, as the universal community of believers, takes precedence over allegiance to one's fellow citizens, which is downgraded to a matter of "geography." "A Muslim first belongs to God," says the same author who also claims a separation and incommensurability of spheres and commitments (p. 155). In one of his taped lectures, Ramadan establishes a hierarchy of religious and worldly belongings, arguing that one should not confound "the sea with a swimming pool" – the "sea" being the *ummah* and the "swimming pool" the paltry citizenry (see Fourest 2004: 221–2).

Crucially, the secular law is only accepted to the degree that it is commanded by Islamic law: "Islamic law and jurisprudence *command* Muslim individuals to submit to the body of positive law," so that "to act according to the law is in itself a way of worshipping" (Ramadan

2004: 95–6). This is no invention of Ramadan's, but inherent in the notion of a "contract of security" (*aman*) that is central to Islamic law's conception of Muslims living under non-Muslim rule. Negatively formulated, if a secular norm conflicts with a religious one, there is no question which one is to be followed: "If for being a good Frenchman you have to be a bad Muslim, then I say no" (Ramadan, quoted in Fourest 2004: 224). But then it cannot be that the choice between being "Muslim" or "European" is a "non-issue insofar as faith and nationality...are not of the same nature" (Ramadan 2002a: 163). Islam's original position as holistic creed that rejects distinction-drawing comes back with a vengeance when a choice has to be made: "To be Muslim is a conception of life....My conception of life comes above everything else" (Ramadan, quoted in Fourest 2004: 221). Caroline Fourest is therefore right to conclude that despite all the talk of being "at home in Europe" (Ramadan 2002a: 223), "citizenship" matters to Ramadan only as an instrumental vessel, a "tool of Islamization" (Fourest 2004: 247).

If Europe and the West "is not in fact a hostile place" (Ramadan 2004: 70), "neither monolithic nor demonic" (p. 171), one also wonders why Muslims should be called upon to "resist." This posture, reminiscent of Marxism's *Totalkritik*, confirms that the adoption of a "citizenship" frame is only instrumental: "Everyday life in Europe, with its modes of thinking and consumption, its conduct of work and of leisure, its culture of cinematography and music has almost unconsciously grown into a second nature that appears much like a prison. We have to escape from it" (Ramadan 2002b: 70). This echoes the Frankfurt School's attack on the "culture industry," much as the critique of alienation under capitalism could be drawn from the pages of the young Marx: "At the heart of the new economic order, the human being, once the subject of his or her own history, has the strange feeling of having become an object, a means, a toy in the hands of others" (p. 72). The difference is that this is not an elitist message of despair (as in Horkheimer and Adorno) or of hope in the working class (as in Marx). Instead, for Ramadan, Western Muslims are the new avant-garde, the "conscience of the South" (Ramadan 2004: 171), and the spearhead of "resistance to the neoliberal system" (p. 198). Finally we come face to face with the House of War: a "neoliberal system" and "world order [that] is sanctioning a cynical, silent, global terrorism" (p. 175). If the radical alternative once was Communism, now it is Islam: "When faced with neoliberal economics, the message of Islam offers no way out but resistance" (p. 173). Through the back door of a contemporary critique of capitalist globalization enters a traditionalist Islam as total alternative not *in* but *to* the West. As a "culture of finalities that is absolutely opposed to the culture of means," argues Ramadan (2001: 262), "Muslim culture is fundamentally and essentially opposed to scientist, technical, and economist logics" (p. 261).

Ramadan takes his position to be an integration-minded "middle path between being a Muslim without Islam and a Muslim in Europe out of Europe" (Ramadan 2002a: 196). However, the moderate language of "integration" deflects attention from the fact that only a variant of multiculturalism that asks very little – if anything – of Muslims could suffice for accommodating a purist Islam rebuilt from "the sources" (Ramadan 2004: 26). In a later work, confusingly entitled *Radical Reform* (because it opposes "changing Islam, perverting it to adapt it to current times"; 2009: 11),[11] Ramadan moves on to "postintegration" (p. 268). He describes it as the effort to identify the economic roots of Muslims' malaise in the West, which is commonly and falsely understood in cultural terms. This is a very plausible stance. But why then does all attention go to "recapturing the original essence and 'form' of the message [of the Qur'an]" (p. 13)?

In keeping with the pieties of orthodox multiculturalism, Ramadan asks for "respect" for Muslims rather than mere "toleration": "Muslims should demand more than toleration.... The basic purpose is to achieve respect" (Ramadan 2004: 110). This stance is consistent with the notion that the integration problem for Muslims in the West is not one of flawed institutions but a matter of attitude, that is, the absence of "spirituality" in Western public spheres (p. 70). The attitudinal deficit in the West is portrayed as involving the "[negative] representation of Islam and Muslims," which Ramadan regards as "at the bottom of the difficulties lived by Muslim communities" (p. 71). While it is true that Western publics tend to hold negative views about Muslims,[12] the demand for "respect" is problematic in several ways. If addressed to the state, "respect" is not something that the state as liberal state could express or command, because this state is neutral about religion and ways of life and does not recognize the existence of groups. If addressed to society, how could the latter "respect" a creed that, in a kind of "Occidentalism" (Buruma and Margalit 2004), is opposed to most of it? Thirdly, the call for "respect" is not meant to be returned: how could Muslims "respect" the "impossible universalism of [European] civilization" that they are called upon to "resist" (Ramadan 2002b: 20)?

The Paradox of Liberalism

It is the paradox of liberal institutions that, in being neutral vis-à-vis religion and ways of life, they can still accommodate a creed that is unsympathetic to them and that may even wish to replace them by theocracy. Islam's great opportunity is "political liberalism," which abstains from imposing "comprehensive doctrines" on people, and limits consensus to accepting the procedures of liberal democracy (Rawls 1993). Even a conservative Maliki religious scholar, writing to a traditional Muslim audience in Arabic, can warm to the "great values of secularism and neutrality," because they do not require "submission to a single comprehensive ideological trend which might wish to impose its particular concepts constructed on its own prejudices" (Ibn Bayya, a leading scholar of the European Council for Fatwa and Research, quoted in March 2009b: 2846).[13]

The problem is that, not deriving from a single metaphysical doctrine or religion, the principles of political liberalism are "free-standing" and thus an inherently thin and fragile source of social unity, to which people may be only contingently attached. Rawls (1993) thus adds that a "full justification" of political liberalism can only come from people's "comprehensive doctrines," as grounding an "overlapping consensus" on the principles of political liberalism.

Andrew March claims that a non-instrumentally understood *da'wa* (proselytizing) might provide an Islamic "affirmation of positive relationships to fellow citizens" (March 2009c: 87). But he also concedes that, upon closer examination, "one often finds an express desire to Islamize non-Muslim societies and states and a recognition of non-Muslims only as potential converts" (March 2006: 420). It seems contradictory to argue, on one side, that "the ethics of *da-wa*...incline towards the values of discourse ethics" (March 2009c: 88), being "free from any spirit of aggression or coercion" (p. 83), but to admit, on the other side, that *da'wa* is precisely not "discourse ethics" (à la Habermas) because the result is presumed and no reciprocity is allowed. March thus admits that "[t]he idea cannot be seriously entertained by Muslims that the actual process of debate and dialogue might result in greater ethical knowledge or a change of heart by Muslim 'callers' " (March 2009a: 228). But then the charge by some critics that Muslims display only a "tactical" acceptance of liberal institutions retains its force (see Berman 2003, 2007, 2010).

The most daring (and widely rejected)[14] defense of the secular state from an Islamic perspective is by Abdullahi An-Na'im (2008). He argues that "[i]n order to be a Muslim by conviction and free choice, which is the only way one can be a Muslim, I need a secular state," which is "one that is neutral regarding religious doctrine" (p. 1). Conversely, an Islamic state that enforced Islamic law (sharia) as state law would "in fact promot[e] a European, positivistic view of law and a totalitarian model of the state that seeks to transform society in its image" (p. 20). The very idea of an "Islamic state" is incoherent, argues An-Na'im, because the medium of the state is coercion, whereas the medium of religion is morality (p. 51). As he concludes, "[T]he separation of Islam and the state is necessary for any possibility of belief, as well as for its legitimacy and value over time. By protecting my freedom to disbelieve, a secular state...is necessary for my freedom to believe, which is the only way belief has any meaning and consequences" (p. 279).

An-Na'im (2008) espouses a rather Protestant, Lockean conception of faith as subjective belief and choice that radically diverges from the Islamic dogma of faith as communal submission. However, sharia's requirement of a linkage between religion and politics remains, because only the state but not society needs to be secular. Accordingly, An-Na'im's plea for the secular state still wishes to retain "a public role for religion in influencing public policy and legislation, subject to the requirement of civic reason" (p. 38). "Civic reason" is a demanding proviso, akin to Rawls' condition of "public reason," which requires a non-sectarian language that is "open and accessible to all citizens" (p. 7).[15] And it raises, again, the question of whether Islamic law (sharia), which is to retain a public role, is compatible with the principles of liberal states and societies. An-Na'im's answer is ambivalent: "Shari'a principles are basically consistent with most human rights norms, *with the exception of some very serious aspects of the rights of women and non-Muslims and the freedom of religion and belief*" (p. 111; emphasis added).

The listed three exceptions are "very serious" indeed, affecting the large majority of humankind. We thus must look at them more closely. I will touch on "women" and "non-Muslims" explicitly. What An-Na'im refers to, thirdly, as "freedom of religion," in Jellinek's famous formulation the oldest of all human rights (1904), invites a general reflection on the status of "rights" in the Islamic tradition.

Unresolved Issues: Women, Non-Muslims, Rights

Women

It is no accident that the role of women is the epicenter of the great conflict between Islam and West. Representative here are the notorious headscarf conflicts in several Western European countries (see Joppke 2009a). The conflict over women is fueled on both sides. On the side of Islam, women's separation and seclusion, via concealment of their bodies, "lies at the heart of Islamic Occidentalism" (Buruma and Margalit 2004: 128), shielding the Islamic community from contamination by an infidel and decadent environment. On the side of Western host societies, women's equality, while formally not a reality in many a Western state till well into the 1960s,[16] and substantively a reality not even today in any of them, is nervously held up as sine qua non of Muslim integration. In France, since 2008, veil-wearing Muslim women have even been routinely denied citizenship because the "radical practice" of their religion is deemed "incompatible with the essential values of the French community, especially the principle of the equality between the sexes."[17]

The Organization of the Islamic Conference's Cairo Declaration on Human Rights in Islam (1990) stipulates that "Woman is equal to man in human dignity, and has rights to enjoy as well as duties to perform" (Article 6a). More interesting than what is said is what is omitted: the "rights" that women enjoy are not said to be "equal rights." Certainly, as a universalistic creed, Islam does not allow any status differences between believers – before God, women are equal to men. But this does not imply their equality on the social plane. In his treatise on *The Status of Women in Islam* (1998), Yusuf al-Qaradawi concedes that women enjoy "a share in humanity equal to that of the man." But then he finds "different tasks" to be assigned to both "by virtue of their natural disposition" (section on "refuted misconceptions," p. 1).[18] He lists some major formal-legal inequalities between men and women stated in the Qur'an, and grounds them in what women (and men) are by nature. For instance, if the Qur'an makes the testimony of one man equal to that of two women, or if women are not allowed to testify in major crime cases, this is because of women's "characteristic inattention" to matters outside "motherhood or the household," and their "run[ning] away in panic from a scene of bloodshed" (p. 2). To deny women legal equality in this respect is only to "protect...and distance them from sites of crime and aggressions against souls, honour and property" (p. 2). If, according to the Qur'an, men are the "guardians" of women, this is because of their "greater strength" (p. 6). The ineligibility of women to hold judicial or political office is due to the "natural disposition of the woman as mother" (p. 7). Why does only the husband have the right to initiate a divorce? This is because "[a] man may be less hasty as he is less affected by emotions" (section on "divorce," p. 5). Polygamy is grounded in the fact that "[s]ome men are more sexual and lusty" and that the first wife may "not satisfy the desire of his instinct nor fill his lustful eyes that seek other women," and having several wives is "to protect him from illicit relationships" (section on "polygamy," p. 6). Overall, "Islam considers the home as the great kingdom of the woman," "her supreme function" being the "vocation of motherhood" (section on "women as members of society," p. 3).With an eye on the corrupting West, al-Qaradawi warns: "Every method or system that attempts to remove the woman from her kingdom, take her from her husband, or displace her from her children in the names of freedom, work, art, etc., is in fact the woman's foe" (p. 3).

Tariq Ramadan, a defender of "Islamic feminism" (Ramadan 2009: 229), holds the same patriarchal views. Yes, women enjoy an "absolute equality before God" (Ramadan 2001: 52). But then women's position is one of "social complementarity...within familial priority" (p. 54), which is a euphemism for assigning to them the family roles of " 'daughters,' 'sisters,' 'wives,' or 'mothers' " (Ramadan 2009: 211). "Equality...in complementarity" means "not [to] confuse [women's] equality with resemblance. A man is [not equal to] a woman, just as fundamentally, profoundly and intimately a father is not a mother" (Ramadan 2001: 254). One finds in Ramadan, exactly as in al-Qaradawi, a naturalistic conception of women's role in society, including a cult of motherhood, an aversion to mixing of the sexes, and a defense of veiling in the name of modesty, even an odd celebration of Islamic Iran as model for the "promotion of women" (Ramadan, quoted in Fourest 2004: 198). As Ramadan arrives at his views on women through a "return to the sources" (2009: ch. 13), one must conclude that the "sources" are more liability than asset for Muslim women.

It should be stressed, however, that among American Evangelicals one finds similarly conservative views on women. Christian Smith summarized them in the notion of "male headship," which has Pauline New Testament sources: "Wives, submit to your husbands as to the Lord. For the husband is the head of the wife as Christ is the head of the church" (quoted in Smith 2002: 170). And, just like Ramadan or al-Qaradawi, American Evangelicals find that "headship and equality are entirely compatible" (p. 172), to the degree that "equality" does not mean "sameness" but recognition of natural "difference" (p. 173). (See also the unique comparison of "veiled submission" by Evangelical and Muslim women in the United States, Bartkowski and Read 2003.) As I shall suggest below, the difference is that "Evangelicals" are a radical fringe within Christianity, even in the United States, while conservative Muslim views on women are the mainstream in Islam.

Non-Muslims

The relationship with non-believers is a prickly issue in all monotheisms, where the unicity of God and His ethical demands requires sharp boundaries between believers and non-believers. In the Christian tradition, the Apostle Paul famously warned the Corinthians not to be "unequally yoked" with non-believers (though on other occasions he recommended mixing with the latter). However, only the Islamic tradition developed a systematic code of relating to non-believers, essentially of fighting and subjugating them. As in the Islamic tradition the only access to God is through revelation, the "infidels," who did not live by God's laws, literally had no morality. They could be "freely killed" or enslaved (Crone 2004: 359). Within the category of infidels, however, a distinction was made between "pagans" or polytheists and "People of the Book," the latter bestowed with the relatively privileged if still inferior *dhimma* status. *Dhimmis* were allowed to practice their religion privately, but they were required to pay a poll tax (*jizya*) that was meant to be stigmatizing and humiliating, and they were relegated to second-class status in a Muslim polity.

The premise of this way of relating to non-believers is the mandate of jihad (Holy War), to bring the entire world under Islamic rule so that religious and political boundaries become identical. Jihad means "striving" in the path of God, and apparently can take on a spiritual meaning. However, originally it meant to fight unbelievers quite literally, by use of violence, on the assumption that no real peace with the Abode of War was possible. Jihad was an "obligation comparable to prayer" (Crone 2004: 363), though also a "communal obligation" that could be fulfilled by some "on behalf of all" (p. 364). Jihad, indeed, is a "very tribal notion," reminiscent of the Old Testament, and medieval Christians found it "deeply offensive, both in its postulate of a blatantly partial God and in its unthinking endorsement of violence" (p. 368).

If Bernard Lewis claims that "Islam must dominate" (1993: 52), this cannot be dismissed as just Orientalist demonology. For An-Na'im (2008: 39), the "sovereignty of Muslims over non-Muslims" and "violently aggressive jihad" are two facets of traditional sharia incompatible with human rights law and in need of being rectified. Both stances are a confluence of creed and political history. On the creedal side, Islam is the "last revelation," which "corrects and rectifies the errors and alterations which...had been introduced within earlier Messages" (Ramadan 2002a: 58). This makes the coexistence with other faiths, or what in Europe is referred to as "interreligious dialogue" (see Silvestri 2009),[19] a difficult enterprise. An Egyptian Muslim scholar ridicules the idea: "Could there ever be in reality a dialogue between Islam and Christianity?...In fact, Islam is revealed by Allah as the final revelation and therefore is not simply just a religion among others.... The point is that the politics of religious rapprochement is guided by one intention: To 'destroy Islam'/*tahtim al Islam*" (Anwar al-Jundi, quoted in Tibi 2009a: 211–12).

On the side of political history, Efraim Karsh (2007) argues that Christian universalism, owing to its early political impotence, was immediately channeled into the realm of spirituality. The making of Islam, by contrast, "was inextricably linked with the creation of a world empire and its universalism was inherently imperialist" (p. 6). There is thus an intricate amalgam between Islam's contingent political history and the content of the creed, which Karsh formulates thus: "As a universal religion, Islam envisages a global political order in which all humankind will live under Muslim rule as either believers or subject communities" (p. 66). If the creed requires every Muslim to "command good and forbid evil," the larger political project always lurks in the background.

Another way of putting the matter is that Islam is intrinsically geared to be a majority religion, and it faces persistent difficulties in refashioning itself as one in a minority position. Al-Alwani, the American Muslim leader and champion of "minority *fiqh*," calls the Muslim community a "raised nation": "It is a nation that has been raised in order to lead others" (2003: 27). Even if the martial language of House of War, jihad, and so on, has been largely dropped, the persistent theme of superior peoplehood is still there.

Rights

If non-Muslims suffer disabilities under Islamic law, apostates fare even worse – according to classic sharia, apostasy is punishable by death, even today. For most Islamic jurists, *ridda* (apostasy) has the quasi-constitutional status of a *hudud* offense, for which the script prescribes a specific punishment, as an unalterable "claim of God." Because in the Christian tradition the freedom of religion had a pioneering role for the idea of human rights, it is apposite in this context to address the problem of "rights" in the Islamic tradition.

The Islamic world's central human rights document, the 1990 Cairo Declaration on Human Rights in Islam, opens with the declaration that "[all] human beings form one family whose members are united by submission to God and descent from Adam" (Article 1a). Before the word "right" is even mentioned, the notion of "submission to God" occupies center-stage. In fact, nowhere in the first article of this "rights" declaration does the word "right" appear at all. Instead, there are references to "basic obligations and responsibilities," "true faith," "human perfection," and human beings as "God's subjects" (Article 1a). Earlier in the same document, the preamble's first reference is not to individuals but to the "Islamic Ummah," which is presented as a "well-balanced" and "harmon[ious]" alternative to "this materialistic civilization." One cannot disagree with Ali Allawi (2009: 193) that the "spirit" of the Cairo Human Rights Declaration is "fundamentally different" from that of the 1948 UN Declaration of Universal Human

Rights (which all Islamic states, like the Soviet-controlled states at the time, promptly refused to sign). For Allawi, the Cairo Declaration reflects the Islamic conception of the human being as "fulfilling duties and obligations," which is "deeply antithetical to the modern individualist sensibility" (p. 194).

Tariq Ramadan argues similarly that "balance" not "liberation," and in consequence "justice" not "rights," are the nucleus of Islamic morality: "It [the Islamic concept of human rights] does not formulate rights in function of [sic] a threat of oppression, but rather with the idea that man is from the outset a responsible being who must be accountable for his choices. Human rights exist in Islam, but they are, nevertheless, part of a holistic vision which orientates their scope" (Ramadan 2001: 101). A more direct way of saying this is: "God, the Proprietor, has rights over both the universe and man, who is the gerent [sic]" (p. 88).[20] If "God...has rights," whatever this means, humans cannot have them too, as this would "result in dismantling the sovereignty of Allah" (Tibi 2009a: 134). Tibi explicates the essence of the matter: "In Islam, Muslims...have duties vis-à-vis the collectivity...but no individual rights in the sense of entitlements" (p. 140).

This position has troubling consequences, not the least of which seems to be the poor human rights record in the Islamic world. The 2002 Arab Human Development Report highlighted the "freedom deficit" above all other problems plaguing Islam's historical heartland, the Arab countries having the lowest freedom score of all seven world regions compared in this respect. The human rights scholar Jack Donnelly notes that in an Islamic perspective, individual rights are not "obligation[s] of others" but obligations "of the alleged rights holder[s]" themselves (1982: 306). This view is confirmed by Ali Allawi, who argues that "most rights [recognized as such in the Qur'an] are in the nature of obligations" (2009: 194). From the point of view of Wesley Newcomb Hohfeld's (1919) classic formal analysis of what is a "right," this statement could only be meaningful if the respective right or obligation is held by a different person. Locating both in one person seems to misconstrue what a right is. If a right is attributed to the same individual as obligation at the same time and in the same respect, a choice has to be made: an individual can either be entitled or obliged, but not both at the same time. A right is a legal entitlement of the individual against other individuals or against society and state, and it is nullified if couched as an obligation. According to Allawi, "[T]he right to free expression exists because man has a duty to seek the truth and its fulfillment" (2009: 194). But who determines what "truth" is and what "fulfillment" is? Thus qualified, there no longer is a right to free expression. One must conclude that in Islamic human rights discourse "Islam is not conceived of as offering the basis for protecting rights but solely as the basis for limiting…rights" (Mayer 1999: 71).

Ordinary Muslim Views: "Demos" versus "Eros"[21]

While there seems to be a good deal of "adversarial" elite reasoning, past and present, the question is how much traction it has on the ground. The first thing to mention here is that the "Muslim" label placed on Europe's nearly 20 million immigrant Muslims is deeply problematic, or rather strongly exaggerated to the degree that it identifies people by their religion. This is because only one-third of European Muslims are estimated to practice their religion strictly and thus to be "Muslim" in an Islamic (and not only ethnic) way. The other two-thirds of European Muslims are considered to be either "non-practicing" or "agnostic" (Dassetto et al. 2007: 8).

The available polls to measure the opinions and degree of attitudinal adjustment to and identification with liberal host societies show two things very clearly. First, there is significant variation across European states, reflecting both indigenous features of North African, Turkish, or South Asian Muslims and differential host-society structures. Secondly, and most importantly, the real integration deficit seems to be with respect not to political but to moral-ethical values, especially those related to sex and gender.

To begin with, the widely noted 2006 Pew survey *The Great Divide: How Westerners and Muslims View Each Other* (Pew Research Center 2006) curiously found that the general public was more skeptical than Muslims themselves about the possibility of "being a devout Muslim and living in a modern society." The majority of Germans (70 percent), Spaniards (58 percent), and British (54 percent) said there was "conflict" (with the interesting exception of the French, only 26 percent of whom thought this way), while the majority of German Muslims (57 percent) and French Muslims (72 percent) and nearly half of British Muslims (49 percent)[22] held that there was "no conflict" (p. 3). Host-society publics are hostile, while most Muslims are modern, one could conclude. Moreover, by "lopsided margins," Western European Muslims expressed "favorable opinions" of Christians (91 percent in France, 82 percent in Spain, 71 percent in Britain, and 69 percent in Germany) (p. 11). The only exception to this positive picture were British Muslims, who, when probed specifically about certain character traits of Westerners ("respectful of women," "generous," "tolerant," "honest," "devout"), expressed "much more negative views of Westerners than do the Muslim minorities of Germany, France, and Spain" (p. 15).

Inquiring into European Muslims' identifications with host countries and their trust in democratic institutions, a 2009 Gallup survey came to similarly upbeat conclusions. German and British Muslims were found to identify "very" or "extremely strongly" with their host country in larger numbers (40 percent of German Muslims and a whopping 77 percent of British Muslims) compared to the general public (where only 32 percent of the German and 50 percent of the British public answered this way); only in the case of France was Muslims' identification with the country a bit smaller than that of the public in general (52 as against 55 percent). Religious identifications were slightly higher than host-society identifications in France (58 against 52 percent) but significantly higher in Germany (59 against 40 percent). (All non-Muslim publics unsurprisingly showed strongly inverse attitudes in this respect, being high on national and low on religious identifications.) British Muslims, meanwhile, surprisingly identified more strongly with their country than with their religion (77 against 75 percent) (Gallup 2009: 19). With respect to "confidence" in public institutions, German and British Muslims were found to have more confidence than ordinary Germans or British in the "judicial system and courts," "financial institutions," and the "honesty of elections." When asked whether they had confidence in the "national government," many more German Muslims than ordinary Germans answered with "yes" (61 versus 36 percent), while by a smaller margin more British Muslims than ordinary British answered this way (40 versus 32 percent). On all of these items French Muslims were interestingly more skeptical than the French public, but not by huge margins (p. 23).

These findings resonate with Rahsaan Maxwell's (2010) study of "trust in government" among British Muslims. It found that Muslims were "more likely than Christians" to display such trust (p. 90), while also showing "relatively high levels of positive British identification" (p. 105). Importantly, this pattern was stable before *and* after the Islamist bombing of the London Underground in July 2005, in response to which one might have expected attitudes to darken. Maxwell attributes this sustained optimism to Muslims' greater likelihood of being immigrants (the assumption being that immigrants are naturally more optimistic than settled folk). This might well explain the similar findings in other European countries, cited above. Trying to square these results with the Pew Research Center (2006) survey, which had found British Muslims more likely than their peers in other European countries to express negative views about non-Muslims and to endorse fundamentalist tenets, Maxwell plausibly argues that "it is possible for Muslims (just like any other group) to be critical of British society while accepting its basic political institutions" (2010: 105).

However, the picture is less bright when considering Muslims' attitudes to moral and sexual issues. The 2009 Gallup survey found that especially British Muslims stood out in their moral conservatism, zero percent of whom found homosexual acts "morally acceptable," while at least 19 percent of German Muslims and even 34 percent of French Muslims held that view (Gallup 2009: 31). In this survey, French, German, and British Muslims *all* held significantly more conservative attitudes than non-Muslims toward abortion, pornography, premarital sex, extramarital affairs, and suicide – on each item the British Muslims turning out as the most conservative of all (pp. 31–3). In line with these trends is the finding that 63 percent of British Muslims found the death penalty "morally acceptable," while only 24 percent of French and 27 percent of German Muslims held that view (p. 33). Of course, one must concede that Muslim and non-Muslim views on the death penalty are not far apart from one another in each of these countries (50 percent of the British support it, while much smaller proportions of the French and German publics are in favor).

The importance of "eros" as against "demos" as the real rift separating Muslims from the West is the key finding of Pippa Norris and Ronald Inglehart's analysis of 1995–2001 World Values Study data (2002). Their impressive study of 70 countries on six continents finds a "persistent gap in support for gender equality and sexual liberalization between the West (which proves most liberal), Islamic societies (which prove most traditional), and all other societies (which are in the middle)" (p. 14). Moreover, their analysis of cohort data reveals that the "erotic" gap between Islam and the West is unexpectedly narrowest among the oldest generations, while it "steadily widen[s]" in the younger generations, where Western youngsters grow even more sexually liberal while their peers in Islamic societies "remain as traditional as their parents and grandparents" (p. 14). This suggests more trouble in the future. At the same time, Norris and Inglehart's survey data show that "[s]upport for democracy is surprisingly widespread among Islamic publics, even among those who live in authoritarian societies." Accordingly, the authors conclude, "[t]he most basic cultural fault line between the West and Islam does not concern democracy – it involves issues of gender equality and sexual liberalization" (p. 16).

These findings throw an important light on Europe's protracted and apparently irresolvable struggles over and with Islam, which are particularly intense surrounding the role of women and control over the woman's body, from foulard and burka to honor killings and genital mutilation Christopher Caldwell argues that "[a]dapting to European styles of sexuality and gender relations is the only non-negotiable demand that Europe makes of its immigrants" (2009: 173). Evidently, European Muslims do show considerable reticence in complying. The schism is constantly sustained by not just endogenous but also home-country-oriented marriage patterns. German Interior Ministry data suggest that half of ethnically Turkish German citizens seek spouses in Turkey, and the number of imported spouses since the mid-1980s is estimated at 500,000 (p. 184). In France, the number of foreign spouses has increased from 23,000 in 1990 to 60,000 in 2004, with family migration now constituting about 78 percent of legal immigration (p. 184). In the United Kingdom, 60 percent of Pakistani and Bangladeshi marriages are to a spouse abroad (p. 184). The same pattern is identifiable among the Turkish and Moroccan communities in the Netherlands. The current pan-European movement to restrict family migration or, to the degree that it cannot be prevented, to require "integration from abroad" cannot be decoupled from this "erotic" reality, which is perhaps the central stake in Europe's Islam struggles.

However, when calibrating the "erotic" gap between European Muslims and their host societies, it needs to be reiterated that similar views exist in other religions too. Poll data from the United States, for instance, show that Evangelicals and some Christian sects reject homosexuality by even higher margins than Muslims. When asked whether "homosexuality is a way of life that should be discouraged by society," 61 percent of Muslims agreed, but 64 percent of Evangelicals, 68 percent of Mormons, and 76 percent of Jehovah's Witnesses rejected homosexuality in these terms (Pew Research Center 2008: 128). The conservatism of these Christian groups if compared with Muslims is higher still with respect to abortion: whereas "only" 48 percent of Muslims opined that abortion should be illegal in "most" or "all" cases, 61 percent of Evangelicals, 70 percent of Mormons, and 77 percent of Jehovah's Witnesses rejected abortion in these strong terms (p. 135). While Muslims' views appear not much different from the views of Christians on these matters, there is still one important difference. In the cited poll, "Muslims" comprise the totality of believers in the Islamic faith in America, while "Evangelicals," "Mormons," and "Jehovah's Witnesses," of course, represent only the conservative end of the Christian spectrum. By contrast, clear majorities of "mainline churches," and even larger majorities of American Jews, "accept" homosexuality as a "way of life" (56 and 79 percent, respectively) (p. 128). The same pattern applies to abortion, which should be legal in "most" or "all" cases for 62 percent of mainline church members, and even for 88 percent of Jews (p. 135). In sum, the majority of Muslims in America hold morally conservative views, which cannot be said about the members of the other two monotheisms. Considering the higher level of religiosity and of religious conservatism in the United States, which reduces the "cultural gap" between Muslims and the majority population (see Orgad, forthcoming: ch. 1), the same pattern a fortiori applies to Europe too.

Not quite covered by the demos versus eros distinction are views about the role of religion in public life and possible conflicts with liberal-secular principles. Also here, as with respect to eros, the picture is not so comforting. A poll in April 2006 of Muslims in the United Kingdom, who are predominantly South Asian and known to be more religiously conservative than Muslims in other European countries (see Joppke 2009b), found that 70 percent thought that "people who insult Islam should be arrested and prosecuted," which brings them into direct conflict with free speech laws (Orgad, forthcoming: ch. 1). In Germany, the great majority of whose Muslims are from laicist Turkey, still nearly half of Muslims polled in 2005 ranked obedience to Qur'anic commandments as "more important" than following secular laws, and over 65 percent advocated censorship of newspapers and television to "protect morality and order" (Brettfeld and Wetzels 2007: 141). In the United Kingdom again, about one-third (32 percent) of Muslim students in a 2008 survey believed that killing for the sake of religion is justified; this is a large number, even for impatient youth, considering that only 2 percent of non-Muslim students justified religious killing (Thorne and Stuart 2008: 43).

Why "Eurabia" Will Not Be

If there are illiberal minorities in the liberal state, as a portion of European Muslims apparently are, the decisive question is whether there are enough of them to threaten the viability of liberal institutions. Particularly alarmist is Bernard Lewis's vision of "Eurabia," according to which late twenty-first century Europe "will be part of the Arabic west, of the Maghreb" (quoted in Caldwell 2009: 12). The British celebrity historian Niall Ferguson sings from the same hymn sheet, fathoming that "[a] youthful Muslim society to the south and east of the Mediterranean is poised to colonize – the term is not too strong – a senescent Europe."[23]

A recent study by the Pew Research Center (2011) does not confirm this demographic alarmism. It concludes that "Muslims will remain relatively small minorities in Europe and the Americas" (p. 14). By 2030, the Muslim population in Europe is expected to grow by just 2 percent, from 6 percent in 2010 to 8 percent (while in the United States the Muslim share will increase from 0.8 percent to 1.7 percent). In absolute numbers, there will be ca. 58 million European Muslims by 2030 (including the "national" Muslims in the Balkans), which is a one-third increase from 2010 (44 million) (p. 15). Certainly, in some European countries the Muslim share will touch or surpass the 10 percent mark in 2030, including Britain (8.2 percent), Austria (9.3 percent), Sweden (9.9 percent), Belgium (10.2 percent), and France (10.3 percent). While this is not nothing it is hardly "Eurabia." The alarmists overlook that immigrants (Muslim or not) always and everywhere adjust their fertility to that of their host societies, which in Europe has been dangerously low for many decades. But even Muslim-majority societies, as a result of modernization and women's entry into the labor market, show declining fertility rates (p. 16), which partially disconfirms the alarmist diagnosis of massive Southern population pressures (at least for north of the Sahara). Overall, "Europe's Muslim population is projected to grow at a declining rate, in part because of falling fertility rates and in part because Muslim immigration to Europe is leveling off" (p. 123).

The 2011 Pew Research Center report also shows that in all but one European country (France), Muslim immigrants do not (or no longer) constitute the majority of new immigrants: only 14.7 percent of new immigrants to Germany in 2010 were Muslim; in Denmark, site of the so-called "Cartoon Crisis" and of some of the most virulent populist opposition to Islam and Muslims, the Muslim share among new entrants was a paltry 8 percent in 2010, which suggests the effectiveness of Denmark's uniquely harsh family reunification rules implemented over the past few years. If the trend toward diminishing Muslim migration persists, there may be a simple demographic deflation of the entire "Islam in Europe" *problématique*. Note, however, that the country with by far the highest Muslim share among new immigrants today is France, with 68.5 percent in 2010 (p. 134). This suggests no lessening of the uniquely heated Islam struggles in that country.

Sharia in the West?

As I demonstrated elsewhere, liberal law, constitutional law in particular, has been a major source of integrating Islam into European societies – Islamic integration has to a significant degree been "legal integration" (Joppke and Torpey 2013). The basis has been religious liberty clauses in European state constitutions and international conventions that protect all religious believers equally, be they majority or minority. Wherever the Muslim demand is to be treated equally under the law, there is simply no way to reject this demand in a liberal society. Reviewing some typical, often delicate, issues, such as amended blasphemy laws, the corporate recognition of Islam, religious symbols in state institutions, Islamic instruction in public schools, mosque building, and ritual slaughter, Kay Hafez concludes that "the adaptation of legal systems is well underway," even though this may be "at painfully slow pace and beset by contradictions" (2013: 52).

The situation is more complicated with respect to Muslim demands not for equal but for special rights; *in extremis* to have Islamic law step in for secular law in some critical domains, especially family law. This is surely Islam's major challenge to the secular state in Europe. It brings into the open some of the compatibility issues between Islamic and liberal precepts that we discussed earlier, in particular with respect to the equality of the sexes. In her classic indictment of "multiculturalism" as "bad for women," Susan Moller Okin argued that "most cultures have as one of their principal aims the control of women by men" (1998: 667) – a fact she interestingly refers to the uncertainty of paternity and to the importance of female primary parenting for cultural reproduction. To recognize these cultures under the cloak of multiculturalism raises the thorny issue of "minorities within minorities," especially women, who must bear the brunt of minority recognition. In their quest for legal pluralism, the focus of religious minorities, particularly Orthodox Jews and Muslims, has unfailingly been on family law. This is "precisely because these norms control women and enable the preservation of group-identity through child-rearing" (Malik 2012: 6). Western family laws are not free of such elements,[24] but they could gradually rid themselves of most of them. By contrast, traditional Islamic sharia rules on marriage and the family, which may have been progressive when they were first introduced in tribal societies, contain gross inequities for women with respect to divorce, child custody, and inheritance.[25]

This is why the claim to have sharia law recognized in Western legal systems is controversial. The debate reached fever pitch when the Anglican Archbishop Rowan Williams, in a rather measured and academic speech at the Royal Courts of Justice in London, called for a "just and constructive relationship between Islamic law and the statutory law of the United Kingdom" (2010: 294).[26] The speech is remarkable for including a religious defense of liberal multiculturalism. It was notably *not* a justification for setting up a "parallel legal system," which one could call, with Anthony Appiah, "millet multiculturalism" (see Cumper 2014: 45). The Archbishop did not discard "legal universalism." Instead, he took it to be merely a "negative" protection, a "commitment to human dignity as such," which he incidentally finds "historically rooted in Christian theology." Conversely, "the important springs of moral vision in a society will be in those areas which a systematic abstract universalism regards as 'private' – in religion above all, but also in custom and habit" (Rowan Williams 2010: 300). Apart from this learned argument, the main body of the Archbishop's defense of sharia law was devoted to countering the risk of upgraded "communal identity," which is internal oppression. He did so above all by embracing Canadian jurist Ayelet Shachar's notion of "transformative accommodation" (2001), which seeks to mend the illiberal edges of a merely "supplementary" religious law by including a "market element" and allowing people to choose their jurisdiction, either religious or secular.

The one uncompromising statement that one finds in the Anglican Archbishop's rather qualified defense of sharia law is not normative but factual: he points to the "existence" of "communities which...relate to something other than the British legal system alone" (Rowan Williams 2010: 293). Indeed, privately operated sharia councils, dealing with family affairs, have been in existence in Britain for several decades. Since 2007 there has even been a Muslim Arbitration Council (MAT), which claims to operate under the 1996 Arbitration Act (but still has no power of legally enforcing its decisions)[27] (see Bono 2012: ch. 8).[28] In one of the earliest analyses of this phenomenon, Werner Menski spoke of *angrezi shariat*, "a new hybrid form of shari'a" in England (2001: 140). It is practiced in the shadow of an English law that takes a "polite distance" (p. 158), and it reflects that Muslims "still put God's law above the State law in the first place" (p. 137). Accordingly, British Muslims tend to live double lives to satisfy the demands of two legal systems, the secular English and the Islamic: "[V]irtually all ethnic minorities in Britain marry twice, divorce twice, and do many other things several times in order to satisfy the demands of concurrent legal systems" (p. 152). Menski leaves no doubt that the informal sharia councils, which for the most part handle religious divorce requests, are tilted against Muslim women: they are "patriarchal in nature and tend to put undue pressure on women, either to pay for their freedom or to go back to their husbands, so as to avoid dishonor through the violation of *izzat* [family honor]" (p. 157).

But the fact is that the ca. 30 private sharia councils and seven MATs operating in Britain today (Bono 2012: 85) are mostly approached by women, who seek a religious divorce from abusive husbands. The beast to beat is co-called "limping marriages." These are marriages for which a civil divorce certificate has been obtained, but where husbands refuse the unilateral *talaq* divorce. This makes the still religiously married Muslim woman ineligible for re-marrying religiously in the eyes of her community, while her civilly divorced husband is free to acquire an additional wife in full legality under English law – not an outlandish scenario as under Islamic law men can marry up to four women, and considering the traditionalist inflection of predominantly Pakistani and Bangladeshi Muslims in Britain. If men refuse the *talaq* divorce, women may still seek a *khul* divorce. But, in contrast to the *talaq*, which only requires the husband's say-so, the *khul* has to be issued by an imam, ideally (though most often not) with the husband's agreement. A further drawback of a *khul* divorce is that the wife has to give up the right to her dowry (*mahr*) and to any future financial support by her divorced husband.

For calibrating Muslim women's "choice," one needs to know that almost 60 percent of British South Asian women (between 19 and 50 years) are married to a spouse who migrated to Britain to marry, typically from Pakistan (Bono 2012: 48). The sharia council members interviewed by Samia Bono cite the "rise of forced marriages" as "one of the primary reasons for women seeking a divorce" (p. 117). This increase strangely coincides with the abolition, in 1997, of the much-criticized "primary purpose" rule in British immigration law (which had invalidated marriages contracted for immigration purposes). The five dominant reasons given by women for requesting a religious divorce from sharia councils are "bigamy, domestic violence, adultery, forced marriage and wider familial conflict" (p. 114). Not all is well with Muslim family life in Britain.

The question is how the British state should react to it. For Prime Minister David Cameron it is clear that sharia law for Muslims is the "logical endpoint of the now discredited doctrine of state multiculturalism" and thus to be condemned with the latter (quoted in Cumper 2014: 35). He can draw ammunition for his view from the European Court of Human Rights' wholesale condemnation of sharia law as "stable and invariable," and as incompatible with "pluralism in the political sphere" and "public freedoms."[29] But, as Maleiha Malik points out, a total prohibition of sharia in the West "will not only alienate minorities, it will also undermine the state's claim to possess sovereign power to control its citizens" (2012: 34). This is because an informally practiced sharia law is an obstinate reality that reflects that "Muslim law is still superior and dominant over English law in the Muslim mind" (Yilmaz 2002: 343).

As Malik further observes, the "minority legal orders" that are "already operating" in Britain "mainly accept the supremacy of the state system" (2012: 8, 6). This is borne out by the operation of the sharia councils. First, they explicitly require a prior civil divorce certificate before agreeing to handle a religious divorce request (Bono 2012: 108). Thus the superiority of the secular law is recognized. Secondly, the councils tend to require a spousal separation for one year, which follows the "same logic as the English legal rule" (Bowen 2010b: 420). Thirdly, sharia councils generally do not rule on child residence or the division of assets, "knowing full well that only courts can issue enforceable orders."[30] As Bono concludes her detailed case study of four English sharia councils, "[T]he councils actively sought to avoid any conflict with civil law or procedure in matters of civil law....[Divorce] certificates were issued for the personal use of applicants and not viewed as legal documents" (2012: 141). Moreover, "no community mechanisms or sanctions [are] in place to enforce the terms of the divorce....[That is] left to the good will of the parties concerned" (p. 141).

Instead of being "parallel systems," civil and religious laws seem to operate in a complementary fashion. As Ihsan Yilmaz observed, the fact that nearly all marriages under English divorce law are pronounced decree nisi, that is, by administrative procedure without a hearing, "has allowed Muslims in Britain to maintain their customary procedures of divorce almost unmodified" (2002: 350).

The sharia councils, in "almost always" being addressed by aggrieved wives (Douglas et al. 2011: 39) and in "most likely" complying with a divorce request (Bono 2012: 126), seem to fulfill a vital function for British Muslim women. As there is no official hierarchy in Islam, women may even "forum shop" at various councils until they obtain the desired decision (p. 207). Women also seem to approach the councils with a sense that Islam is "empowering" them (p. 156).

However, there is no doubt that the sharia councils are conservative and male-dominated. In the typical case of a divorce request, the primary attempt of council imams is at reconciliation, because "[i]n Islam women must obey their husbands" (an imam quoted in Bono 2012: 210). Bono thus describes the reconciliation phase as "male dominated with the presence of male family members, male witnesses and the male 'judge'" (p. 140), and a failure to reconcile on the part of reluctant women is "equated with female disobedience" (p. 141). Drawing on his own extensive fieldwork on English sharia councils, Bowen similarly observes that "some councils seem out of touch with gender roles in the UK."[31]

Considering the conflicting realities of conservative sharia councils approached mainly by Muslim women to escape even more distressing family situations, and most often successfully, Malik reasonably concludes that the proper state response should be to make the councils "more 'women friendly' rather than prohibiting them," in an approach she dubs "progressive multiculturalism" (2012: 29). English civil courts are actually moving in this direction, flexibly accepting sharia-based rules that happen to be conformant with English law[32] while rejecting others that are not.[33] This "pick and choose" approach (see p. 7) is certainly short of a formal recognition of sharia law, which would open up complicated issues of demarcating jurisdictions and formalizing and thus freezing group membership (issues that plague Shachar's otherwise cogent proposal of multicultural jurisdictions [2001]). But it is also remarkable that an Equality Bill, proposed by Baroness Cox in the House of Lords, has been lingering for several years without making any headway. It would go in the opposite direction of amending the Arbitration Act to formally prohibit discriminatory aspects of sharia law and force Muslim Arbitration Tribunals to explicitly "acknowledge the primacy of English law." This private member's bill, unsupported by any party, is widely criticized for its "failure to appreciate cultural sensitivities," not to mention that it would duplicate certain prohibitions and protections that already exist (Maret 2013: 276). According to an angry sharia council member, "[I]t [was] morally wrong to comment on [the issue of the testimony of a woman being half of that of a man] without any knowledge of [it]," and the bill was chided as "an effort to undermine the work of the shariah councils.... [S]he [Baroness Cox] deserves little praise" (p. 276). In sum, the English state wishes neither to formalize its de facto acceptance of parts of sharia, nor to unnecessarily antagonize its Muslim population by putting undue constraints on the sharia councils. The approach taken is a very English one of pragmatism and muddling through.

The sharia councils are a "singular British development" for which there is no direct parallel on the European continent (German jurist Mathias Rohe, quoted in Glazer 2012: 10). But there exist close equivalents in continental civil law systems, in terms either of private international law or of "optional" civil law (Rohe 2003). Let me comment on each in turn.

With respect to private international law, in Anglo-Saxon countries "domicile" constitutes the "connecting factor" for adjudicating civil law disputes between immigrants who are foreign nationals – also therefore the need for something like the sharia councils, because otherwise English law would immediately apply. By contrast, in continental Europe the parties' "nationality," and thus the law of their countries of origin, typically controls family law disputes (see Foblets 2000). This way, without ever subscribing to a multicultural ideology, continental European courts "have traditionally favoured preservation of the cultural distinctiveness of foreigners and newcomers" (p. 17). Rohe even argues, for the case of Germany, that with the help of a nationality-based private international law, "Islamic law...has largely preserved its dominant position especially within the area of personal status (marital and family law)" (2003: 48).

In continental Europe, this makes for an extreme de facto multiculturalism that often is "disadvantageous to Muslim women" (Büchler 2012). In a case study of Moroccan women in Belgium, Marie-Claire Foblets (2000) observes the dismal workings of an unwittingly multicultural Belgian family law: with elderly first-generation wives struggling with husbands who took other wives in their origin countries; second-generation women forced into arranged marriages with men from their origin country; and an "intermediate generation" of women entering through family unification, who have "high expectations" of being protected under Belgian law but are left empty-handed. However, in response to these problems, continental European courts are gradually shifting to more protective "domicile"-based, "better law," or "autonomy"-based "conflict of law" approaches in family law that are more attuned to a situation where "guestworkers" have permanently settled in Europe (pp. 22–5).

Next to private international law, a second way in which sharia law has been de facto acknowledged in continental Europe is through "optional" civil law, which is the direct equivalent of *angrezi shariat* in England (Rohe 2003). The Islamic dowry (*mahr*), for instance, is "accepted in general" by German courts. Even the *talaq* divorce is accepted, if "the prerequisites for a judicial divorce according to German family law [are] equally fulfilled," such as separation of the spouses for more than a year or the wife having been adequately informed about the *talaq* (p. 8). Rohe thus concludes that the "application of Islamic family law – within the limits of public order – has become everyday business in German courts" (pp. 4–5). However, the public order proviso indicates that this is no unconditional acceptance, but that a "balancing" has to be performed between fulfilling the requirements of German law and "fulfilling individual needs for legal 'difference'" (p. 10).

Sharia in the West is not fiction but reality. It is an ambiguous reality, torn between disadvantaging *and* helping out Muslim women. Already by the standards of secular law, which must partially acknowledge the laws of other (Muslim) states through the international law principle of "comity of nations" (Rohe 2004: 335), there is no return to an idealized "one law for all" (MacEoin 2009). In fact, such a monistic situation has never existed, either in Europe or elsewhere. A modicum of "legal pluralism" has *always* been the reality *everywhere* (Merry 1988). For Europe, it is apposite to cite again the classic study of Catholic canon law by Harold Berman, who called legal pluralism the Western legal tradition's "perhaps most distinctive characteristic" and "source of freedom" (1983: 10). This does not mean that *any* legal pluralism is freedom-enhancing. (For an astute indictment of "legal group-ism" in personal law, see Cohen 2012.) However, in particular the experience of English sharia councils, which seem to be more advantageous than disadvantageous for the Muslim women who mostly make use of them, suggests that the accommodation of Islam in Europe and the West will have to occur, to a degree, from within Islam, irrespective of the many ways in which Islam is an irritation to liberal societies.

Conclusion

This chapter started darkly, by laying out some incompatibilities between Islam and Europe, but ended lightly, by stressing the integrative powers of liberal institutions, which even include the selective recognition of sharia law. Both realities are often denied. On the one side, academic etiquette eschews the notion of "Islam" for fear of "essentializing" or even "Orientalizing" it. On the other side, a widespread perspective on Muslims as victims obscures the successes achieved by liberal law in integrating Islam. Certainly, to be upbeat about legal integration does not mean that Muslims are not among Europe's most disadvantaged minorities, only that Muslims' socioeconomic and educational woes are mainly not related to their religion (Hansen 2012).

One should have no illusion about the chimera of "liberal Islam" and the fact that Islamic elite doctrine is deeply conservative, even hostile to secularism. It does not have to stay this way but currently it is so. Sociologist Charles Kurzman's authoritative anthology *Liberal Islam* shows the feebleness of this "contradiction in terms" (1998: 3), which flowered only briefly in the first two decades of the twentieth century and remains an "unpromising position" today (p. 12). Kurzman sharply lays out three ways in which Islam *could* be liberal, only to refute each possibility in turn. First, one might argue that sharia itself is liberal. Yet this is a "difficult intellectual venture" by "autodidacts venturing into textual analysis for which others are better prepared" (p. 14), indeed requiring the rolling back of the accumulated wisdom in Islam's four legal schools, "this thousand-year-old sacred folly" (Rahman 1998: 314). Secondly, one might argue that Muslims may be liberal where the sharia is silent. This is the project of ethicizing Islam, of cutting off its legal and political dimension, of privatizing it. Its early twentieth-century pioneer was Abdel al-Raziq, the Egyptian sharia judge and religious scholar at Al-Azhar University, Sunni Islam's most prestigious academy. He took the Prophet to be a spiritual "messenger" but not a political "ruler" (al-Raziq 1998: 32). However, al-Raziq lost his religious posts for his heretical view that "Islam has nothing to do with the State" (Binder 1988: 147). As Kurzman points out, the "silent sharia" view immediately raises the "counterargument that religion and politics are not separate in Islam" (1998: 1), and – perhaps more importantly still – this view leaves little room for challenging illiberal elements in sharia that are not silent at all. Finally, one might argue that sharia, even the divine revelation in the Qur'an itself, is interpreted and thus subject to human imagination (which is the famous claim of the Iranian cleric Abdolkarim Soroush [2002]). However, this is heresy as it "reduces revelation to the level of fallible human interpretation" (Kurzman 1998: 17), and it made its prominent Iranian proponent the target of a deadly *fatwa*. The conservatism of mainstream Islam is nowhere more visible than in the dogma, shared by all except a persecuted few, of the Qur'an as "eternal and revealed" (Ramadan 2009: 17), "the word of God ... revealed to mankind as such in clear Arabic language" (p. 14). One wonders: why didn' t God speak Swiss German?

Islamic elite doctrine's hostility to secularism is over-determined by creed and history. With respect to creed, Bernard Lewis noted that "[t]he words for 'secular' and 'secularism' in modern Islamic languages are either loanwords or neologisms. There are still no equivalents for the words 'layman' and 'laity'" (1996: 62). With respect to history, the notion of "secularism" is deeply identified with and tainted by Western colonialism and dominance, and in opposition to the latter "a rejection of the idea that religion and state should be separate has morphed into a core aspect of Islamic identity" (Hashemi 2009: 143). Accordingly, to the degree that liberal democracy "requires a form of secularism" (p. 1), there is a need for "indigenizing" secularism from within Islam (ch. 4).

Something akin to this is occurring in Europe. In his ethnography of rapprochements between French *banlieue* Islam and local state institutions, John Bowen (2010a: ch. 8) defined the mutual mindset on the ground as "social pragmatism." On the Islamic side, it accepts liberal-secular principles and institutions, such as civil marriage (the only type of marriage recognized under French law), not for their own sake but for their "positive social consequences" for Muslims, and if they can be justified from within Islam. The Islamic basis for this is the so-called *maqasid* approach, which looks for the "purposes" behind a scriptural obligation to flexibly, that is, non-literally, implement the latter. Bowen explicates its workings: "Marrying in city hall is thus indicated by scripture, because scripture's passages on marriage have as their purpose to make marriage a stable contract" (p. 166). Key to social pragmatism is to stay always within an Islamic framework, with Muslims "defin[ing] the space as Islamic, rather than French or European or 'modern' or 'liberal'" (p. 155). If the outcome is "integration," it is by stealth, happening *despite* the intentions of the involved Muslims rather than *because* of them. And it may fail, because Muslims are never forced to step out of their religion – or, rather, they will follow secular law only to the degree that their religion permits.

Social pragmatism is applied "political liberalism," which stipulates the possibility of reaching an "overlapping consensus" about joint legal–political rules from within one's "comprehensive doctrine," be it religious or not (Rawls 1993). However, as Andrew March pointed out, there is an inherent weakness to political liberalism: it "cannot require as part of a minimal doctrine of citizenship any robust or emotional attachment to one's community of citizenship" (2007a: 249). Because it wisely does not touch upon people's souls, political liberalism allows for merely thin – ultimately, contingent and tactical – attachments, which last as long as people's primordial commitments are not compromised.

If "social pragmatism" is the way Islam becomes part of Europe and the West, that is, only from within its religious framework, one concedes that "Islam" and "Europe" are bound to remain extraneous to one another, at least for the time being. One could say that social pragmatism and its philosophical cousin, political liberalism, are the default position in the legal system with its strong religious rights provisions. In the political system, a different logic applies: there is a good deal less patience here and more populist pressure. Thus it is no surprise that European governments have recently stepped up their efforts to domesticate or nationalize Islam. The immediate triggers are obvious: the terrorist attacks early in the millennium, often committed by homegrown second-generation Muslims; the entry into most European polities of radical right parties that are openly hostile to Muslims and Islam; and a widespread perception that "multiculturalism" has failed. Two American observers call the new European agenda the "institutionalization of a moderate, Euro-friendly Islam" (Haddad and Golson 2007). That agenda includes the state-aided creation of representative Islamic bodies, facilitation of mosque construction and Islamic schooling, and the local education of imams. The novelty, argue Haddad and Golson, not without sarcasm, is a "religion-change" agenda (p. 487), aiming to "recreate Islam as a Westernized, liberal, manageable religion on par with other faiths" (p. 499).

Such an endeavor would be unthinkable in the United States, despite the mellowing of the "wall of separation" recently (see Chapter 3). And it is not compatible with a strict neutrality stance that requires the liberal state to be agnostic and hands-off with respect to religion. However, one must ask: is there an alternative? A friendlier view of the same policy sees it as European states, however whipped by security concerns and populism, becoming more proactive in molding Islam into historically established and necessarily particular church–state regimes, notably on a basis of equality with the Christian and Jewish faiths. The foremost chronicler of "neo-corporatist" Islam inclusion in Europe identified a "dual movement" of "expanding religious liberty *and* increasing control exerted over religion" (Laurence 2012: 6). This is a very accurate description of the relationship between Islam and Europe today. At the discursive level, the nationalization of Islam is framed by spelling out more explicitly the values and principles that define liberal societies and that Muslims, like everyone else, are expected to adopt, or at least accept – nationalization in this respect is identical with liberalization. This implies, in some European countries (like France or the Netherlands), a thickening of political into ethical liberalism, or the rise of "liberal identities" that are exclusive and repressive (see Joppke 2010: 137–42). In this mold, Bassam Tibi is not content with the "ideological neutrality of the legal state"; instead he finds it necessary to "defend liberty in an ideologically active way" (2009b: 41). Examples of this are not difficult to find. France had always done it in term of its Republicanism, and the latter is emulated today in some smaller European states, like Denmark or the Netherlands (see Mouritsen 2006). In Germany, the ethical thickening of liberalism goes under the name of *Leitkultur*, a term that was, incidentally, invented by Tibi.

Interestingly, both Tariq Ramadan and Bassam Tibi defend "Euro-Islam." But they attribute very different meanings to it. For Ramadan, Euro-Islam is integration on Islamic terms: "[W]hat Islam will contribute to the West is Islam" (quoted in Caldwell 2009: 245). For Tibi, Euro-Islam is integration on European terms, which would yield an Islam that is laic and secular: "Laicity and secularism in the limited sense of separating religion and politics has to be built into Islamic thinking" (Tibi 2009b: 93). What is notably absent in both scenarios is any appreciation of the role of liberal institutions, which neither require theological reform nor are likely to leave the religions processed by them unaffected. If Islam in Europe is a "challenge to the secular state," it is one in principle, perhaps, but very little in reality. In particular, one searches in vain for something similar to the holes bitten into the American "wall of separation" by the Christian Right. The absence of any comparable constitutional change in Europe suggests, indeed, that Islam has been a lesser challenge to the secular state in the West.

Conclusion
Islam and Christianity in the Secular State

Since the axial age, to legitimize power and to challenge power have been the two oldest, most elementary, if rather contradictory, ways for religion to relate to politics (see Chapter 1). However, neither notion is helpful to an understanding of the less central, less dramatic relationship of religion to the state in Europe and America today. On the one side, the Western secular state rests on democratic, not divine, legitimacy, which rules out the possibility of religion to legitimize power, at least as directly as it once did under a divine monarchy. On the other side, the secular state is so firmly entrenched and broadly supported in the West that the notion of religion as a "challenge" to power is just a touch too grand to be meaningful. If, in the last two chapters, we referred to the Christian Right in America and Islam in Europe as a "challenge to the secular state," it was only to signal where "the action is" in religion–state relations on both sides of the Atlantic. It was not, of course, to claim that the secular state is at risk of being replaced by something else.

There is still an enduring element of truth in the notion of religion as legitimizing or challenging power. This is because both religion and state are "models of authority," each by itself constituting "a totalizing order capable of regulating every aspect of life" – the propensity to which Roger Friedland tellingly finds stronger in "religions other than

Christianity, which began as a stateless faith" (2002: 390). Still, their being "models of authority" (Friedland) makes for the possibility of a special intimacy *or* friction between religion and state, even in Christian settings, which could never exist between the state and any other sphere of a differentiated social order.

If we compare European Islam's and the American Christian Right's claims toward the secular state, they differ in interesting, because historically inverted, ways. Even in its stronger quest for legal pluralism, "Islam" (as shorthand for Islamic claims-makers) essentially asks for "the free exercise of religion, according to the dictates of conscience," to quote Article 16 of the 1776 Virginia Bill of Rights (which points to the religious, more precisely sectarian-Protestant, origins of the idea of constitutionally protected individual rights, as argued by Jellinek 1904). Apart from certain complications surrounding sharia law, the free religious exercise claim is difficult to reject in a liberal-constitutional state, which owes its existence precisely to the protection of religious freedoms. By contrast, the typical Christian claim in a secular state goes a bit further, to fill the "naked public square" (Neuhaus 1984) with Christian symbolism that would be imperative and binding for all, even for nonbelievers and other believers. This is an ironic reversal of roles, considering Christianity's historical function as premier secularizing force, the "religion for departing from all religion," to quote again Gauchet (1997 [1985]: 4), whereas Islam has always been imbued with a much stronger totalizing and political ambition. However, this reversal of roles simply reflects Islam's modest status as minority religion and Christianity's more exalted status as majority religion in the West. Demography limits Islamic claims to the unhindered exercise of religion itself, while Christian claims often go beyond the latter to define the public square and to shape public policy.

Representative of Islam's and Christianity's rather different types of claims-making in the Western secular state, self-limiting for Islam but other-imposing for Christianity, are recent legal and political conflicts about the Islamic veil and the Christian crucifix (see Joppke 2013c). Both symbols and surrounding conflicts are instances of "public religion" (Casanova 1994), in that not the private practice of religion but its visibility and presence in the public sphere are contested, though with interestingly different meanings and outcomes that merit further attention.

The Islamic Veil

As Muslims are a minority in Western societies, it is no accident that courts have been largely protective of them, true to their function to "protect those who can't protect themselves politically" (Ely 1980: 152). The main source of this protection has been religious liberty rights, but also parental education rights, which are guaranteed by Western state constitutions and international conventions. One critical Islam scholar thus mused that "the future of the Muslim minority...depends not so much on how the law might be expanded to accommodate its concerns but on a larger transformation of the cultural and ethical sensibilities of the majority Judeo-Christian population that undergird the law" (Mahmood 2009: 860).

However, the one limit to Muslims' religious liberty in Western lands has been the protracted and often successful attempts to restrict the Islamic headscarf, which may also be seen as political backlash against a self-propelling legal inclusion (see Joppke 2013a: 428–30). Interestingly, the United States has been immune from this dynamic (see Elver 2012: ch. 8), much as there has been little conflict surrounding the integration of Muslim and Islam in America in general (Joppke and Torpey 2013: ch. 4). Only in Europe has there been chronic conflict over the headscarf, for a quarter-century now, recently reaching new heights in laws prohibiting extreme veiling ("burkas") in France and Belgium. The headscarf conflict is as old as European colonialism, where the forced unveiling of Muslim women for the sake of equality between the sexes was responded to with the political insistence on the veil as a symbol of resistance against Western domination (see Ahmed 1992: ch. 8). Ever since, there has been a political dimension to the veil, on *both* sides of the conflict. The political dimension attributed to the veil, in fact, often (not always)[1] served as justification for a legislative clamp-down (which would be much more difficult to justify against religious symbols proper).[2]

In this minefield, where the symbol of female subordination in Islam to some is the badge of Islamic feminism to others, it is important to differentiate. In Round One of the European headscarf struggles, the main issue was restricting the ordinary headscarf (which covers the hair but not the face) in public institutions, especially state schools, and it applied mostly to civil servants (especially teachers) whose religious attire was taken to be in conflict with the state's mandate to be "neutral" on religion. Only France went further, legislating against the headscarves worn by school girls in 2004, thus politically over-turning a court-driven liberal toleration of the headscarf since 1989 (see Joppke 2009a: 37–52). One American observer found the 2004 Law on Laicity expressive of a "racist" animus of the French against Muslims (Scott 2007: ch. 2), but it is better seen as continuing a Republican state legacy of holding religion at bay, whether Catholicism in the nineteenth century or Islam today. The 2004 law entailed a new, expansive definition of *laïcité*, in being extended from the providers to the beneficiaries of state services. However, in keeping with the traditional practice of school uniforms in many countries (including liberal Britain and France itself), this restriction may be justified by the exclusion of disturbing group influences from public education, much as other functional sectors (like the workplace) have always required similar moderation.

In Round Two of the European headscarf struggles, the target of restriction is both more specific and more general: more specific, because only the more extreme form of covering ("burka" or "veil" proper), which hides the Muslim woman's face and thus her identity, is targeted; but also more general, because the veil is now meant to be suppressed not just in public institutions but in public space at large (see Joppke and Torpey 2013: ch. 2). Apparently, one needs a more precise taxonomy of the spatial dimension of the public sphere to make sense of this restriction. At a minimum one must distinguish between the *common* space of streets and squares and the *institutional* space of courts and schools (where the state is constitutively present and accordingly impartiality and neutrality considerations apply). To prescribe what (not) to wear in the streets makes for the most drastic restriction of liberty waged by a Western state today. How can it be justified?

Interestingly, the French 2010 anti-burka law is notionally restricting not a religious symbol but a political one, however implausible this attribution may appear. To justify this restriction still required considerable legal acrobatics. In the end, the law was justified by the notion that life in public requires a "reciprocity" of seeing and being seen that is impaired by the veil (which allows seeing without being seen in turn). "Reciprocity" is an entirely new concept in French law grafted onto the "morality" dimension of "public order," which had been dwindling under an increasingly rights- rather than morality-enforcing understanding of public law in the past half-century (see the classic statement by Hart 1963). For some, it is consistent to outlaw veiling for public morality reasons, much as the exact opposite of the veil, nudity, is also prohibited. However, the better compass is the gradual retreat of public morality restrictions, or rather their reinterpretation in individual rights terms. For instance, long-standing morality laws against bigamy, incest, or bestiality today do not protect religious norms (which had traditionally been the core of public morality)[3] but vulnerable people or organisms, in the mentioned cases women, children, or animals. It is obvious that the French anti-burka law departs from this trend, marking a resurgence of unreconstructed "legal moralism" (Feinberg 1985: xiii) that cannot be reduced to the protection of an individual interest (least of all the interest of veiled women, who mostly claim the veil to be their choice) (see also Joppke forthcoming). Instead, this latest and most radical of all headscarf laws in Europe signals that the bigger threat to liberty today is not Islam but laws for the protection of morality, however "liberal" the latter may fashion themselves as.

The Christian Crucifix

As a religious symbol, the Christian crucifix differs from the Islamic veil in interesting ways. First, whereas the veil as such is only textile and has no intrinsic religious meaning, or rather can be invested with many meanings (religious, political, and other[4]), the crucifix is more intrinsically religious, and other than religious meanings are not as easily attributed to it. This makes the crucifix in principle less vulnerable to political attack than the veil, namely, protected by religious liberty clauses in a constitutional state. Secondly, however, the veil is always an attribute of the person wearing it, whereas the crucifix is often part of an institutional environment, such as public buildings or squares, detached from persons. In fact, only in this institutional respect, not as something attached to people, has the crucifix become controversial recently. But outside the church, its cultic home ground, such as in a public school or courtroom, the crucifix is an awkward thing for the secular state to protect, which owes its name precisely to separating what it now sometimes claims to be identifying with, if only in terms of history and culture and not, of course, religion.

The propriety of the Christian crucifix if entangled with the state has recently been subject to controversial high court rules, interestingly both in Europe and in the United States. In Europe, the leading case is *Lautsi v. Italy*, adjudicated by the European Court of Human Rights twice, in 2009 and 2011. The case concerned an Italian policy, based on a fascist-era administrative decree, of mandating the hanging of crucifixes in its public schools. Two opposite decisions by the European Court of Human Rights (ECtHR), which watches over the European Convention of Human Rights (ECHR), display a considerable uncertainty about the meaning of secularism in Europe, and whether and in what ways the state could be partial toward, or even identify with, the majority religion (in this case, Catholicism as Italy's predominant religion).

In 2009, the ECtHR's lower chamber decided that the crucifix had to be removed for the sake of "secularism," which required the state to be equidistant from all religions, even that of the majority: "The concept of secularism required the State to be neutral and keep an equal distance from all religions, as it should not be perceived as being closer to some citizens than to others."[5] This decision (henceforth: Lautsi I) caused uproar in Italy. The prime minister himself called it "not acceptable for us Italians" (Berlusconi, quoted in Mancini 2010a: 6–7). It also came to be opposed by a "holy alliance" of American Evangelicals, the Russian Orthodox Church, and the Vatican, alongside the government of Italy and 10 Eastern European states (all with doubtful secular or liberal credentials) (Annicchino 2011). As one liberal Italian observer commented on this dubious alliance, many of whose members had been repeatedly condemned by the ECtHR for their oppression of minority religions: "From today, Italy is the country which has defended the Central-Eastern Europe of traditions against the Western Europe of pluralistic neutrality."[6] The intervening states were delicately represented by the famous American–Israeli constitutional lawyer Joseph Weiler, a specialist in European Union law, and a major academic operator on both sides of the Atlantic. He called Lautsi I an "embarrassment" because it allegedly mistook "neutrality" for "secularism," rendering illegitimate, if not illegal, the many European church–state regimes, including Italy's, where the secular and the religious were not strictly separated, as in France or America, but meshed (Weiler 2010). Weiler conveniently overlooked the very first high court decision on the crucifix in Europe, which had been issued by the German Federal Constitutional Court in 1995.[7] It was decided much like Lautsi in 2009, the German high court outlawing a mandatory crucifix on Bavarian public school walls for the sake of secularism. But this judgment was no indictment of the German approach of "open" neutrality in favor of French-type "separationist" neutrality. Instead, the German high court simply asked the secular state to be equidistant from all religions, including that of the majority, which is the norm even in a regime, like the German, that invites religion into the public sphere. Still, for a Catholic Church lobbyist to the Strasbourg court Lautsi I amounted to nothing less than "outlaw[ing] Italian identity," which he – rather questionably[8] – grounds in the Catholic religion.[9]Adding insult to injury, this outcome was achieved through the religious liberty clause of the ECHR, which also protects *negative* religious liberty, in this case the liberty of the son of a Finnish-born atheist not to have to learn under the Catholic cross.[10]

When the Grand Chamber of the ECtHR surprisingly overturned the lower-instance decision in 2011[11] (henceforth: Lautsi II), now defending the right of the Italian state to place Christian crucifixes in its public schools, the Strasbourg court espoused a rather different understanding of secularism than in its 2009 decision. To be sure, the court explicitly refused to take a position on the "principle of secularism" in the Italian context,[12] construing the case narrowly as one of whether the "right to education" of the pupil's parent, under Article 2 of the ECHR, had been harmed by the Italian crucifix policy. That is, legally the court took as the only question to be answered in Lautsi II whether the plaintiff was prevented from passing on her atheistic leanings to her son. But in assuring fair treatment to the plaintiff, the court also qualified "secularism" as a "conviction" (more precisely: a "philosophical conviction") protected by the convention, much like a religious belief.[13] Secularism was thus demoted to one of the many beliefs or ideologies that compete in a pluralistic society. As the court opinion was rather short on this, two concurring opinions made clear that "secularism" was now understood in narrowly French terms as one possible state ideology among others, even equating it with religion itself. In one concurring opinion, Judge Bonello from Malta strangely argued that "secularism, pluralism, the separation of Church and State, religious neutrality, religious tolerance...are not values protected by the Convention."[14] This even undercut the court opinion, and it is plainly nonsensical: how then could the ECHR protect the freedom of religion, in its Article 9, which includes a *negative* religious freedom? This protection would be inconceivable without a modicum of state "secularism" and "neutrality." In a second concurring opinion, Judge Power from Britain claimed that secularism is "one ideology among others," contrasting it with "neutrality" and "pluralism."[15] She thus, much like the majority court in its chalk-eating protection of the "supporters of secularism,"[16] bought into Joseph Weiler's poisonous critique of the lower chamber's 2009 interdiction of the crucifix: "[F]avouring secularism was a political position that, whilst respectable, was not neutral."[17] If one buys into this, "secularism," in being non-neutral, is rendered formally equivalent to a religious stance itself[18] – a view not far from that of American Evangelicals who take "secularism" and "humanism" to be just another "religion." Lorenzo Zucca rightly objects that in this way "secularism is demoted from an overarching principle of the constitutional state to one possible philosophical conviction amongst others" (2013: 222). Or rather, the militant French version of secularism, in terms of *laïcité*, is confounded with secularity, a minimal distancing of the state from religion, without which it could not be a liberal state, and both – secularism and secularity – are dispensed with jointly.

What makes this dismissal of secularism even more dubious is that Italian courts were divided on the issue. The Italian Constitutional Court had long established that "secularism" (even referred to as *laicità*) was one of the "fundamental principles of the Italian legal system" (Mancini 2014: 122, fn. 81), and it ruled internally that in Italian courtrooms the crucifix had to be removed. This fact alone disproves

Weiler's implicit equating of "secularism" with a foreign (French) impo-sition, and it (among other, more historical facts) also throws a strange light on any facile equation of "Italian identity" with Catholicism. However, the Italian Constitutional Court refused to rule on the class-room crucifix, simply because it lacked the competence to rule on a decree that was only administrative and short of the status of statutory law. The Court of Cassation (Italy's highest civil court), which is not liable to such constraints, explicitly deemed the crucifix in violation of the principle of secularism and the neutrality of the state. Only the State Council (Italy's highest administrative court), concurring with the lower-level Italian administrative courts in this matter, defended the crucifix. It did so, bizarrely, by taking the crucifix as a "universal value" that supported the secular state abstracted from any religious creed (Zucca 2013). This was a kind of "confessional secularism" (Mancini 2006: 187) that, if valid, would also oblige India or Turkey to hold high the cross. When the Strasbourg court okayed the cross in Lautsi II, this amounted to factual support for the controversial right-wing government at the time (of Berlusconi's populist Popolo della Libertà and the radical rightist and anti-immigrant Lega Nord) and to disagree-ing with a good part of Italy's legal establishment, including the Italian Constitutional Court.

The Strasbourg Court's Lautsi II decision has important ramifications, because it seems to affirm the license for the liberal state to embrace a Christian identity (see Joppke 2013b). It is thus apposite to look at its justification more closely. In particular, the court adduced two arguments in favor of the crucifix, one substantive and one formal.

On the substantive side, the crucifix was declared a "passive symbol" that could not influence school children in the same manner as "didactic speech or participation in religious activities."[19] Therefore there could not be an infringement of the parents' educational rights (in this case, to educate their children in a non-religious mode), protected by Article 2 of the ECHR. Interestingly, the court conceded that the crucifix was at heart a "religious symbol," but that in certain contexts – as in this case – it could also take on an "identity-linked" connotation, which the state was entitled to "perpetuate" in terms of a "tradition."[20] While this is a reasonable and politically prudent position to take (as I argue in Joppke 2013b), it still contrasts with the same court's previous, much less lenient, judgments on the Islamic headscarf, in one of which the headscarf was taken to be, without closer examination, a "powerful external symbol" with the potential to disturb young and unformed minds.[21] To make things worse, all of this was rather random herme-neutics, because in Lautsi I the same court had explicitly taken *both* symbols, that is, the veil *and* the crucifix, as "powerful external symbols" that could not but "be interpreted by pupils of all ages as...religious sign[s]."[22] Not bothering to elaborate why suddenly one religious symbol was merely "passive" while the other was still "powerful," Europe's human rights court obviously espouses a "double standard" in its judgments on majority and minority religions, to the detriment of the latter, particularly Islam (see Joppke 2013c).

On the formal side, rather than adjudicating in a more principled way how the secular state should reconcile the competing claims of majority and minority religions in an age of religious pluralism, the court preferred to hide behind its traditional "margin of appreciation" doctrine. This is a legal term for letting national governments prevail on sensitive questions pertaining to national culture and identity. Of course, the "margin of appreciation" reasoning automatically kicked in once the court had decided that, in this case, the issue was less religious indoctrination than "to perpetuate a tradition."[23]

Lautsi II vindicates the possibility for the liberal state to favor the majority religion in society, but only to the degree that the latter is transformed into a cultural tradition. Only in this way is the secularity of the state retained. By contrast, Joseph Weiler denounced the demotion of the crucifix from religious to cultural symbol (which had already been the Italian government position during Lautsi I in 2009) as a "disingenuous secular canard," the "opposite of pluralism," because religion was thus expelled from the public sphere (2010: 2). However, this is still a necessary transformation for making Christianity an identity option, because the state's outright identification with religion as religion would clearly be a violation of its secularity.

The demotion of religion to the status of culture plays on the fact that there is a difference in kind between separating state and religion, which is the touchstone of liberalism, and separating state and culture, which is impossible. Only with respect to religion, but not with respect to culture, is "benign neglect" on part of the state possible, as one could argue with Will Kymlicka (1995: 111; see also Scheffler 2007). Tellingly, when some German Länder outlawed the wearing of Islamic headscarves by public school teachers a few years ago, explicitly exempting from the reach of the prohibition Catholic nun teachers in certain schools, this rested on the same premise that this was not a religious discrimination but a matter of recognizing the "Christian-Occidental tradition" (Joppke 2009a: ch. 3). While clearly an indirect discrimination against Islam, this was also an unacknowledged victory of secularism because Christianity could only be favored to the degree that it was not a religion.

The crucifix's "culturalization" makes for an interesting parallel with the Islamic veil's (at least partial) "politicization," except that "culturalization" was construed as a license for the secular state to identify with this central symbol of Christianity, while the veil's "politicization" (sometimes) was a pretext for its exclusion from the public sphere. One may find both moves equally implausible, but there is still an undeniable logic to them – qua religious symbol, the crucifix could never be embraced by the state, much as the veil, which is always claimed by an individual as expressive of her religious beliefs, would enjoy much higher protection if seen as a straightforwardly religious symbol.[24]

There is also a noteworthy parallel between the ECtHR's "culturalist" preference for Christianity in Lautsi II and recent US Supreme Court decisions that favor the Christian-majority religion through the selfsame prism of "culturalizing" it.[25] The culturalization of Christian symbols is the gist of turning the Christian crèche into a "holiday" display in Lynch v. Donnelly (1984), and of having to stress that the "nonreligious aspects" of a Ten Commandments monolith are "predominant" to let it pass constitutional muster in Van Orden v. Perry (2005) (see Chapter 3). And just between the two European Lautsi decisions, the United States had its own crucifix case, which was argued and decided in a strikingly similar way to Lautsi II. In its Salazar v. Buono (2010) decision, the US Supreme Court found compatible with the Establishment Clause the placing of a huge Latin cross in a national park in the Californian Mojave desert. The cross had many possible meanings, the American court argued, not unlike the European Lautsi II court, and in this particular context it happened to be merely a "national memorial," to "honor our Nation's fallen soldiers" (in World War I). Accordingly, its placement on public land (where it had quietly stood for eight decades without anyone taking offense!) could not be taken as "attempt to set the imprimatur of the state on a particular creed."[26] Of course, a cross in the desert is a rather more marginal affair than one in each classroom, and a mandatory classroom crucifix, even under a post-separationist Supreme Court, would be anathema in the United States.

In an American peculiarity, however, one also finds on its Supreme Court, even in the opinions of its previous Chief Justice, calls for the state to identify itself with religion qua religion, which would be unthinkable in secular Europe (see again Chapter 3). Accordingly, in McCreary County v. ACLU of Kentucky (2005), Justice Scalia (joined in full or in part by three other justices, that is, short of just one justice to constitute the court majority in this case!), defended a deliberately provocative Ten Commandments exhibit in a Kentucky courthouse, which had been strangely put there in "honor of Jesus Christ" (for biblical consistency, it should have been in honor of God the Father or His prophet

Moses), and which was found to be the "acknowledgment of a single Creator" that was perfectly legitimate for the government to make. In *Elk Grove Unified School District v. Newdow et al.* (2004), Justice Thomas coolly pointed out that the meaning of "under God" in the Pledge of Allegiance *had* to be religious, and that this was no problem anyway because the states were free under the Constitution to declare themselves "Christian" if they so wished, even in twenty-first-century multicultural America. And Chief Justice Rehnquist upped the ante when bluntly stating in his plurality opinion in *Van Orden v. Perry* (2005) that "[o]ur institutions presuppose a Supreme Being" (see Chapter 3). Most of this was in the denominationally anonymous (and thus fairly but not perfectly inclusive) mode of American deism, which had been the nucleus of American "civil religion" (Bellah 1967) all along. However, when Joseph Weiler ridiculed the European "secular canard" of culturalized Christianity in Lautsi, one wonders: did he prefer a US-style open endorsement of theocracy?

The Intractable Dilemma: Religion versus Liberalism

Public religion eventually founders on the rock of the liberal-democratic state: religion qua religion is only open to its believers and thus must discriminate against all others, to a degree even against some of its own members (especially women), whereas the liberal-democratic state is open to all comers and stipulates a perfect equality of membership.[27] This, one must know, is a tension further aggravated by the process of secularization, because its reverse side, often ignored, is a growing reluctance of the state to intervene in the internal affairs of religion (see Rémond 1998: ch. 12). But in the end, a choice has to be made, between respecting religious rights and human rights. *Tertium non datur*. The intractable dilemma between religion and liberalism may be illustrated by two recent high court decisions, one from the United States and one from Britain.

In *Christian Legal Society v. Martinez* (2010), the US Supreme Court upheld the right of a public university to withhold official recognition from a Christian group on campus that denied membership to practicing homosexuals. This was, notably, not a prohibition of the group, only a denial of official status that made it ineligible for certain privileges, especially financial support. The denial of official status was in reference to the conservative (if not fundamentalist) Evangelical beliefs of the group, which required its members to abstain from "participation in or advocacy of a sexually immoral lifestyle,"[28] including premarital sex, adultery, and homosexual conduct. Giving in to this restriction for the sake of religious freedom and "viewpoint neutrality" (the prevailing Supreme Court doctrine for accommodating religious groups on public university campuses) would mean that the university in question, the University of California–Hastings College of Law, which is legally and philosophically obliged to follow the principle of non-discrimination, would be forced to publicly recognize and hand out state money to a group that openly denied the non-discrimination principle. Siding with the university administration in this case, liberal Supreme Court Justice Ruth Bader Ginsburg pretended that the court majority's repudiation of the Evangelical campus group only targeted its discriminatory "conduct" but not its "Christian perspective."[29] However, this was an academic (or liberal Protestant) distinction that denied the reality of a necessary fusion between belief and conduct for certain religious groups, such as the one in question – the Evangelical group would just lose its distinct character if it included everyone, including gays. It was thus understandable that an amicus brief filed by a coalition of Muslim, Christian, Sikh, and Jewish groups found it "fundamentally confused to apply a rule against religious discrimination to a religious association."[30] But it is equally understandable that for the university "[i]t would be an odd constitutional rule that prohibited public educational institutions from discriminating but required them to subsidize discrimination by student groups," as the opposite ACLU's amicus brief put it.[31] The university, much like any public institution committed to liberal-universalistic principles, was in an "impossible position,"[32] either honoring the group's religious right to determine its membership but violating the university's commitment to non-discrimination *or* discriminating against the group but remaining faithful to its own liberal-universalistic principles.

As Stanley Fish put it in a trenchant discussion of *Christian Legal Society v. Martinez*, "The liberal state and its institutions face a choice between being faithful to the democratic principle of open access or closing the liberal door to those who are illiberal."[33] In dissent, Justice Alito (joined by Justices Scalia and Thomas) correctly identified the principle animating the majority opinion: "[N]o freedom for expression that offends prevailing standards of political correctness in our country's institutions of higher learning."[34] It was, indeed, an "ideology of liberal multiculturalism,"[35] of endorsing diversity as long as it did not hurt or discriminate, that drove the Supreme Court's decision in *Christian Legal Society v. Martinez*. But the alternative of supporting illiberal groups with state funds appears equally unattractive, if not more so, because it undermines the liberal principles on which the state rests and thus is potentially self-destructive. Sometimes a decision must be made – for the liberal state or for religion.

The intractable dilemma between religion and liberalism is equally visible in a recent British high court case, *R. v. The Governing Body of Jewish Free School (JFS)* (2009).[36] This case involved a state-funded ("voluntary aided") religious school, incidentally one of the best-performing schools in the United Kingdom, but one that warded off the flood of comers through only admitting students who were recognized Jews under strict Orthodox rules (that is, either descending from a Jewish mother or converted according to Orthodoxy). In particular, the school had excluded a student ("M") whose mother was Italian and Catholic by origin and, before his birth, had converted to Judaism under the less exacting procedures of the Masorti branch of Judaism. The refusal to admit M had distressing consequences for him: a deeply religious practicing Jew, he had no other secondary Jewish school in the entire London area to which he could turn instead. More gallingly, "atheists or even...practising Christians or practising Muslims"[37] would be admitted by Jewish Free School, as long as they met the matrilineal descent test that defined them as Jewish according to Orthodoxy.

Curiously, the House of Lords (Britain's Supreme Court) judged that the school's admissions policy, applying the maternal descent test on M, was based not on religion but on ethnicity, and therefore in violation of the 1976 Race Relations Act.[38] The act prohibits a person's "less favourabl[e]" treatment on "racial grounds," the latter defined in terms of "colour, race, nationality or ethnic or national origins,"[39] *irrespective* of its motivation, that is, even if the intention is benign or, as in this case, religious. As Lord Phillips expressed the rigid workings of British race relations law, "A person who discriminates on the ground of race, as defined by the Act, cannot pray in aid the fact that the ground of discrimination is mandated by his religion."[40] While the majority judges in this case bent over backward to stress that the religious admissions policy of Jewish Free School was, of course, not "'racist' as that word is generally understood,"[41] which would be a strange charge to throw against the proverbially persecuted people, this is still what it came down to: "[T]hese requirements of Jewish law are racial as defined by section 3 of the 1976 Act."[42]

The *R. v. The Governing Body of JFS* case may well reflect a "defect" in British antidiscrimination law, as it provides "no defence of justification"[43] and thus prescribes a "rigid adherence to formal symmetry,"[44] irrespective of who discriminates with what intention. Antidiscrimination law is not necessarily so, as attested by the experience of other countries that subscribe to a more substantive (rather than strictly formal) view of equality (see Fredman 2011: 248–58). But the more important matter is that, as in the US *Christian Legal*

Society v. Martinez case, religious rights clashed with human rights (perceptively diagnosed by Ferrari 2011: 6). Certainly, one may find fault with the court's mandating of an alternative admissions procedure that was based on individual belief and self-definition, instead of descent – this "mirror[ed] a Christian understanding of membership" (Mancini 2010b: 3). Indeed, it was factually true that an admissions procedure putting a premium on "faith" and "individual commitment" corresponded to a "Christian, universalistic, logic of belonging" (p. 10). But this critique dodges the fact that any other approach would discriminate on the basis of descent, which the liberal state just cannot condone, at least to the degree that it is asked by a religious organization for benefits or status under public law. This is a predicament from which there is no rescue. It does not help to deplore this fact as a "homogenization of behaviours and values" (p. 17), even a forced "incorporation of Christian attributes" as the "price to pay for religious minorities to be 'equal' in the public sphere" (p. 16) – in this case, as the price of being included among the 7,000 state-funded religious schools in England. A Jewish leader still complained with good reason that, "[e]ssentially, we must now apply a non-Jewish definition of who is Jewish" (p. 16). However, as in the American *Christian Legal Society v. Martinez* case, the alternative looked less desirable still: give public funds and recognition to a school that was in violation of the state's antidiscrimination law. Note that "no other faith schools" in England would screen on the basis of ethnicity, and the "Christian Church will admit children regardless of who their parents are."[45] In these other cases, there was a happy coincidence of religion with the inclusiveness that liberal education requires. Jonathan Sacks, Britain's eloquent Chief Rabbi at the time of the *JFS* case, credibly characterized Judaism as "not a mere creed" but "a distinctive, detailed way of life,"[46] closed to most. And Jeff Spinner-Halev is right that "liberalism" and "religion" cannot be expected to become "congruent," also because religions are "generally hierarchically structured" (2008: 557).

However, it is still fact that in the English *R. v. The Governing Body of JFS* case, much as in the American *Christian Legal Society v. Martinez* case, religious rights clashed with human rights, and the two things could not be equally had. The two cases, similarly adjudicated under very different religion–state regimes, point to the limit of public religion in the liberal-democratic state: this state is faithful either to its own priorities or to those of religion, because sometimes both cannot be followed at the same time. Or, as Silvio Ferrari put it succinctly: "[T]he price religions have to pay to be admitted to the public sphere is the respect for human rights within their own doctrinal and organizational system" (2011: 10). Importantly, this does not amount to the suppression of religion. Instead, religion is merely asked to make concessions in return for taking advantage of public resources. If it refuses to do so, religion is still free to step back to the private realm. The private realm is thus confirmed as religion's inevitable but unassailable default position in the secular state.

Courts, Courts, Courts...and Politics?

Throughout the preceding chapters, which compared majority and minority religions as claims-makers in Western Europe and North America, it sprang to the eye that courts and legal systems, more than legislatures and political systems, were the primary arena in which many of these claims and surrounding conflicts came to be articulated and addressed. The theme of this part of the book is really "religion and the law" rather than "religion and politics." The prominence of the law, especially constitutional law, in the articulation and resolution of religious conflict is due to the settled nature of the secular state in the West, which is challenged at best at its fringes but not at its core by religious actors. Moreover, the prominence of courts and the law reflects that religion is firmly institutionalized and protected in the form of rights. These are above all individual rights, to believe and to practice one's beliefs freely and equally. To a lesser degree and notably not in America, these are also corporate rights that, in Europe, reflect contingent settlements of the historical struggle between church and state as competing systems of authority. But even when majority religions became contested, this was either because secular or atheistic minorities insisted on their negative religious liberty rights (as in the European crucifix cases), or because in a radical separation regime, like the American, religionists could fashion themselves as a besieged minority. In both instances, one would expect that constitutional courts as minority protector would become the main arena in which to carry out the conflict.

The last moment in Western Europe when religion was high politics was the nineteenth-century struggle between a secularizing state and a recalcitrant Catholic Church, its remnants continuing to exist in some countries as the thoroughly secularized (and once profoundly secularizing) Christian Democratic parties. The United States went through an acute moment of religious politics more recently, though this became immediately deflected to the legal sphere, which mostly cut the Christian Right down to liberal size. On both sides of the Atlantic, secularism, succinctly defined by Lorenzo Zucca as "precondition for coexistence through law" (2012: xxii), became challenged, either by majorities unhappy to see their religion diminished or evacuated from the public sphere, or by new minorities clamoring to have their religions included, which often amounts to a shock to a latently Christian system. As Silvio Ferrari confirms, there is no best practice in this vexed terrain that asks for a pragmatic and case-by-case approach commensurate with the "specificities of each national Church–State system" (2011: 12). The prominent involvement of courts and lawyers in this process does not guarantee the right outcome but at least one that is tamed by the civility and impersonality that is the hallmark of liberal law.

Notes

Introduction: Religion as Structure and as Actor

1 For a *cri de coeur* about an American sociology of religion being at the "lower end" of the academic pecking order, and a call to "identify and focus on big questions," see Smith et al. (2013: esp. 913 and 928). For a more sanguine state-of-the-art review of the European scene, see Koenig and Wolf (2013).

2 To put myself in flattering company, I mention only Rogers Brubaker, Ruud Koopmans, or John Torpey. Then, of course, there are those who had been "into religion" from the start, such as the admirable Philip Gorski, who has brought religion into macrosociology and political sociology like no one else of my generation.

Chapter 1   Religion in Social and Political Theory

This chapter profited from a careful reading by Gianfranco Poggi.

1 Some would prefer a narrower view of secularism, according to which anything short of a strict and categorical separation between state and majority religion would mark a state as non-secular. The problem of such a narrow definition is that it cannot distinguish Iran from Britain.

2   A recent overview of the development and different uses of the "axial age" concept is Boy and Torpey (2013).

3   The key work is Ludwig Feuerbach's *Das Wesen des Christentums* (*The Essence of Christianity*) (1978 [1849]): "In the personality of God, human beings are celebrating the spirituality (*Übernatürlichkeit*), immortality, independence, and universalism (*Unbeschränktheit*) of their own personality" (p. 168).

4   Marx borrowed this phrase almost verbatim from Feuerbach (1978 [1849]: 66): "Religion has no own, particular content."

5   Though McLellan finds this "surely to overstate the case" (1987: 15).

6   It is similarly laid out in *Totem und Tabu* (*Totem and Taboo*) (1912–13) and *Der Mann Moses und die monotheistische Religion* (*Moses and Monotheism*) (1939), Freud's first and last writings on religion, respectively.

7   Of course, a serious deficiency of Freudian psychoanalysis is its exclusively male perspective. Attempts to repair this are, among many others, Chodorow (1999) and, with respect to religion, Riesebrodt (2007: 241–3) (following the work of Ana-Maria Rizzuto).

8   By the same token, Riesebrodt (2007: 118) finds that the classical sociologists showed "almost no interest in religion itself," that is, in religion from the view of its practitioners. In this spirit, he develops a compelling theory of religion as "liturgy," according to which religion is "communication with supra-human powers" for the sake of "salvation."

9   From a "Neo-Durkheimian" perspective, the British Coronation is "ritual," in which "society reaffirms the moral values which constitute it as a society and renews its devotion to those values by an act of communion" (Edward Shils and Michael Young, quoted in Lukes 1975: 293). But is this "religion"?

10 This is a questionable assumption, because "the magician and his clientele also constitute a certain kind of moral community" (Goody 1961: 146). A compelling critique of expelling "magic" from the ambit of religion is Riesebrodt (2007: 112).

11 For the effects of Calvinism's "disciplinary revolution" on the early modern state, see Gorski (2003).

12 For a good reflection on the different possible linkages between religion and nationalism, see Brubaker (2012).

13 On Max Weber's complicated, if not pathological, sex life, see the biography by Radkau (2009).

14 My discussion of Durkheim does not include this sociology of knowledge aspect of his work on religion, because this does not directly pertain to the relationship between religion and politics.

15 See their joint classic *The Social Construction of Reality* (Berger and Luckmann 1967).

16 The rational-choice literature on American religion has become so vast that it is impossible to survey. Particularly fruitful applications for the comparative-historical study of religions, also outside the American context, are Gill (2008) and Kalyvas (1996). A sound rebuttal that "religious pluralism" is always good for "religious participation" is Chaves and Gorski (2001).

17   See also Joas (2004: 17), who closely follows Otto in this respect.

18   Interestingly, Otto argues that in Islam one could still find the "numen, without the temperature of the rational moments," which he finds responsible for the "'fanatical' edge of this religion" (1963 [1917]: 112).

19   "Political theology" is defined rather flatly as "the set of ideas that a religious actor holds about what is legitimate political authority" (Toft et al. 2011: 27)

20   For instance, in their chapter on "religious terrorism," Toft et al. (2011: ch. 3) do not hold back that, indeed, "religion" drives such practice, and in a "more deadly" way than secular terror (p. 122). But instead of delving more deeply into this motivational source, they usefully highlight that religious terrorism is driven by an institutional context of "integration" of a particular religion (usually that of the majority) in combination with "exclusion" of another religion that also wants its own integration with the state.

Chapter 2   Secularization and the Long Christian Exit

1   Unless otherwise specified, the following discussion takes the notions "secularization," "secularism," and "secular" as closely related – the first being a process term, the second the condition that results from the process, the third being this condition in adjectival form. In this sense, the three terms are exchangeable.

2   Charles Taylor calls the Enlightenment critique of religion a "subtraction story": "slough off" religion, and you will find "modernity" or "secularity" as "underlying features of human nature which were there all along, but had been impeded by what is now set aside" (2007: 22).

3   See also evolutionary biologist Stephen Jay Gould (1997), who considered science and religion as "nonoverlapping magisteria" (NOMA) belonging to two separate knowledge spheres, the first dealing with the "empirical universe" and the second with "questions of moral meaning and value" (discussed in de Waal 2013: 105).

4   The empirical-cum-normative argument that democracy does not necessitate a "complete separation" between religion and state, but only a "twin toleration" between the two, has been influentially made by Stepan (2001).

5   Asad quoting Clifford Geertz (Asad 2003: 188).

6   "Rawls has not explained why people who are communitarians in private life should be liberals in political life," as Kymlicka objects to "political liberalism" (1995: 162).

7   Here as throughout this chapter, the notion of "Christian" mostly refers to developments in "Western" or "Latin" Christianity. Eastern or Orthodox Christianity with its "cesaropapist" legacy of subordinating the church to the state took a different direction that is outside the purview of this analysis. A compelling broad-brush comparison of the different political logics of the Christian West, the Christian East, and Islam is Black (2008).

8   The central source is the entry *Säkularisation, Säkularisierung,* in Conze et al. (1984), a classic exercise in German *Begriffsgeschichte* (history of concepts). Another valuable discussion is Lübbe (1965). A concise account in English is included in Gorski and Altinordu (2008: 59–61).

9   " 'The secular' should not be thought of as the space in which *real* human life gradually emancipates itself from the controlling power of 'religion,' " but rather as "part of a doctrine called secularism" (Asad 2003: 191).

10 *Tawhid,* or the "seamlessness of Islam," argues Peter Beyer, "contains the express negation of the conditions for a primacy of functional differentiation" (2006: 158).

11 For the conflict between the "rationalist" Mu'tazilites and the "voluntarist" Ash'aris, see also El Shakankiri (1981). Fadel (2008), however, argues that "rational judgment" and "rational investigation" are not altogether foreign to al-Ghazali and the Ash'aris, and that even a Rawlsian "overlapping consensus" and agreement on the principles of "political liberalism" can be reached from within their conservative theological position.

12 One-third of the states in Muslim-majority societies define themselves as "Islamic," and more than half include sharia among the sources of state law (Ferrari 2012b: 15).

13 The Investiture Struggle came to an end in 1170, with the slaying of Thomas Becket in Canterbury Cathedral by the henchmen of the English king, Henry II. Henry had previously reasserted royal supremacy over the church against Pope Gregory VII's declaration of papal independence, appointing his close friend, Becket, as Archbishop of Canterbury. Becket, however, switched sides. The main sources of the conflict were two articles in Henry's Constitutions of Clarendon: Article 3, which amounted to "double jeopardy" for clerics (who if accused of felony were to be first tried in an ecclesiastical court and then in the king's court); and Article 8, which made the king, not the pope, the supreme arbiter of canon law in England. Becket's heinous murder in Canterbury Cathedral, until recently known to every school child in Britain, generated so much public outrage that Henry II had to repent. See Berman (1983: ch. 7).

14 Of course, the immediate target of Luther's scorn was not the confession as such, but the late medieval practice of selling "indulgences," the profit from which was used to finance the building of St. Peter's Basilica in Rome. But there was also a deeper concern that the church's complete absolution of sin through the sacrament of confession conflicted with the dogma of original sin, which Luther took very seriously.

15 The mentioned German authors are peculiarly oblivious of Foucault; only Gorski (2003) is emphatically not.

16 A slightly different, if still tripartite, typology can be found in Monsma and Soper (1997), who distinguish between a "strict church–state separation model," an "established church model," and a "pluralist model." This is more an analytical than a formal-legal typology, with "established" denoting a modicum of recognition and partnership on the part of the state, while "pluralist" denotes the state's evenhandedness toward and equidistance

from society's religions, which are still accorded important public functions. Accordingly, Germany is classified as both (informally) "established," because the state cooperates with religion, and "pluralist," because this cooperation extends to several religions on the premise of "equal justice" (p. 12).

17   The word "concordatarian" flags that the countries in this category have made formal agreements ("concordats") with the Roman Catholic Church, extending similar state contracts (*Kirchenverträge* in German parlance) to other denominations.

18   Ferrari (2002: 6) mentions the curious fact that, formally speaking, Ireland also is "separationist," much like France, in that the churches enjoy only private law status. At the same time, the Irish Constitution invokes the Holy Trinity and Catholicism is unquestionably the fundament of Irish nationalism.

19   A later version of the "Western European model" claim, which discusses in particular how Islam is accommodated by it, stresses that the collective-level "co-operation" between state and religious groups is "selective and graduated," whereby the "religious groups that share the principles and values upheld by the majority receive more support than the groups that are based on a different *ethos*" (Ferrari 2002: 11). Now the selectivity or inequity built into the model obviously shifted from religious versus non-religious to majority religious versus minority religious. Whatever its emphasis, collective-level selectivity and inequity reflect the "history of Europe" and the "historical predominance of a little group of Churches" (p. 11). However, the "inborn degree of unequal treatment" is counteracted by the "extension of...basic liberties to all religious groups," which moves to the fore in the modern context of "pluralism" (p. 11).

20   Ferrari (1995) claims that France is part of the common Western European model because there is "cooperation" in certain areas: for instance, state-paid chaplains in prisons, hospitals, and the army, privileged tax status for churches, or a public school schedule that, while not providing religious education itself, leaves time for its external provision, traditionally on Wednesday afternoons (p. 424). However, in my view, this still does not amount to "preferential treatment" of "religious subjects" over "nonreligious subjects" (p. 422).

21   See also Doe, who argues that the "dominant model in Europe is that of cooperation between State and religion" (2011: 2). According to him, the similarities of state–religion relations in Europe outweigh their differences, which the "classical doctrine" had summarized in terms of three distinct models: "state–church," "separation," and "cooperation" (p. 2).

22   For the meaning of this proviso, and recent legal developments under the influence of the Christian Right, see Chapter 3.

23   German Emperor Wilhelm describing the "prime object" of the *Volksschulon* (McLeod 2000. 79).

24   For other, narrower typologies of secularism, see Kura (2007), who distinguishes within the "laicist" camp between the "passive" secularism of the

United States and the "assertive" secularism of France and Turkey (the difference being the absence or presence, respectively, of an "ancien régime" that had to be combatted); and Hurd (2008: ch. 2), who distinguishes between a "laicist" secularism in France or Turkey and a "Judeo-Christian" variant in the United States.

25 The most detailed history of European Christian Democracy remains Fogarty (1957). A third important work, covering the postwar period, is Warner (2000).

Chapter 3   Challenge to the Secular State (I): The Christian Right in America

1 The "Christian Right," as referred to in this chapter, is an umbrella term for a movement led by (but not limited to) Protestant Evangelicals to bring to bear conservative religious precepts in public policy and law-making, and to overcome the "wall of separation" between church and state that had distinguished America from Europe from the start. The Christian Right rose to prominence with (but is not exhausted by) the "Moral Majority" of Baptist Evangelical Jerry Fawell in the late 1970s, followed by Pentecostal Evangelical Pat Robertson's "Christian Coalition," and has since become closely associated with the Republican Party, including the recent Tea Party movement (for the latter, see Formisano 2012). Among the summary accounts that I found helpful are Goldberg (2007), Lambert (2008: ch. 8), Phillips (2006), Wald and Calhoun-Brown (2011: ch. 8), Daniel Williams (2010), and – covering the movement's first decade – Bruce (1988). Richard John Neuhaus, though distancing himself from the shriller Evangelicals and their "revivalist politics of the camp meeting" (1984: 104), is an intellectual leader of the Christian Right (as are Carter [1994] and McConnell [1985], to whom the same proviso applies). That Neuhaus, Carter, and McConnell, all three thoughtful and noted public intellectuals or academics, still belong to the Christian "Right" is immediately apparent when contrasting their anti-separationist views with the rather pro-separationist views of the advocates of a "Religious Left," who "oppose tight connections between church and state in accordance with their religious premises" (Shiffrin 2009: 1; see also Dionne 2008). Excluded from the ambit of this chapter is the "militant" Christian Right, which operates outside mainstream politics, is overtly racist, and practices terrorist violence (see Armstrong 2000: 360–4; Juergensmeyer 2008: 182–92).

2 In this chapter, as throughout this book, the concepts of church–state regime and religion–state regime are used interchangeably.

3 Only from the eighteenth century on were church taxes extracted for the dissenters' *own* churches.

4   It must be conceded, however, that the main cause of factionalism and strife according to Madison's Federalist Letter no. 10 is "property," not "religion."

5   Carter argues that the First Amendment and its "separation of church and State originated in an effort to protect religion from the State, not the State from religion" (1994: 105). He cites as evidence James Madison's famous *Memorial and Remonstrance Against Religious Assessments* (1785), which opposed a bill for a new tax in Virginia to support the teachers of religion. Madison's call upon Virginia lawmakers to kill the bill (it eventually was defeated) indeed is stronger in pointing to its threat to religious liberty than to the "health and prosperity of the State" (which, by the same token, does not go unmentioned). However, one must also take into account the strategic dimension of such an intervention, as the threat of immediate liberty restrictions evidently is more urgent than more indirect and remote stability concerns.

6   As the English-language edition notes, this citation is English in the French original (Tocqueville 1969 [1835–40]: 293, fn. 3).

7   In 2008, the proportion of "nones" was 17 percent (Chaves 2011: 19). For the "churching" of America, see Finke and Stark's classic study (2006).

8   The Due Process Clause of the Fourteenth Amendment states that "No State shall deprive any person of…liberty…without due process of law."

9   Since 1780, Massachusetts had had a law requiring every citizen to be a member of a church and to pay church taxes, without specifying the denomination. In effect this amounted to the establishment of the majority church, Congregationalism.

10 Under American federalism, public schools are regulated and financed at the state or even local levels.

11 In his concurring opinion to *Elk Grove Unified School District v. Newdow et al.* (542 U.S. [2004]), Justice Thomas argued that the Establishment Clause "is a federalism provision intended to prevent Congress from interfering with state establishments." Accordingly, as the Establishment Clause (unlike the Free Exercise Clause) does not protect an individual right, it cannot be "incorporated" and used against states by the Fourteenth Amendment's Due Process Clause. However, Thomas's argument is historically dubious (see Greenawalt 2009).

12 See the historical review by Justice Souter (dissenting), *Lee et al. v. Weisman*, 505 U.S. 577 (1992), at 612–15.

13 This formulation is more specific in naming religion; and more encompassing in containing a reference to practice ("exercise"), not only belief.

14 Justice Kennedy (dissenting), *County of Allegheny v. ACLU*, 492 U.S. 573 (1989), at 659.

15 *Everson v. Board of Education of the Township of Ewing*, 330 U.S. 1 (1947), at 16.

16 *Everson v. Board of Education*, at 18.

17 *Everson v. Board of Education*, at 18.
18 *Everson v. Board of Education*, at 13.
19 *Everson v. Board of Education*, at 18.
20 Justice Douglas (majority opinion), *Zorach v. Clauson*, 343 U.S. 306 (1952), at 313.
21 Justice Douglas (majority opinion), *Zorach v. Clauson*, at 313–14.
22 Justice Douglas (majority opinion), *Zorach v. Clauson*, at 314.
23 Justice Douglas (majority opinion), *Zorach v. Clauson*, at 312.
24 *Engel v. Vitale*, 370 U.S. 421 (1962), at 422.
25 *Engel v. Vitale*, at 425.
26 *Engel v. Vitale*, at 425.
27 *Engel v. Vitale*, at 429.
28 *Van Orden v. Perry*, 545 U.S. (2005).
29 *Engel v. Vitale*, at 431.
30 *Engel v. Vitale*, at 445.
31 *School District of Abington Township v. Schempp*, 374 U.S. 203 (1963), at 216.
32 *School District of Abington Township v. Schempp*, at 219.
33 *School District of Abington Township v. Schempp*, at 219.
34 *School District of Abington Township v. Schempp*, at 220.
35 *School District of Abington Township v. Schempp*, at 222.
36 *Epperson v. Arkansas*, 393 U.S. 97 (1968), quoted from syllabus.
37 Justice Fortas, *Epperson v. Arkansas*, at 102.
38 *Lemon v. Kurtzman*, 403 U.S. 602 (1971), at 619.
39 *Lemon v. Kurtzman*, at 622.
40 *Lemon v. Kurtzman*, at 624.
41 *Lemon v. Kurtzman*, at 625.
42 *Lemon v. Kurtzman*, at 612–13.
43 The Supreme Court declared in *Zorach v. Clauson*: "The First Amendment, however, does not say that in every and all respects there shall be a separation of Church and State," whereupon the mundane examples of "police" and "fire protection" are mentioned (at 312).
44 *Lemon v. Kurtzman*, at 614.
45 *Sherbert v. Verner*, 374 U.S. 308 (1963).
46 Justice Brennan (majority opinion), *Sherbert v. Verner*, at 404 and 406.
47 Justice Brennan (majority opinion), *Sherbert v. Verner*, at 409.
48 According to Hout et al. (2001: 470), higher birth rates and earlier child-bearing among religiously conservative women explain three-quarters of the growth of conservative denominations and of the decline of liberal ones, for cohorts born between 1903 and 1970. By contrast, conversion from mainline to conservative denominations had no effect.
49 Feldman dates the appearance of a minority posture in the Christian Right only to the "early 1990s" (2005: 206), but it had been there from the beginning.
50 However, the American figure, based on image-boosting self-reporting, is known to be exaggerated, and the actual figure of weekly church attendance is estimated to be at 25 percent (Chaves 2011: 45).

51   But see Finke and Stark, who argue that "the trend of growing upstart sects and declining mainline denominations has been in place since at least 1776" (2006: 3). They ground this trend in a perennial "sect–church process," according to which there is a continuous process, favored by America's open market for religion, between fervent sects, in tension with their environment, turning into self-satisfied, worldly churches, which in turn creates the conditions for renewed sectarianism. However, this approach is agnostic about the content and social implications of faith, and it dodges the fact that previously liberal, democracy-affirming religion has in the meantime turned conservative and anti-secular.

52   Greeley and Hout (2006: 4) point out, however, that this equation is mistaken because African-American Evangelicals are predominantly aligned with the Democratic Party.

53   But see Greeley and Hout, whose estimates are more cautious: according to them, only 10 percent of "white Americans" are "strictly 'evangelical,'" defined by them as "believ[ing] in the literal, word-for-word inerrancy of the Bible" (2006: 178). Another, less friendly word for this would be "fundamentalist."

54   For the readiness of Southern Baptists to allow freed slaves to build their own churches under their umbrella, see Finke and Stark (2006: 190).

55   Incidentally, none of the three was Protestant, at least not originally: Paul Weyrich (who died in 2008) was Catholic, as is Richard Viguerie, and Howard Phillips (who died in 2013) was originally Jewish, later converting to Evangelical Protestantism.

56   In *Hein v. Freedom From Religion Foundation* (551 U.S. 587 [2007]), the US Supreme Court rejected an Establishment Clause challenge to the Faith-Based Initiative, arguing procedurally that taxpayers lack standing to challenge the constitutionality of expenditures by the federal government.

57   When campaigning for the presidency, Democratic candidate Barack Obama had promised to undo the discriminations and proselytizing associated with the Faith-Based Initiative. But out of fear of antagonizing the religionists, much of this continues under his reign. See Laurie Goodstein, "White House Director of Faith-Based Office is Leaving His Post," *New York Times*, February 7, 2013.

58   Based on data from the late 1990s, already Hout and Fischer estimated that "[f]or 5 to 7 percent of American adults, holding no religious preference...was a political act, a dissent from the affinity that had emerged between conservative politics and organized religion" (2002: 188). This amounted to almost half of the 14 percent of Americans declaring a preference for "no religion" in 1998, which was already a doubling of the "nones" between 1991 and 1998. According to Chaves (2011: 20), the backlash-driven rise of the nones underwent an "acceleration" after 2000.

59   See *Lemon v. Kurtzman*, at 614.

60   Michael McConnell has put it well: "Taken together, the Religion Clauses can be read most plausibly as warding off two equal and opposite threats to religious freedom – government action that promotes the majority's

brand of religion and government action that impedes religious practices not favored by the majority" (1992: 690).

61 Justice Brennan (majority opinion), *Edwards v. Aguillard*, 482 U.S. 578 (1987), at 587.

62 Justice Brennan (majority opinion), *Edwards v. Aguillard*, at 589.

63 Justice Powell (concurring opinion, joined by O'Connor), *Edwards v. Aguillard*, at 608.

64 Louisiana Senator Bill Keith, quoted in *Edwards v. Aguillard*, at 592.

65 Justice Powell summarizing the key tenet of Creation Science, *Edwards v. Aguillard*, at 600.

66 Justice Scalia (dissenting, joined by Rehnquist), *Edwards v. Aguillard*, at 627.

67 Justice Scalia (dissenting), *Edwards v. Aguillard*, at 634.

68 Justice Souter (majority opinion), *McCreary County v. ACLU of Kentucky*, 545 U.S. (2005), at 4.

69 Justice Souter (majority opinion), *McCreary County v. ACLU of Kentucky*, at 4.

70 Justice Souter (majority opinion), *McCreary County v. ACLU of Kentucky*, at 25.

71 Justice Souter (majority opinion), *McCreary County v. ACLU of Kentucky*, at 30.

72 Justice Souter (majority opinion), *McCreary County v. ACLU of Kentucky*, at 28.

73 Justice Scalia (dissenting, joined by Rehnquist, Thomas, and in part by Kennedy), *McCreary County v. ACLU of Kentucky*, at 3.

74 Justice Scalia (dissenting), *McCreary County v. ACLU of Kentucky*, at 4.

75 Justice Scalia (dissenting), *McCreary County v. ACLU of Kentucky*, at 6.

76 "The First Amendment mandates governmental neutrality between religion and religion, and between religion and nonreligion" (*Epperson v. Arkansas*, at 104).

77 Justice Scalia (dissenting), *McCreary County v. ACLU of Kentucky*, at 9–10.

78 Justice Scalia (dissenting), *McCreary County v. ACLU of Kentucky*, at 10.

79 Justice Scalia (dissenting), *McCreary County v. ACLU of Kentucky*, at 17.

80 Justice Scalia (dissenting), *McCreary County v. ACLU of Kentucky*, at 10.

81 This first part of Scalia's dissent in *McCreary County v. ACLU of Kentucky* was notably *not* endorsed by Justice Kennedy, a conservative who often took centrist lines on religion–state issues.

82 Justice Kennedy (dissenting), *County of Allegheny v. ACLU*, 492 U.S. 573 (1989), at 659.

83 Justice Kennedy (dissenting), *County of Allegheny v. ACLU*, at 657.

84 *Lee et al. v. Weisman*, 505 U.S. 577 (1992), at 581.

85 *Lee et al. v. Weisman*, at 590 and 592, respectively.

86 *Lee et al. v. Weisman*, at 593.

87 *Lee et al. v. Weisman*, at 593.

88 Justice Souter (concurring) refers to fellow judge Rehnquist in this respect, *Lee et al. v. Weisman*, at 612.

89   Justice Souter (concurring), *Lee et al. v. Weisman*, at 610.

90   Justice Scalia (dissenting), *Lee et al. v. Weisman*, at 642.

91   Justice Scalia (dissenting), *Lee et al. v. Weisman*, at 646.

92   Justice Scalia (dissenting), *Lee et al. v. Weisman*, at 646.

93   As do, of course, many other religio-national symbolisms, such as the very national motto "In God we trust," which is also imprinted on all coins and paper money.

94   The plaintiff, Michael Newdow, the divorced father of a Californian school girl subjected to the Pledge, was declared to lack "standing" in this case because he was not the legal custodian of his daughter. See *Elk Grove Unified School District v. Newdow et al.*, 542 U.S. (2004).

95   *Elk Grove Unified School District v. Newdow et al.*, at 3.

96   Justice Thomas (concurring), *Elk Grove Unified School District v. Newdow et al.*, at 4.

97   Justice Rehnquist (concurring), *Elk Grove Unified School District v. Newdow et al.*, at 14.

98   Justice O'Connor (concurring), *Elk Grove Unified School District v. Newdow et al.*, at 9.

99   Justice O'Connor (concurring), *Elk Grove Unified School District v. Newdow et al.*, at 3.

100   Justice O'Connor (concurring), *Elk Grove Unified School District v. Newdow et al.*, at 5.

101   Justice O'Connor (concurring), *Elk Grove Unified School District v. Newdow et al.*, at 9. O'Connor mentions in this context that teachers, not chaplains, are employed for the recital of the Pledge.

102   Justice O'Connor (concurring), *Elk Grove Unified School District v. Newdow et al.*, at 10–11.

103   *Rosenberger et al. v. Rector and Visitors of University of Virginia et al.*, 515 U.S. 819 (1995), at 868.

104   Justice Souter (dissenting), *Rosenberger et al. v. University of Virginia*, at 868.

105   "Who does not see that...the same authority which can force a citizen to contribute three pence only of his property for the support of any one establishment, may force him to conform to any other establishment in all cases whatsoever?" (James Madison, quoted in *Rosenberger et al. v. University of Virginia*, at 868).

106   Stanley Fish, "Is Religion Special?" *New York Times*, July 26, 2010 (*opiniator.blogs.nytimes.com/2010/07/26/is-religion-special/*).

107   Justice Souter (dissenting), *Rosenberger et al. v. University of Virginia*, at 885.

108   Justice Thomas (plurality opinion), *Mitchell et al. v. Helms et al.*, 530 U.S. (2000), at 31. However, *Mitchell et al. v. Helms et al.* was decided only by a "plurality," not a "majority," of the court, and so it is not legally binding on further case law.

109   "[P]eyote plant embodies their deity, and eating it is an act of worship and communion" (Justice Blackmun, dissenting, *Employment Division, Oregon Department of Human Resources v. Smith*, 494 U.S. 872 [1990], at 919).

110 Justice Scalia (majority opinion), *Employment Division v. Smith*, at 878–9.
111 Justice Scalia (majority opinion), *Employment Division v. Smith*, at 890.
112 Justice Burger (majority opinion), *Lynch v. Donnelly*, 465 U.S. 668 (1984), at 681.
113 Justice Burger (majority opinion), *Lynch v. Donnelly*, at 685.
114 Justice O'Connor (concurring), *Lynch v. Donnelly*, at 688.
115 Justice Brennan (dissenting), *Lynch v. Donnelly*, at 700.
116 Justice Brennan (dissenting), *Lynch v. Donnelly*, at 701.
117 Justice Brennan (dissenting), *Lynch v. Donnelly*, at 718.
118 Justice Brennan (dissenting), *Lynch v. Donnelly*, at 725.
119 Justice Blackmun (majority opinion), *County of Allegheny v. ACLU*, 492 U.S. 573 (1989), at 598.
120 Justice Blackmun (majority opinion), *County of Allegheny v. ACLU*, at 614.
121 Justice Blackmun (majority opinion), *County of Allegheny v. ACLU*, at 587.
122 Justice Brennan (dissenting), *County of Allegheny v. ACLU*, at 641, 654, 655.
123 Justice Kennedy (dissenting), *County of Allegheny v. ACLU*, at 674, 676.
124 Justice Kennedy (dissenting), *County of Allegheny v. ACLU*, at 655.
125 A photograph of the monolith is annexed to the dissent by Justice Stevens. *Van Orden v. Perry*, 545 U.S. (2005) (Appendix to opinion of Stevens J.).
126 Syllabus, *Van Orden v. Perry*, at 3. This was one reason cited by "swing" Justice Breyer to be lenient toward the Texas monument, but to say "nay" to the rather more recent Kentucky exhibit.
127 Justice Breyer (concurring), *Van Orden v. Perry*, at 4.
128 Justice Rehnquist (plurality opinion, joined by Justices Scalia, Kennedy, and Thomas), *Van Orden v. Perry*, at 5, fn. 3). A "plurality opinion" is that opinion joined by most other judges in a particular case, though it stays short of a majority. It is thus not binding for further case law.
129 Justice Stevens (dissenting), *Van Orden v. Perry*, at 7.
130 Justice Rehnquist (plurality opinion), *Van Orden v. Perry*, at 11.
131 Justice Scalia (concurring), *Van Orden v. Perry*, at 1.
132 Justice Breyer (concurring), *Van Orden v. Perry*, at 6.
133 This line was affirmed in the Supreme Court's so far last religious symbol case, *Salazar, Secretary of the Interior, et al. v. Buono*, 559 U.S. (2010). I briefly discuss this case in the Conclusion.

Chapter 4   Challenge to the Secular State (II): Islam in Europe

1 In 2010, there were 19 million Muslims in the European Union, amounting to 3.8 percent of its population (Pew Research Center 2011).
2 As Jean Cohen of Columbia University put it in a private conversation.

3   Giovanni Sartori, "L'integrazione degli islamici," *Corriere della Sera*, December 9, 2009; Sartori, "Una replica ai pensabenisti sull'Islam," *Corriere della Sera*, January 10, 2010.

4   Apart from Huntington's famous polemic (1996), there has been a resurgence of more sober academic reasoning in civilizational terms (Collins 2004; Katzenstein and Checkel 2009; Meyer 1989).

5   "Culture" is "the overall way of life of a people" (Huntington 1996: 41).

6   See the convincing critique of "civilizationalism" as "the last refuge of scoundrels" by Huntington's Harvard colleague Mottahedeh (1995: 14).

7   See also Paul Starr: "Liberalism values various kinds of separation (separation of powers, of church and state, of knowledge and politics) as a means of protecting values specific to particular institutions and spheres of life" (2007: 54).

8   I quote from a written commentary by Samuel Heilman (2011) on my presentation of a previous version of this section at CUNY Graduate Center, New York, May 5, 2011.

9   Yusuf al-Qaradawi, "Duties of Muslims Living in the West," *IslamOnline. net*, May 27, 2007.

10   However, al-Qaradawi later qualified his position, advocating "integration without assimilation," which includes "positively interacting with non-Muslim communities" (2003: 6, 8).

11   There *is* a "radical" element in *Radical Reform* (2009), which consists at the theoretical level of replacing "law" by "ethics" and even integrating elements of natural law. However, Ramadan still arrives at practical conclusions that are "not particularly radical or challenging" (March 2010: 256).

12   See a survey commissioned by *Le Monde*, according to which 68 percent of the French and 75 percent of the Germans polled found that Muslims "are not well integrated" in their respective societies ("Islam et intégration," *Le Monde*, January 5, 2011, p. 1). 42 percent of the French, who in European comparison had always held moderate to positive views of Muslims, even think that Muslims are "rather a threat" (p. 9).

13   For an unambiguously liberal adoption of political liberalism, which even concedes that it requires Muslims' "self-restraint in public discourses," see Abou El Fadl (1996).

14   Even fellow liberal Muslim scholars have expressed "doubts regarding the Islamic plausibility of An-Na'im's arguments," pointing to the fact that the revelation "could also provide a plausible basis for a religious state" (Fadel 2009: 103).

15   "By civic reason, I mean that the rationale and the purpose of public policy or legislation must be based on the sort of reasoning that most citizens can accept or reject" (An-Na'im 2008: 7).

16   Consider, for instance, that Switzerland introduced the female right to vote as late as 1971.

17   Conseil d'État, June 27, 2008, Mme Faiza M., req. No. 286/98. This rule has since been generalized into a requirement that applicants for French citizenship must not wear a burka or niqab (hiding the face of the woman).

18   Al-Qaradawi (1998) is structured according to non-enumerated sections. Quotes from the text are identified by section titles followed by page numbers.

19   For a rather one-sided "inter-religious dialogue," not reciprocated by Islam, see Jenkins (2007: 269–71).

20   Ramadan (2001) is a suboptimal translation of the French original. The French word "gerent," used without explication in the English translation, means "agent" (as against "principal").

21   This section and the one following build and expand on parts of Joppke (2014).

22   The percentage of British Muslims saying that there is "conflict" is slightly smaller (47 percent) (Pew Research Center 2006: 3).

23   Niall Ferguson, "Eurabia?" *New York Times*, April 4, 2004, p. 13.

24   Note, for instance, that until 1988, the Swiss Civil Code stated that the husband was the head of the family; that the wife's duty was to run the household; and that in the case of divorce she was entitled to only one-third of any increase in the couple's joint wealth during their marriage (see Büchler 2012).

25   The unilateral divorce by *talaq* is available only to men; in case of divorce, child custody is to be automatically transferred to the father when the child turns seven years old; and girls inherit only half as much as boys.

26   Williams' speech does not contain the controversial notion that the adoption of sharia in the United Kingdom was "unavoidable." It apparently stemmed from an interview given by the Archbishop (see Tucker 2008: 463).

27   This claim is contested, because the Arbitration Act mostly applies to commercial (and not family) disputes. A government minister confirmed in 2008 that "[r]eligious courts are always subservient to the established family courts of England and Wales," and their decisions thus have no legal effect (quoted in Grillo 2012: 224).

28   Apparently, since September 2007, the British government, under Labour Prime Minister Tony Blair, had been "quietly sanctioning" Muslim Arbitration Councils operating under the Arbitration Act, on the condition that the involved parties agreed to them and that their decisions were approved by civil courts (see Moore 2010: 105).

29   European Court of Human Rights, *Case of Refah Partisi and Others v. Turkey*, decision of February 13, 2003, at para. 124.

30   John Bowen, "Panorama's Exposé of Sharia Councils Didn't Tell the Full Story," *Guardian*, April 26, 2013.

31   Bowen, "Panorama's Exposé of Sharia Councils."

32   In *Uddin v. Choudhury* (2009), the English Court of Appeal recognized the Islamic law concept of *mahr* (the case is discussed in Bowen 2010b).

33   In *EM (Lebanon) v. Home Secretary* ([2008] UKHL), the House of Lords denounced as "arbitrary and discriminatory" a (Lebanese) sharia rule that requires a child to be turned over to its father's custody at age seven, and on this basis granted its Lebanese mother asylum in the United Kingdom.

Conclusion: Islam and Christianity in the Secular State

1   The French 2004 Law on Laicity, which prohibits "ostensible religious symbols" in public schools, obviously restricts religious symbols proper.

2   Cases in point are the German anti-veiling laws in some *Länder*, which single out the Islamic headscarf for its political dimension (which Catholic veils do not share) (Joppke 2009a: 72–4); or the French anti-burka law of 2010, which rests on the notion of the extreme veil as a political symbol of oppressing females that is not prescribed by Qur'an (Joppke and Torpey 2013: 25–6).

3   For a classic statement, see Devlin: "No society has yet solved the problem of how to teach morality without religion" (1963: 25). The dramatic retreat of religion-based public morality since the 1960s is shown by McLeod (2010: ch. 10).

4   Including fashion, which, however, in the Islamic world is premised on a religious meaning (see "Hijab Couture," *The Economist*, April 26, 2014, p. 54).

5   ECtHR, *Case of Lautsi v. Italy*, decision of November 3, 2009, at para. 32.

6   Marco Ventura in the *Corriere della Sera* (Italy's leading newspaper), quoted by Annicchino (2011: 214).

7   German Federal Constitutional Court, decision of May 16, 1995 (*Crucifix*), 1 BvR 1087/91.

8   Only consider that the Vatican had fiercely opposed the founding of the first Italian nation-state in the late nineteenth century, mandating Italian Catholics to stay away from it. After all, the Vatican, to the present day, is its own "state," with no interest in seeing itself diminished by an Italian state. Italy is a typical mono-Catholic country deeply divided between religionists and secularists (see Martin 1978). For the nineteenth century, even into the early twentieth century, René Rémond speaks of a "conflict between patriotism and Catholicism" (1998: ch. 7). It is true, however, that Lautsi I was rejected by the large majority of Italians (see Joppke 2013c: 115).

9   Patrick Gregor Puppinck, "Lautsi v. Italy: An Alliance Against Secularism," *L'Osservatore Romano*, July 28.

10 The same irony, of course, marks the German crucifix case, which was decided on the basis of the negative religious liberty clause in the German Basic Law (Article 4). The latter thus protected the son of atheist parents from having to "learn under the cross," as the German Federal Constitutional Court put it.

11 ECtHR (Grand Chamber), *Lautsi and Others v. Italy*, decision of March 18, 2011.

12 *Lautsi and Others v. Italy*, at para. 57.

13 *Lautsi and Others v. Italy*, at para. 58.

14 *Lautsi and Others v. Italy*, at p. 27.

15 *Lautsi and Others v. Italy*, at p. 30.

16 *Lautsi and Others v. Italy*, at para. 58.

17 *Lautsi and Others v. Italy*, at para. 47.

18   At least this is what one must conclude from his parable of Marco and Leonardo, told to the Strasbourg court during Lautsi II. See the critical discussion by Pajno (2011).

19   *Lautsi and Others v. Italy*, at para. 72.

20   *Lautsi and Others v. Italy*, at para. 67.

21   ECtHR, *Dahlab v. Switzerland*, decision of February 15, 2001.

22   ECtHR, *Case of Lautsi v. Italy*, decision of November 3, 2009, at para. 55.

23   *Lautsi and Others v. Italy* (2011), at para. 68.

24   Apart from the veil, particularly the vitriolic exclusions of Islam from Western public spheres have rested on its "politicization." A pertinent example is minarets, which in Switzerland's successful 2009 referendum were rejected as a "symbol of political and aggressive Islam" (quoted by Liviatan 2012: 110).

25   See the instructive comparison between recent European and American high court decisions on "religious symbols on government property," revealing a "growing convergence" between Europe and America (Witte and Arold 2011).

26   US Supreme Court, *Salazar, Secretary of the Interior, et al. v. Buono*, 559 U.S. 700 (2010), decision of April 28, 2010, at 11 (majority opinion of Justice Kennedy).

27   Of course, this statement is only valid abstracted from the state's immigration powers, that is, within its borders.

28   Justice Alito (dissenting, joined by Scalia and Thomas), *Christian Legal Society v. Martinez*, 561 U.S. (2010), US Supreme Court decision of June 28, 2010, at 3.

29   Justice Ginsburg (majority opinion), *Christian Legal Society v. Martinez*, at 30.

30   Justice Alito (dissenting, joined by Scalia and Thomas), *Christian Legal Society v. Martinez*, at 22.

31   As summarized by Stanley Fish, "Is Religion Special?" *New York Times*, July 26, 2010 (*opiniator.blogs.nytimes.com/2010/07/26/is-religion-special/*).

32   Fish, "Is Religion Special?"

33   Fish, "Is Religion Special?"

34   Justice Alito (dissenting, joined by Scalia and Thomas), *Christian Legal Society v. Martinez*, at 1.

35   See Stanley Fish, "Being Neutral Is Oh So Hard to Do," *New York Times*, July 19, 2010 (*opinionator.blogs.nytimes.com/2010/07/19/being-neutral-is-oh-so-hard-to-do/*).

36   *R. v. The Governing Body of Jewish Free School* (JFS) (2009 UKSC 15).

37   Lord Hope (minority judgment), *R. v. The Governing Body of JFS*, at 60.

38   Faith schools are exempted by the 2010 Equality Act from the prohibition against discrimination on grounds of religion; but this does not exempt them from the prohibition of discrimination on ethnic or racial grounds (see Lord Mance, *R. v. The Governing Body of JFS*, at 27).

39   Lord Phillips (President), *R. v. The Governing Body of JFS*, at 5.

40   Lord Phillips (President), *R. v. The Governing Body of JFS*, at 13.

41 Lord Phillips (President), *R. v. The Governing Body of JFS*, at 4.
42 Lord Phillips (President), *R. v. The Governing Body of JFS*, at 11.
43 As conceded by Lord Phillips (President), *R. v. The Governing Body of JFS*, at 4.
44 Lady Hale, *R. v. The Governing Body of JFS*, at 24.
45 Lady Hale, *R. v. The Governing Body of JFS*, at 24.
46 Quoted by Lord Phillips (President), *R. v. The Governing Body of JFS*, at 3.

References

Abou El Fadl, Khaled. 1996. "Muslim Minorities and Self-Restraint in Liberal Democracies," *Loyola of Los Angeles Law Review* 29: 1525–42.

Ahmed, Leila. 1992. *Women and Gender in Islam.* New Haven: Yale University Press.

al-Alwani, Tahar Jabir. 2003. *Towards a Fiqh for Minorities.* London: The International Institute of Islamic Thought.

al-Qaradawi, Yusuf. 1960. *The Lawful and the Prohibited in Islam* (*www.witness-pioneer.org/vil/Books/Q_LP/*).

al-Qaradawi, Yusuf. 1987. *Islamic Awakening between Rejection and Extremism.* Herndon, VA: The International Institute of Islamic Thought.

al-Qaradawi, Yusuf. 1998. *The Status of Women in Islam* (*www.witness-pioneer.org/vil/Books/Q_WI/*).

al-Qaradawi, Yusuf. 2003. *Fiqh of Muslim Minorities.* Cairo: Al-Falah Foundation.

al-Raziq, Ali Abd. 1998. "Message Not Government, Religion Not State," in Charles Kurzman, ed., *Liberal Islam: A Sourcebook.* New York: Oxford University Press.

Allawi, Ali A. 2009. *The Crisis of Islamic Civilization.* New Haven: Yale University Press.

An-Na'im, Abdullahi. 1990. *Toward an Islamic Reformation: Civil Liberties, Human Rights, and International Law.* Syracuse, NY: Syracuse University Press.

205

An-Na'im, Abdullahi. 2008. *Islam and the Secular State*. Cambridge, MA: Harvard University Press.

Anidjar, Gil. 2012. "On the European Question," *Forum Bosnae* 55: 13–27.

Annicchino, Pasquale. 2011. "Winning the Battle by Losing the War: The *Lautsi* Case and the Holy Alliance between American Conservative Evangelicals, the Russian Orthodox Church and the Vatican to Reshape European Identity," *Religion and Human Rights* 6: 213–19.

Armstrong, Karen. 2000. *The Battle for God*. New York: Knopf.

Asad, Talal. 2003. *Formation of the Secular: Christianity, Islam, Modernity*. Stanford: Stanford University Press.

Bartkowski, John P. and Jen'nan Ghazal Read. 2003. "Veiled Submission: Gender, Power, and Identity among Evangelical and Muslim Women in the United States," *Qualitative Sociology* 26(1): 71–92.

Bedi, Sonu. 2007. "What Is So Special About Religion? The Dilemma of the Religious Exemption," *Journal of Political Philosophy* 15(2): 235–49.

Bellah, Robert N. 1964. "Religious Evolution," *American Sociological Review* 29(3): 358–74.

Bellah, Robert N. 1967. "Civil Religion in America," *Daedalus* 96: 1–21.

Bellah, Robert N. 2005. "What Is Axial About the Axial Age?" *European Journal of Sociology* 46: 69–87.

Bellah, Robert N. 2011. *Religion in Human Evolution*. Cambridge, MA: Harvard University Press.

Bellah, Robert N., Richard Madsen, William M. Sullivan, Ann Swidler, and Steven M. Tipton. 1985. *Habits of the Heart*. Berkeley: University of California Press.

Berger, Peter L. 1967. *The Sacred Canopy*. New York: Random House.

Berger, Peter L. 1999. "The Desecularization of the World: A Global Overview," in Peter L. Berger, ed., *The Desecularization of the World*. Washington, DC: Ethics and Public Policy Center.

Berger, Peter L. and Thomas Luckmann. 1967. *The Social Construction of Reality*. New York: Doubleday.

Berman, Harold J. 1983. *Law and Revolution: The Formation of the Western Legal Tradition*. Cambridge, MA: Harvard University Press.

Berman, Paul. 2003. *Terror and Liberalism*. New York: Norton.

Berman, Paul. 2007. "Who's Afraid of Tariq Ramadan?" *New Republic*, June 4.

Berman, Paul. 2010. *The Flight of the Intellectuals*. New York: Melville House.

Beyer, Peter. 2006. *Religions in Global Society*. London: Routledge.

Bhargava, Rajeev. 1998. "What is Secularism For?" in Rajeev Bhargava, ed., *Secularism and Its Critics*. New Delhi: Oxford University Press.

Bhargava, Rajeev. 2010. "States, Religious Diversity, and the Crisis of Secularism," *Hedgehog Review* Fall: 8–22.

Binder, Leonard. 1988. *Islamic Liberalism*. Chicago: University of Chicago Press.

Black, Antony. 2008. *The West and Islam: Religion and Political Thought in World History*. Oxford: Oxford University Press.

Black, Antony. 2011. *The History of Islamic Political Thought*. Edinburgh: Edinburgh University Press.

Blaschke, Olaf. 2000. "Das 19. Jahrhundert: Ein Zweites Konfessionelles Zeit-alter?" *Geschichte und Gesellschaft* 26: 38–75.

Bono, Samia. 2012. *Muslim Women and Shari'ah Councils*. Basingstoke: Palgrave.

Bowen, John. 2010a. *Can Islam be French?* Princeton: Princeton University Press.

Bowen, John. 2010b. "How Could English Courts Recognize Shariah?" *University of St. Thomas Law Journal* 7(3): 411–35.

Boy, John D. and John Torpey. 2013. "Inventing the Axial Age: The Origins and Uses of a Historical Concept," *Theory and Society* 42(3): 241–59.

Brettfeld, Katrin and Peter Wetzels. 2007. *Muslime in Deutschland*. Berlin: Bundesministerium des Inneren.

Brown, Carl. 2000. *Religion and State: The Muslim Approach to Politics*. New York: Columbia University Press.

Brubaker, Rogers. 2012. "Religion and Nationalism: Four Approaches," *Nations and Nationalism* 18(1): 2–20.

Brubaker, Rogers. 2013a. "Language, Religion and the Politics of Difference," *Nations and Nationalism* 19(1): 1–20.

Brubaker, Rogers. 2013b. "Categories of Analysis and Categories of Practice: A Note on the Study of Muslims in European Countries of Immigration," *Ethnic and Racial Studies* 36(1): 1–8.

Bruce, Steven. 1988. *The Rise and Fall of the New Christian Right: Conservative Protestant Politics, 1978–1988*. Oxford: Oxford University Press.

Bruce, Steven. 2011. *Secularization: In Defence of an Unfashionable Theory*. Oxford: Oxford University Press.

Büchler, Andrea. 2012. "Islamic Family Law in Europe?" *International Journal of Law in Context* 8 (*http://www.rwi.uzh.ch/oe/cimels/IslamicLawInEurope .pdf*).

Buruma, Ian and Avishai Margalit. 2004. *Occidentalism*. New York: Penguin.

Caldwell, Christopher. 2009. *Reflections on the Revolution in Europe*. New York: Penguin.

Carter, Stephen. 1994. *The Culture of Disbelief*. New York: Anchor.

Casanova, José. 1994. *Public Religion in the Modern World*. Chicago: University of Chicago Press.

Casanova, José. 2006. "Rethinking Secularization: A Global Comparative Approach," *Hedgehog Review* Spring and Summer: 7–22.

Casanova, José. 2011. "The Secular, Secularization, Secularisms," in Craig Calhoun, Mark Juergensmeyer, and Jonathan VanAntwerpen, eds, *Rethinking Secularism*. New York: Oxford University Press.

Cavanaugh, William T. 1995. "'A Fire Strong Enough to Consume the House': The Wars of Religion and the Rise of the State," *Modern Theology* 11(4): 397–420.

Champion, Françoise. 1993. "Entre laïcisation et sécularisation," *Le débat* 77: 46–72.

Chaves, Mark. 2011. *American Religion: Contemporary Trends*. Princeton: Princeton University Press.

Chaves, Mark and Philip S. Gorski. 2001. "Religious Pluralism and Religious Participation," *Annual Review of Sociology* 27: 261–81.

Chodorow, Nancy. 1999. *The Reproduction of Mothering: Psychoanalysis and the Sociology of Gender*. Berkeley and Los Angeles: University of California Press.

Cohen, Jean. 2012. "The Politics and Risks of the New Legal Pluralism in the Domain of Intimacy," *International Journal of Constitutional Law* 10(2): 380–97.

Cohen, Jean. 2013a. "Political Religion vs. Non-Establishment: Reflections on 21st-Century Political Theology. Part I," *Philosophy and Social Criticism* 39(4–5): 443–69.

Cohen, Jean. 2013b. "Political Religion vs. Non-Establishment. Part II," *Philosophy and Social Criticism* 39(6): 507–21.

Colley, Linda. 1994. *Britons*. New Haven: Yale University Press.

Collins, Randall. 1998. *The Sociology of Philosophies*. Cambridge, MA: Harvard University Press.

Collins, Randall. 2004. "Civilizations as Zones of Prestige and Social Contact," in Said Arjomand and Edward Tiryakian, eds, *Rethinking Civilizational Analysis*. London: Sage.

Conze, Werner, Hans-Wolfgang Strätz, and Hermann Zabel. 1984. "Säkularisation, Säkularisierung," in Otto Brunner, Werne Conze, and Reinhard Koselleck, eds, *Geschichtliche Grundbegriffe*. Vol. 5, Stuttgart: Klett-Cotta.

Coulson, Noel J. 1957. "The State and the Individual in Islamic Law," *International and Comparative Law Quarterly* 6(1): 49–60.

Crone, Patricia. 2004. *Medieval Islamic Political Thought*. Edinburgh: Edinburgh University Press.

Cumper, Peter. 2014. "Multiculturalism, Human Rights and the Accommodation of Sharia Law," *Human Rights Law Review* 14(1): 31–57.

Dahrendorf, Ralf. 1968. *Gesellschaft und Demokratie in Deutschland*. Munich: DTV.

Dassetto, Felice, Silvio Ferrari, and Brigitte Maréchal. 2007. *Islam in the European Union*. Brussels: European Parliament.

Dawkins, Richard. 2006. *The God Delusion*. London: Bantam Press.

de Waal, Frans. 2013. *The Bonobos and the Atheist*. New York: Norton.

Devlin, Patrick. 1963. *The Enforcement of Morals*. Oxford: Oxford University Press.

Dionne, E.J., Jr. 2008. *Souled Out: Reclaiming Faith and Politics after the Religious Right*. Princeton: Princeton University Press.

Dobbelaere, Karel. 2009. "The Meaning and Scope of Secularization," in Peter Clarke, ed., *The Oxford Handbook of the Sociology of Religion*. Oxford: Oxford University Press.

Dobbelaere, Karel and Jan Lauwers. 1973/4. "Definition of Religion: A Sociological Critique," *Social Compass* 20: 535–51.

Doe, Norman. 2011. *Law and Religion in Europe*. Oxford: Oxford University Press.

Donnelly, Jack. 1982. "Human Rights and Human Dignity: An Analytic Critique of Non-Western Conceptions of Human Rights," *American Political Science Review* 76(2): 303–16.

Douglas, Gillin, Sophie Gilliat-Ray, Norman Doe, Russell Sandberg, and Asma Khan. 2011. *Social Cohesion and Civil Law: Marriage, Divorce and Religious Courts*. Cardiff: University of Cardiff.

Durkheim, Émile. 1960 [1912]. *Les formes élémentaires de la vie religieuse*. Paris: Presses Universitaires de France.

Eisenstadt, S.N. 1999. *Fundamentalism, Sectarianism, and Revolution*. Cambridge: Cambridge University Press.

Eisenstadt, S.N. 2000. "Multiple Modernities," *Daedalus* 129(1): 1–29.

Eisgruber, Christopher and Lawrence Sager. 2007. *Religious Freedom and the Constitution*. Cambridge, MA: Harvard University Press.

El Shakankiri, Mohammed. 1981. "Loi divine, loi humaine, et droit dans l'histoire juridique de l'Islam," *Revue Internationale de droit comparé* 33(3): 767–86.

Elver, Hilal. 2012. *The Headscarf Controversy*. New York: Oxford University Press.

Ely, John Hart. 1980. *Democracy and Distrust*. Cambridge, MA: Harvard University Press.

Fadel, Mohammad. 2008. "The True, the Good and the Reasonable," *Canadian Journal of Law and Jurisprudence* 21(1): 1–65.

Fadel, Mohammad. 2009. "Islamic Politics and Secular Politics: Can They Co-Exist?" *Journal of Law and Religion* 25: 101–18.

Feinberg, Joel. 1985. *The Moral Limits of the Criminal Law*. Vol. 2. New York: Oxford University Press.

Feldman, Noah. 2002a. "The Intellectual Origins of the Establishment Clause," *New York University Law Review* 72: 346–428.

Feldman, Noah. 2002b. "From Liberty to Equality: The Transformation of the Establishment Clause," *California Law Review* 90(3): 673–731.

Feldman, Noah. 2005. *Divided by God*. New York: Farrar, Straus and Giroux.

Feldman, Noah. 2007. "Shari'a and Islamic Democracy in the Age of Al-Jazeera," in Abbas Amanat and Frank Griffel, eds, *Shari'a: Islamic Law in the Contemporary Context*. Palo Alto, CA: Stanford University Press.

Ferrari, Silvio. 1995. "The Emerging Pattern of Church and State in Western Europe: The Italian Model," *Brigham Young University Law Review* 2: 421–37.

Ferrari, Silvio. 2002. "Islam and the Western European Model of Church and State Relations," in W.A.R. Shadid and P.S. van Koningsveld, eds, *Religious Freedom and the Neutrality of the State: The Position of Islam in the European Union*. Leuven: Peeters.

Ferrari, Silvio. 2011. "Religion and the Public/Private Divide in the European Legal System." Typescript (in author's possession).

Ferrari, Silvio. 2012a. "The Christian Roots of the Secular State." Typescript (in author's possession).

Ferrari, Silvio. 2012b. "Constitution et religion," in Dominique Chagnollaud and Michel Troper, eds, *Traité international de droit constitutionnel*. Vol. 3. Paris: Dalloz.

Feuerbach, Ludwig. 1978 [1849]. *Das Wesen des Christentums*. Stuttgart: Reklam.

Finer, Samuel E. 1997. *The History of Government*. Vol. 2. Oxford: Oxford University Press.

Finke, Roger. 1990. "Religious Deregulation: Origins and Consequences," *Journal of Church and State* 32(1): 609–26.

Finke, Roger and Rodney Stark. 2006. *The Churching of America, 1776–2005*. New Brunswick: Rutgers University Press.

Fish, Stanley. 1997. "Mission Impossible: Settling the Just Bounds between Church and State," *Columbia Law Review* 97(8): 2255–333.

Foblets, Marie-Claire. 2000. "Migrant Women Caught between Islamic Family Law and Women's Rights," *Maastricht Journal of European and Comparative Law* 7: 11–34.

Fogarty, Michael P. 1957. *Christian Democracy in Western Europe 1820–1953*. London: Routledge and Kegan Paul.

Formisano, Ronald. 2012. *The Tea Party*. Baltimore, MD: Johns Hopkins University Press.

Fourest, Caroline. 2004. *Frère Tariq*. Paris: Grasset.

Fredman, Sandra. 2011. *Discrimination Law* (2nd edition). Oxford: Oxford University Press.

Freud, Sigmund. 1974 [1912–13]. "Totem und Tabu," in Sigmund Freud, *Studienausgabe*. Vol. 9. Frankfurt am Main: Fischer Verlag.

Freud, Sigmund. 1974 [1927]. "Die Zukunft einer Illusion," in Sigmund Freud, *Studienausgabe*. Vol. 9. Frankfurt am Main: Fischer Verlag.

Freud, Sigmund. 1974 [1930]. "Das Unbehagen in der Kultur," in Sigmund Freud, *Studienausgabe*. Vol. 9. Frankfurt am Main: Fischer Verlag.

Freud, Sigmund. 1974 [1939]. "Der Mann Moses und die monotheistische Religion: Drei Abhandlungen," in Sigmund Freud, *Studienausgabe*. Vol. 9. Frankfurt am Main: Fischer Verlag.

Friedland, Roger. 2002. "Money, Sex, and God: The Erotic Logic of Religious Nationalism," *Sociological Theory* 20(2): 381–425.

Gallie, W.B. 1956. "Essentially Contested Concepts," *Proceedings of the Aristotelian Society* 56: 167–98.

Gallup. 2009. *The Gallup Coexist Index 2009: A Global Study of Interfaith Relations*. Washington, DC.

Gambetta, Diego and Steffen Hertog. 2009. "Why Are There So Many Engineers among Islamic Radicals?" *European Journal of Sociology* 50(2): 201–30.

Gauchet, Marcel. 1997 [1985]. *The Disenchantment of the World: A Political History of Religion*. Princeton: Princeton University Press.

Gellner, Ernest. 1978. *Nations and Nationalism*. Ithaca, NY: Cornell University Press.

Gellner, Ernest. 1992. *Postmodernism, Reason and Religion*. London: Routledge.

Gey, Steven G. 2007. "Life After the Establishment Clause," *West Virginia Law Review* 110: 1–49.

Gill, Anthony. 2008. *The Political Origins of Religious Liberty*. New York: Cambridge University Press.

Glazer, Sarah. 2012. "Sharia Controversy," *Global Researcher* 6(1): 1–28.

Goldberg, Michelle. 2007. *Kingdom Coming: The Rise of Christian Nationalism*. New York: W.W. Norton.

Goody, Jack. 1961. "Religion and Ritual: The Definitional Problem," *British Journal of Sociology* 12(2): 142–64.

Goody, Jack. 2004. *Islam in Europe.* Cambridge: Polity.

Gorski, Philip S. 2000a. "Historicizing the Secularization Debate: Church, State, and Society in Late Medieval and Early Modern Europe, ca. 1300 to 1700," *American Sociological Review* 65: 138–67.

Gorski, Philip S. 2000b. "The Mosaic Moment," *American Journal of Sociology* 105(5): 1428–68.

Gorski, Philip S. 2003. *The Disciplinary Revolution: Calvinism and the Rise of the State in Early Modern Europe.* Chicago: University of Chicago Press.

Gorski, Philip S. and Ates Altinordu. 2008. "After Secularization?" *Annual Review of Sociology* 34: 55–85.

Gould, Stephen Jay. 1997. "Nonoverlapping Magisteria," *Natural History* 106: 16–22.

Graf, Friedrich Wilhelm. 2007. "Protestantismus," in Hans Joas and Klaus Wiegandt, eds, *Säkularisierung und die Weltreligionen.* Frankfurt am Main: Fischer.

Greeley, Andrew and Michael Hout. 2006. *The Truth About Conservative Christians.* Chicago: University of Chicago Press.

Greenawalt, Kent. 2009. *Religion and the Constitution. Volume 2: Establishment and Fairness.* Princeton: Princeton University Press.

Greenfeld, Liah. 2001. *The Spirit of Capitalism: Nationalism and Economic Growth.* Cambridge, MA: Harvard University Press.

Greenhouse, Linda and Reva B. Siegel. 2011. "Before (and After) *Roe v. Wade*: New Questions about Backlash," *Yale Law Journal* 120: 2028–87.

Grillo, Ralph. 2012. "In the Shadow of the Law: Muslim Marriage and Divorce in the UK," in Rubya Mehdi, Werner Menski, and Jorgen S. Nielsen, eds, *Interpreting Divorce Laws in Islam.* Copenhagen: DJOF Publishing.

Habermas, Jürgen. 1980. *Theorie des kommunikativen Handelns.* 2 vols. Frankfurt am Main: Suhrkamp.

Habermas, Jürgen. 1985. *Der philosophische Diskurs der Moderne.* Frankfurt am Main: Suhrkamp.

Habermas, Jürgen and Jacques Derrida. 2005. "February 15, or, What Binds Europeans Together: Plea for a Common Foreign Policy, Beginning in Core Europe," in Daniel Levy, Max Pensky, and John Torpey, eds, *Old Europe, New Europe, Core Europe: Transatlantic Relations After the Iraq War.* New York: Verso (originally in *Frankfurter Allgemeine Zeitung*, May 31, 2003).

Haddad, Yvonne Yazbeck and Tylor Golson. 2007. "Overhauling Islam," *Journal of Church and State* 49(3): 487–515.

Hafez, Kai. 2013. "Liberty, Equality and Intolerance: Islam in Liberal Europe." Typescript (in author's possession).

Hansen, Randall. 2011. *The Centrality of Employment in Immigrant Integration in Europe.* Washington, DC: Transatlantic Council on Migration.

Harding, Susan Friend. 2000. *The Book of Jerry Falwell.* Princeton: Princeton University Press.

Hart, H.L.A. 1963. *Law, Liberty, and Morality.* Oxford: Oxford University Press.

Hashemi, Nader. 2009. *Islam, Secularism, and Liberal Democracy.* New York: Oxford University Press.

Hastings, Adrian. 1997. *The Construction of Nationhood.* Cambridge: Cambridge University Press.

Heclo, Hugh. 2007. *Christianity and American Democracy.* Cambridge, MA: Harvard University Press.

Heilman, Samuel. 2011. "Comments on Joppke." Written comment provided at CUNY Graduate Center, New York, May 5.

Herberg, Will. 1960. *Protestant-Catholic-Jew* (revised edition). Garden City, NY: Anchor.

Hobbes, Thomas. 1996 [1651]. *Leviathan.* Oxford: Oxford University Press.

Hohfeld, Wesley Newcomb. 1919. *Fundamental Legal Concepts.* New Haven: Yale University Press.

Hout, Michael and Claude Fischer. 2002. "Why More Americans Have No Religious Preference: Politics and Generations," *American Sociological Review* 67(2): 165–90.

Hout, Michael, Andrew Greeley, and Melissa J. Wilde. 2001. "The Demographic Imperative in Religious Change in the United States," *American Journal of Sociology* 107(2): 468–500.

Hout, Michael, Claude S. Fischer, and Mark A. Chaves. 2013. *More Americans Have No Religious Preference: Key Finding from the 2012 General Social Survey.* University of California, Berkeley: Institute for the Study of Societal Issues, March.

Hunter, James Davison and Alan Wolfe. 2006. *Is There a Culture War?* Washington, DC: Pew Research Center, Brookings Institution Press.

Huntington, Samuel. 1996. *The Clash of Civilizations.* New York: Simon and Schuster.

Hurd, Elizabeth Shakman. 2008. *The Politics of Secularism in International Relations.* Princeton: Princeton University Press.

Jefferson, Thomas. 1802. *Letter to the Danbury Baptists* (http://www.loc.gov/loc/lcib/9806/danpre.html).

Jellinek, Georg. 1904. *Die Erklärung der Menschen- und Bürgerrechte.* Berlin: Duncker and Humblot.

Jenkins, Philip. 2007. *God's Continent.* New York: Oxford University Press.

Joas, Hans. 2004. *Warum braucht der Mensch Religion?* Munich: Herder.

Johnson, Paul E. 1978. *A Shopkeeper's Millennium.* New Haven: Yale University Press.

Joppke, Christian, ed. 1998. *Challenge to the Nation-State: Immigration in Western Europe and the United States.* Oxford: Oxford University Press.

Joppke, Christian. 2009a. *Veil: Mirror of Identity.* Cambridge: Polity.

Joppke, Christian. 2009b. "Limits of Integration Policy: Britain and Her Muslims," *Journal of Ethnic and Migration Studies* 35(3): 453–72.

Joppke, Christian. 2010. *Citizenship and Immigration.* Cambridge: Polity.

Joppke, Christian. 2013a. "Islam in Europa. Integration durch Recht und ihre Grenzen," *Kölner Zeitschrift für Soziologie und Sozialpsychologie* 65 (special issue 53 on "Religion und Gesellschaft," edited by Christoph Wolf and Matthias Koenig): 409–35.

Joppke, Christian. 2013b. "A Christian Identity for the Liberal State?" *British Journal of Sociology* 64(4): 597–616.

Joppke, Christian. 2013c. "Double Standards? Veils and Crucifixes in the European Legal Order," *European Journal of Sociology* 54(1): 97–123.

Joppke, Christian. 2014. "Europe and Islam: Alarmists, Victimists, and Integration by Law," *West European Politics* 37(6): 1314–35.

Joppke, Christian. Forthcoming. "Islam and the Legal Enforcement of Morality." *Theory & Society.*

Joppke, Christian and John Torpey. 2013. *Legal Integration of Islam: A Transatlantic Comparison.* Cambridge, MA: Harvard University Press.

Juergensmeyer, Mark. 2008. *Religious Challenges to the Secular State, from Christian Militias to al Qaeda.* Berkeley and Los Angeles: University of California Press

Kagan, Robert. 2003. *Of Paradise and Power.* New York: Knopf.

Kahn, Paul. 2011. *Political Theology.* Ithaca, NY: Cornell University Press.

Kalyvas, Stathis N. 1996. *The Rise of Christian Democracy in Europe.* Ithaca, NY: Cornell University Press.

Kalyvas, Stathis N. 2003. "Unsecular Politics and Religious Mobilization," in Thomas Kselman and Joseph A. Buttigieg, eds, *European Christian Democracy.* Notre Dame, IN: University of Notre Dame Press.

Karsh, Efraim. 2007. *Islamic Imperialism.* New Haven: Yale University Press.

Katzenstein, Peter and Jeffrey Checkel. 2009. "European Identity in Context," in Jeffrey Checkel and Peter Katzenstein, eds, *European Identity.* New York: Cambridge University Press.

Koenig, Matthias and Christoph Wolf. 2013. "Religion und Gesellschaft: Aktuelle Perspektiven," *Kölner Zeitschrift für Soziologie und Sozialpsychologie* 65 (special issue 53 on "Religion und Gesellschaft," edited by Christoph Wolf and Matthias Koenig): 1–23.

Kramnick, Isaac and R. Laurence Moore. 2005. *The Godless Constitution.* New York: W.W. Norton.

Kura, Ahmet. 2007. "Passive and Assertive Secularism," *World Politics* 59(4): 568–94.

Kurzman, Charles. 1998. "Liberal Islam and Its Islamic Context," in Charles Kurzman, ed., *Liberal Islam: A Sourcebook.* New York: Oxford University Press.

Kymlicka, Will. 1995. *Multicultural Citizenship.* Oxford: Oxford University Press.

Laborde, Cécile. 2013. "Political Liberalism and Religion: On Separation and Establishment," *Journal of Political Philosophy* 21(1): 67–86.

Lacorne, Denis. 2011. *Religion in America.* New York: Columbia University Press.

Lambert, Frank. 2008. *Religion in American Politics: A Short History.* Princeton: Princeton University Press.

Lasswell, Harold D. 1936. *Politics: Who Gets What, When, How.* New York: McGraw-Hill.

Laurence, Jonathan. 2012. *The Emancipation of Europe's Muslims.* Princeton: Princeton University Press.

Lehmann, Kardinal Karl. 2007. "Das katholische Christentum," in Hans Joas and Klaus Wiegandt, eds, *Säkularisierung und die Weltreligionen*. Frankfurt am Main: Fischer.

Leiken, Robert S. 2012. *Europe's Angry Muslims*. New York: Oxford University Press.

Lewis, Bernard. 1993. *Islam and the West*. New York: Oxford University Press.

Lewis, Bernard. 1996. "Islam and Liberal Democracy," *Journal of Democracy* 7(2): 52–63.

Lewis, Bernard. 2002. *What Went Wrong? Western Impact and Middle Eastern Response*. New York: Oxford University Press.

Lilla, Mark. 2007. *The Stillborn God: Religion, Politics, and the Modern West*. New York: Knopf.

Liviatan, Ofrit. 2012. "From Abortion to Islam: The Changing Function of Law in Europe's Cultural Debates," *Fordham International Law Journal* 36: 93–135.

Locke, John. 1689. *A Letter Concerning Toleration* (*www.constitution.org/jl/tolerati.htm*).

Löwith, Karl. 1953. *Weltgeschichte als Heilsgeschehen*. Stuttgart: Kohlhammer.

Lübbe, Hermann. 1965. *Säkularisierung*. Freiburg: Karl Alber.

Lübbe, Hermann. 2004. *Religion nach der Aufklärung*. Munich: Fink.

Luckmann, Thomas. 1991 [1967]. *Die unsichtbare Religion*. Frankfurt am Main: Suhrkamp.

Luhmann, Niklas. 1982. *Funktion der Religion*. Frankfurt am Main: Suhrkamp.

Lukes, Steven. 1975. "Political Ritual and Social Integration," *Sociology* 9(2): 289–308.

Lukes, Steven. 1985. *Marxism and Morality*. Oxford: Oxford University Press.

Lupu, Ira C. 1994. "The Lingering Death of Separationism," *George Washington Law Review* 62: 230–79.

Lynch, Marc. 2010. "Veiled Truths," *Foreign Affairs* 89(4) (*www.foreignaffairs.com/articles/66468/marc-lynch/veiled-truths*).

McConnell, Michael W. 1985. "Accommodation of Religion," *Supreme Court Review*: 1–59.

McConnell, Michael W. 1992. "Accommodation of Religion: An Update and a Response to Critics," *George Washington Law Review* 60(3): 685–742.

MacCulloch, Diarmaid. 2010. *A History of Christianity*. London: Penguin.

MacEoin, Denis. 2009. *Sharia Law or "One Law For All"?* London: Civitas.

McLellan, David. 1987. *Marxism and Religion*. London: Macmillan.

McLeod, Hugh. 2000. *Secularisation in Western Europe, 1848–1914*. Basingstoke: Macmillan.

McLeod, Hugh. 2010. *The Religious Crisis of the 1960s*. Oxford: Oxford University Press.

Madeley, John T.S. 2009. "Unequally Yoked: The Antinomies of Church–State Separation in Europe and the USA," *European Political Science* 8(3): 273–88.

Madison, James. 1785. *Memorial and Remonstrance Against Religious Assessments* (*http://press-pubs.uchicago.edu/founders/documents/amendl_religions43.html*).

Mahmood, Saba. 2009. "Religious Reason and Secular Affect: An Incommensurable Divide?" *Critical Inquiry* 35: 836–62.

Malik, Maleiha. 2012. *Minority Legal Orders in the UK.* London: British Academy.

Mancini, Susanna. 2006. "Taking Secularism (Not Too) Seriously: The Italian 'Crucifix' Case," *Religion and Human Rights* 1: 179–95.

Mancini, Susanna. 2010a. "The Crucifix Rage," *European Constitutional Law Review* 6: 6–27.

Mancini, Susanna. 2010b. *To Be Or Not To Be Jewish: The UK Supreme Court Answers the Question.* University of Bologna School of Law and SAIS Johns Hopkins University, Bologna Center. October 16.

Mancini, Susanna. 2014. "The Tempting of Europe, the Political Seduction of the Cross," in Susanna Mancini and Michel Rosenfeld, eds, *Constitutional Secularism in an Age of Religious Revival.* New York: Oxford University Press.

Mann, Michael. 1986. *The Sources of Social Power.* Vol. 1. New York: Cambridge University Press.

March, Andrew F. 2006. "Liberal Citizenship and the Search for an Overlapping Consensus: The Case of Muslim Minorities," *Philosophy and Public Affairs* 34(4): 373–421.

March, Andrew F. 2007a. "Islamic Foundations for a Social Contract in Non-Muslim Liberal Society," *American Political Science Review* 101(2): 235–52.

March, Andrew F. 2007b. "Reading Tariq Ramadan," *Ethics and International Affairs* 21(4): 399–413.

March, Andrew F. 2009a. *Islam and Liberal Citizenship.* New York: Oxford University Press.

March, Andrew F. 2009b. "Are Secularism and Neutrality Attractive to Religious Minorities?" *Cardozo Law Review* 30(6): 2821–54.

March, Andrew F. 2009c. "Sources of Moral Obligation to Non-Muslims in the 'Jurisprudence of Muslim Minorities' (Fiqh al-aqalliyyat) Discourse," *Islamic Law and Society* 16: 34–94.

March, Andrew F. 2010. "The Post-Legal Ethics of Tariq Ramadan," *Middle East Law and Governance* 2: 253–73.

March, Andrew F. 2011. "Theocrats Living Under Secular Law," *Journal of Political Philosophy* 19(1): 28–51.

Maret, Rebecca E. 2013. "Mind the Gap: The Equality Bill and Sharia Arbitration in the United Kingdom," *Boston College International and Comparative Law Review* 36(1): 255–83.

Martin, David. 1978. *A General Theory of Secularization.* New York: Harper and Row.

Marty, Martin. 1969. *The Modern Schism: Three Paths to the Secular.* London: SCM Press.

Marty, Martin. 2000. "Religious Fundamentalism: Cultural Concerns," in *International Encyclopedia of the Social and Behavioral Sciences.* New York: Elsevier.

Marx, Anthony. 2005. *Faith in Nation.* New York: Oxford University Press.

Marx, Karl. 1964 [1843–4]. "Zur Kritik der Hegelschen Rechtsphilosophie: Einleitung," in Karl Marx and Friedrich Engels, *Werke*. Vol. 1, Berlin (East): Dietz Verlag.

Marx, Karl. 1975 [1867]. *Das Kapital*. Vol. 1. Berlin (East): Dietz Verlag.

Marx, Karl. 1978 [1843]. "Zur Judenfrage," in Karl Marx and Friedrich Engels. *Werke*. Vol. 1. Berlin (East): Dietz Verlag.

Marx, Karl. 1979 [1859]. "Vorwort zur Kritik der politischen Ökonomie," in Karl Marx and Friedrich Engels, *Ausgewählte Schriften in zwei Bänden*. Berlin (East): Dietz Verlag.

Maxwell, Rahsaan. 2010. "Trust in Government among British Muslims: The Importance of Migration Status," *Political Behavior* 32: 89–109.

Mayer, Ann-Elizabeth. 1999. *Islam and Human Rights*. Boulder, CO: Westview.

Menski, Werner F. 2001. "Muslim Law in Britain," *Journal of Asian and African Studies* 62: 127–63.

Merry, Sally Engle. 1988. "Legal Pluralism," *Law and Society Review* 22: 869–96.

Meyer, John W. 1989. "Conceptions of Christendom: Notes on the Distinctiveness of the West," in Melvin L. Kohn, ed., *Cross-National Research in Sociology*. Newbury Park, CA: Sage.

Milward, Alan. 1992. *The European Rescue of the Nation-State*. London: Routledge.

Monnerot, Jules. 1949. *Sociologie du communisme*. Paris: Gallimard.

Monsma, Stephen and Christopher Soper. 1997. *The Challenge of Pluralism: Church and State in Five Democracies*. Lanham, MD: Rowman and Littlefield.

Moore, Kathleen. 2010. *The Unfamiliar Abode: Islamic Law in the United States and Britain*. New York: Oxford University Press.

Mottahedeh, Roy P. 1995. "The Clash of Civilizations: An Islamicist's Critique," *Harvard Middle Eastern and Islamic Review* 2(2): 1–26.

Mouritsen, Per. 2006. "The Particular Universalism of a Nordic Civic Nation," in Tariq Modood, Anna Triandafyllidou, and Ricard Zapata-Barrero, eds, *Multiculturalism, Muslims and Citizenship*. London: Routledge.

Nasr, Vali. 2005. "The Rise of 'Muslim Democracy,'" *Journal of Democracy* 16(2): 13–27.

Neuhaus, Richard John. 1984. *The Naked Public Square*. Grand Rapids, MI: William B. Eerdmans Publishing.

Nisbet, Robert. 1966. *The Sociological Tradition*. New York: Basic Books.

Norris, Pippa and Ronald Inglehart. 2002. "Islam and the West: Testing the 'Clash of Civilizations' Thesis." Working Paper, John F. Kennedy School of Government, Harvard University.

Nussbaum, Martha. 2008. *Liberty of Conscience*. New York: Basic Books.

O'Brien, Conor Cruise. 1988. *God Land: Reflections on Religion and Nationalism*. Cambridge, MA. Harvard University Press.

Oestreich, Gerhard. 1969. "Strukturprobleme des europäischen Absolutismus," in Gerhard Oestreich, *Geist und Gestalt des frühmodernen Staates*. Berlin: Duncker and Humblot.

Okin, Susan Muller. 1998. "Feminism and Multiculturalism: Some Tensions," *Ethics* 108(4): 661–84.

Orgad, Liav. Forthcoming. *Cultural Defense of Nations*. New York: Oxford University Press.

Osterhammel, Jürgen. 2009. *Die Verwandlung der Welt: Eine Geschichte des 19. Jahrhunderts*. Munich: C.H. Beck.

Otto, Rudolf. 1963 [1917]. *Das Heilige*. Munich: C.H. Beck.

Pagden, Anthony. 2008. *Worlds at War*. New York: Oxford University Press.

Pajno, Simone. 2011. "The Apologue of Marco and Leonardo: A Response to Joseph Weiler," *Italian Journal of Public Law* 3(1): 163–8.

Parsons, Talcott. 1963. "Christianity and Modern Industrial Society," in Edward A. Tiryakian, ed., *Sociological Theory, Values, and Sociocultural Change*. New York: Free Press.

Parsons, Talcott. 1964. "Evolutionary Universals in Society," *American Sociological Review* 29(3): 339–57.

Peters, F.E. 2004. *The Children of Abraham: Judaism, Christianity, Islam*. Princeton: Princeton University Press.

Pew Research Center. 2006. *The Great Divide: How Westerners and Muslims View Each Other*. Washington, DC.

Pew Research Center. 2008. *US Religious Landscape Survey*. Washington, DC.

Pew Research Center. 2011. *The Future of the Global Muslim Population: Projection for 2010–2030*. Washington, DC.

Phillips, Kevin. 2006. *American Theocracy*. New York: Penguin.

Philpott, Daniel. 2000. "The Religious Roots of Modern International Relations," *World Politics* 52: 206–45.

Philpott, Daniel. 2009. "Has the Study of Global Politics Found Religion?" *Annual Review of Political Science* 12: 183–202.

Pirenne, Henri. 1970 [1939]. *Mahomet et Charlemagne*. Paris: Presses Universitaires de France.

Pollack, Detlef. 1995. "Was ist Religion?" *Zeitschrift für Religion* 3: 163–90.

Preuss, Ulrich. 1995. "Problems of a Concept of European Citizenship," *European Law Journal* 1(3): 267–81.

Putnam, Robert D. and David E. Campbell. 2010. *American Grace*. New York: Simon and Schuster.

Radkau, Joachim. 2009. *Max Weber: A Biography*. Cambridge: Polity.

Rahman, Fazlur. 1998. "Islam and Modernity," in Charles Kurzman, ed., *Liberal Islam: A Sourcebook*. New York: Oxford University Press.

Ramadan, Tariq. 2001. *Islam, the West and the Challenge of Modernity*. Leicester: The Islamic Foundation.

Ramadan, Tariq. 2002a. *To be a European Muslim*. Leicester: The Islamic Foundation.

Ramadan, Tariq. 2002b. *La foi, la voie et la résistance*. Lyon: Tawhid.

Ramadan, Tariq. 2004. *Western Muslims and the Future of Islam*. Oxford: Oxford University Press.

Ramadan, Tariq. 2009. *Radical Reform*. Oxford: Oxford University Press.

Rawls, John. 1993. *Political Liberalism*. New York: Columbia University Press.

Reinhard, Wolfgang. 1981. "Konfession und Konfessionalisierung in Europe," in Wolfgang Reinhard, ed., *Bekenntnis und Geschichte: Die Confessio Augustana im historischen Zusammenhang*. Munich: Ernst Vögel.

Reinhard, Wolfgang. 1989. "Reformation, Counter-Reformation, and the Early Modern State: A Reassessment," *Catholic Historical Review* 75(3): 383–404.

Reinhard, Wolfgang. 1992. "Die lateinische Variante von Religion und ihre Bedeutung für die politische Kultur Europas," *Saeculum* 43: 231–55.

Reinhard, Wolfgang. 1997. "Sozialdisziplinierung-Konfessionalisierung-Modernisierung," in Nada Boskovska Leimgruber, ed., *Die Frühe Neuzeit in der Geschichtswissenschaft*. Paderborn: Ferdinand Schöningh.

Reinhard, Wolfgang. 1999. *Geschichte der Staatsgewalt*. Munich: Beck.

Rémond, René. 1998. *Religion et société en Europe au XIXe et XXe siècles*. Paris: Éditions du Seuil.

Riesebrodt, Martin. 2007. *Cultus und Heilsversprechen: Eine Theorie der Religionen*. Munich: Beck.

Rohe, Mathias. 2003. "Islamic Law in German Courts," *Hawwa* 1 (*http://www.zr2.jura.uni-erlangen.de/islamedia/publikation/Hawwa%20-%20Islamic%20Law%20in%20German%20Courts.pdf*).

Rohe, Mathias. 2004. "Application of Shari'a Rules in Europe – Scope and Limits," *Die Welt des Islams* 44(3): 323–50.

Roy, Olivier. 2002. *L'Islam mondialisé*. Paris: Seuil.

Roy, Olivier. 2010. *Holy Ignorance: When Religion and Culture Part Ways*. New York: Columbia University Press.

Roy, Olivier. 2013. "Secularism and Islam: The Theological Predicament," *International Spectator* 48(1) (special issue on "Europe and Islam," edited by Erik Jones and Saskia van Genugten): 5–19.

Ryan, Alan. 2012. *On Politics: A History of Political Thought from Herodotus to the Present* Vol. 1. New York: Norton.

Schacht, Joseph. 1964. *An Introduction to Islamic Law*. Oxford: Oxford University Press.

Scheffler, Samuel. 2007. "Immigration and the Significance of Culture," *Philosophy and Public Affairs* 35(2): 93–125.

Schluchter, Wolfgang. 1991. *Religion und Lebensführung*. Vol. 2. Frankfurt am Main: Suhrkamp.

Schluchter, Wolfgang. 2009. *Grundlegungen der Soziologie*. Vol. 1. Tübingen: Mohr Siebeck.

Schmitt, Carl. 2005 [1922]. *Political Theology*. Chicago: University of Chicago Press.

Scott, Joan. 2007. *The Politics of the Veil*. Princeton: Princeton University Press.

Shachar, Ayelet. 2001. *Multicultural Jurisdictions*. New York: Cambridge University Press.

Shiffrin, Steven. 2009. *The Religious Left and Church–State Relations*. Princeton: Princeton University Press.

Shils, Edward. 1972. "Center and Periphery," in Edward Shils, *The Constitution of Society*. Chicago: University of Chicago Press.

Silvestri, Sara. 2009. "Islam and Religion in the EU Political System," *West European Politics* 32(6): 1212–39.

Simmel, Georg. 1912. *Die Religion*. Frankfurt am Main: Rütten & Loening.

Smelser, Neil J. 1998. "The Rational and the Ambivalent in the Social Sciences," *American Sociological Review* 63(1): 1–16.

Smith, Christian. 1998. *American Evangelicalism*. Chicago: University of Chicago Press.

Smith, Christian. 2002. *Christian America? What Evangelicals Really Want*. Berkeley: University of California Press.

Smith, Christian et al. 2013. "Twenty-Three Theses on the Status of Religion in American Sociology," *Journal of the American Academy of Religion* 81(4): 903–38.

Soroush, Abdolkarim. 2002. *Reason, Freedom and Democracy in Islam*. New York: Oxford University Press.

Spinner-Halev, Jeff. 1999. "Cultural Pluralism and Partial Citizenship," in Christian Joppke and Steven Lukes, eds, *Multicultural Questions*. Oxford: Oxford University Press.

Spinner-Halev, Jeff. 2008. "Liberalism and Religion: Against Congruence," *Theoretical Inquiries in Law* 9: 553–72.

Stark, Rodney. 1999. "Secularization, RIP," *Sociology of Religion* 60(3): 249–73.

Stark, Rodney. 2003. *For the Glory of God*. Princeton: Princeton University Press.

Starr, Paul. 2007. *Freedom's Power*. New York: Basic Books.

Stepan, Alfred. 2001. "The World's Religious Systems and Democracy: Crafting the 'Twin Tolerations,'" in Alfred Stepan, *Arguing Comparative Politics*. New York: Oxford University Press.

Stepan, Alfred. 2011. "The Multiple Secularisms of Modern Democratic and Non-Democratic Regimes," in Craig Calhoun, Mark Juergensmeyer, and Jonathan VanAntwerpen, eds, *Rethinking Secularism*. New York: Oxford University Press.

Strayer, Joseph. 1955. *Western Europe in the Middle Ages*. New York: Appleton-Century-Crofts.

Strayer, Joseph. 1958. "The State and Religion: An Exploratory Comparison in Different Cultures (Greece and Rome, the West, Islam)," *Comparative Studies in Society and History* 1(1): 38–43.

Strayer, Joseph. 1970. *On the Medieval Origins of the Modern State*. Princeton: Princeton University Press.

Taylor, Charles. 1998. "Modes of Secularism," in Rajeev Bhargava, ed., *Secularism and Its Critics*. New Delhi: Oxford University Press.

Taylor, Charles. 2007. *A Secular Age*. Cambridge, MA: Harvard University Press.

Taylor, Charles. 2011. "Western Secularity," in Craig Calhoun, Mark Juergensmeyer, and Jonathan VanAntwerpen, eds, *Rethinking Secularism*. New York: Oxford University Press.

Thorne, John and Hannah Stuart. 2008. *Islam on Campus: A Survey of UK Student Opinions*. London: Centre for Social Cohesion.

Tibi, Bassam. 2006. "Europeanizing Islam or the Islamization of Europe: Political Democracy vs. Cultural Difference," in Timothy A. Byrnes and Peter J. Katzenstein, eds, *Religion in an Expanding Europe*. New York: Cambridge University Press.

Tibi, Bassam. 2009a. *Islam`s Predicament with Modernity*. London: Routledge.

Tibi, Bassam. 2009b. *Euro-Islam*. Darmstadt: Wissenschaftliche Buchgesellschaft.

Tocqueville, Alexis de. 1969 [1835–40]. *Democracy in America* (edited by J.P. Mayer). Garden City, NY: Anchor Books.

Toft, Monica Duffy, Daniel Philpott, and Timothy Samuel Shah. 2011. *God's Century: Resurgent Religion and Global Politics*. New York: Norton.

Trevor-Roper, H.R. 1965. "Religion, the Reformation, and Social Change," *Historical Studies* 4: 18–45.

Troeltsch, Ernst. 1906. "Die Bedeutung des Protestantismus für die Entstehung der modernen Welt," *Historische Zeitschrift* 97(1): 1–66.

Troeltsch, Ernst. 1994 [1912]. *Die Soziallehren der christlichen Kirchen und Gruppen*. 2 vols. Tübingen: Mohr Siebeck.

Tucker, Adam. 2008. "The Archbishop's Unsatisfactory Legal Pluralism," *Public Law* Autumn: 463–9.

Tyrell, Hartmann. 2008. "Kulturkämpfe in Frankreich und Deutschland und die Anfänge der Religionssoziologie," in Matthias Koenig and Jean-Paul Willaime, eds, *Religionskontroversen in Frankreich und Deutschland*. Hamburg: Hamburger Edition.

van der Veer, Peter. 2001. *Imperial Encounters*. Princeton: Princeton University Press.

Wald, Kenneth D. and Allison Calhoun-Brown. 2011. *Religion and Politics in the United States* (6th edition). Lanham, MD: Rowman and Littlefield.

Walter, Christian. 2006. *Religionsverfassungsrecht*. Tübingen: Mohr Siebeck.

Walzer, Michael. 1984. "Liberalism and the Art of Separation," *Political Theory* 12(3): 315–30.

Warner, Carolyn M. 2000. *Confessions of an Interest Group: The Catholic Church and Political Parties in Europe*. Princeton: Princeton University Press.

Warner, Michael, Jonathan VanAntwerpen, and Craig Calhoun, eds. 2010. *Varieties of Secularism in a Secular Age*. Cambridge, MA: Harvard University Press.

Warner, R. Stephen. 1993. "Work in Progress toward a New Paradigm for the Sociological Study of Religion in the United States," *American Journal of Sociology* 98(5): 1044–93.

Weber, Max. 1976 [1921]. *Wirtschaft und Gesellschaft*. Tübingen: Mohr Siebeck.

Weber, Max. 1977 [1926]. *Politik als Beruf*. Tübingen: Mohr Siebeck.

Weber, Max. 1978 [1920]. *Gesammelte Aufsätze zur Religionssoziologie*. Vol. 1. Tübingen: Mohr Siebeck.

Weber, Max. 1979 [1919/20]. "Die protestantischen Sekten und der Geist des Kapitalismus," in Max Weber, *Die Protestantische Ethik I: Eine Aufsatzsammlung*. Gütersloh: Gerd Mohn.

Weiler, Joseph. 2010. "Lautsi: Crucifix in the Classroom Redux," *European Journal of International Law* 21(1): 1–6.

Whitman, James Q. 2008. "Separating Church and State: The Atlantic Divide," *Historical Reflections* 34(3): 86–104.

Williams, Daniel K. 2010. *God's Party: The Making of the Christian Right*. New York: Oxford University Press.

Williams, Rowan. 2010. "Civil and Religious Law in England: A Religious Perspective," in Rex Ahdar and Nicholas Aroney, eds, *Shari'a in the West*. Oxford: Oxford University Press.

Witte, John, Jr. and Nina-Louisa Arold. 2011. "Lift High the Cross? Contrasting the New European and American Cases on Religious Symbols on Government Property," *Emory International Law Review* 25: 5–55.

Witte, John, Jr. and Joel A. Nichols. 2011. *Religion and the American Constitutional Experiment* (3rd edition). Boulder, CO: Westview Press.

Yilmaz, Ihsan. 2002. "The Challenge of Post-Modern Legality and Muslim Legal Pluralism in England," *Journal of Ethnic and Migration Studies* 28(2): 343–54.

Zolberg, Aristide and Long Litt Woon. 1998. "Why Islam is Like Spanish," *Politics and Society* 27(1): 5–38.

Zolberg, Aristide, Astrid Suhrke, and Sergio Aguayo. 1989. *Escape from Violence*. New York: Oxford University Press.

Zoller, Elisabeth. 2006. "*Laïcité* in the United States or the Separation of Church and State in a Pluralist Society," *Indiana Journal of Global Legal Studies* 13(2): 561–94.

Zubaida, Sami. 1995. "Is there a Muslim Society?" *Economy and Society* 24(2): 151–88.

Zubaida, Sami. 2004. "Islam and Nationalism," *Nations and Nationalism* 10(4): 407–20.

Zucca, Lorenzo. 2012. *A Secular Europe*. Oxford: Oxford University Press.

Zucca, Lorenzo. 2013. "Lautsi – On a Decision by the ECtHR Grand Chamber," *International Journal of Constitutional Law* 11(1): 218–29.

Index